PUSHING BOUNDARIES in POSTGRADUATE SUPERVISION

EDITORS

ELI BITZER
RUTH ALBERTYN
LIEZEL FRICK
BARBARA GRANT
FRANCES KELLY

Pushing Boundaries in Postgraduate Supervision

Published by SUN PRESS
www.africansunmedia.co.za
www.sun-e-shop.co.za

All rights reserved.

Copyright © 2014 AFRICAN SUN MeDIA and the authors.

No part of this book may be reproduced or transmitted in any form or by any electronic, photographic or mechanical means, including photocopying and recording on record, tape or laser disk, on microfilm, via the Internet, by e-mail, or by any other information storage and retrieval system, without prior written permission by the publisher.

Views expressed in this publication are those of the authors and do not necessarily reflect the views of the publisher.

First edition 2014
ISBN (printed version) 978-1-920689-15-5
ISBN (electronic version) 978-1-920689-16-2

Set in Futura Lt BT 10/13
Cover design by SUN MeDIA Stellenbosch
Typesetting by SUN MeDIA Stellenbosch

SUN PRESS is an imprint of AFRICAN SUN MeDIA. Academic, professional and reference works are published under this imprint in print and electronic format. This publication may be ordered directly from www.sun-e-shop.co.za.

Packaging, reproduction, printing and binding by SUN MeDIA Stellenbosch.

ACKNOWLEDGEMENTS

The editors are very pleased to acknowledge all the authors who have contributed so generously to this book and made its publication possible. Those colleagues who acted as critical readers to the different chapters are thanked sincerely for their inputs and valuable comments. We also want to acknowledge our three external reviewers, Professors Ann Austin (Michigan State University), Judy Backhouse (University of the Witwatersrand) and Jane Castle (University of the Witwatersrand) for their highly appreciated reviewing of the book which added valuable perspectives to its content and its individual chapters. Last, but not least, we thank Ella Belcher who language edited the text of the book with meticulous accuracy.

The National Research Foundation in South Africa is acknowledged for contributing financially to this publication through incentive funding and SUN MeDIA for their excellent efforts to get the book published. In particular we would like to thank the managing editor, Liezel Meintjes, for her support and advice throughout.

The Editors

March 2014

CONTENTS

Contributing authors ix

1 Candidates, supervisors and institutions: Pushing postgraduate boundaries –
   An overview 1
   Liezel Frick, Eli Bitzer and Ruth Albertyn

PART ONE • Knowledge Boundaries

2 Knowledge questions and doctoral education 11
   Sue Clegg

3 Doctoral work as boundary-riding and boundary-breaking 25
   Terry Evans

PART TWO • Expansion and Risk

4 The South African doctorate: Where to now? 39
   Chaya Herman

5 Conceptualising risk in doctoral education: Navigating boundary tensions 53
   Liezel Frick, Ruth Albertyn and Eli Bitzer

PART THREE • Doctoral Writing

6 Doctoral writing as an affective practice: Keep calm and carry on? 69
   James Burford

7 Integrating authoritative disciplinary voices in postgraduate writing 85
   Pia Lamberti and Arnold Wentzel

PART FOUR • Supervision Strategies

8 Pushing the boundaries of postgraduate supervision: Theorising
   research learning in community 109
   Callie Grant

9 Coursework in Australian PhD programmes: Why is this a boundary and
   how is it being pushed? 123
   Margaret Kiley, Joe Luca and Anna Cowan

10 The cohort supervision model: To what extent does it facilitate
   doctoral success? 133
   Nonnie Botha

11 The journeyman as a metaphor for developing skills in postgraduate education:
   Experience, feedback and role models 153
   Khalid El Gaidi

PART FIVE • Supervision across Cultures

12 A coordinated framework for developing researchers' intercultural competency 169
    Cally Guerin, Michelle Picard and Ian Green

13 More than agency: The multiple mechanisms affecting postgraduate education 185
    Puleng Motshoane and Sioux McKenna

PART SIX • Doctoral Experiences and Identities

14 First-generation students aspiring to live the academic dream: The role of
    supervisor support 203
    Catherine Mitchell

15 Evolving doctoral identities: Understanding 'complex investments' 215
    Susan van Schalkwyk

CODA • Beyond the end of the book

Research as openings into new spaces of thought and practice 229
    Frances Kelly and Barbara Grant

A tribute to Alison Lee by Sue Clegg 233

Index 239

CONTRIBUTING AUTHORS

Ruth Albertyn is currently involved in research and development in the field of postgraduate supervision, doctoral education, research methodology and academic writing. She is a research associate in the Centre for Higher and Adult Education in the faculty of Education, Stellenbosch University. She lectured and supervised postgraduate students for seventeen years in the faculty of Community and Health Sciences at the University of the Western Cape. She teaches research methodology in various disciplines and supervises students on a Master's and doctoral level. She has published in the field of adult and higher education both nationally and internationally.

Eli Bitzer is Director of the Centre for Higher and Adult Education in the faculty of Education, Stellenbosch University (SU). He has worked for nineteen years in academic staff development at Free State University and for the past fifteen years he has taught at the master's level and supervised a substantial number of master's and PhD students at SU in higher education studies. He has published extensively in the field of higher education and his current fields of interest are postgraduate supervision, doctoral education and different aspects of quality promotion in higher education.

Nonnie Botha is professor and head of the Intercultural Education Unit (ICEDU) in the Faculty of Education, Nelson Mandela Metropolitan University (NMMU), South Africa. She has worked previously as librarian, Mathematics teacher, trainer of Mathematics teachers and education planner for school Mathematics. She subsequently turned to academia, working in faculties of Education at several South African universities for the past thirty years. She has published on a wide range of topics in the field of education and has also supervised a significant number of MEd and PhD studies. Her current research focuses on intercultural issues and postgraduate pedagogies, policies and practices.

James Burford is a doctoral candidate at the University of Auckland and visiting research fellow at the Contemplative Education Centre, Mahidol University. His doctoral research examines the relationship between affect and doctoral writing. James previously worked as a diversity practitioner in universities, most recently as a facilitator of diversity workshops at Auckland University. He has completed projects examining sexuality/gender diversity interventions in secondary schools, and LGBT development practice in Thailand. His current research interests range from doctoral be(com)ing, experimental genres for academic writing, and LGBT intergenerational practice in higher education, to transgender experiences of schooling and embodiment.

Sue Clegg is Emeritus Professor of Higher Education Research at Leeds Metropolitan University. She is a sociologist of higher education whose research is informed by critical realism and feminist theory. She has published widely on substantive policy and pedagogical issues including learning and teaching strategies, personal development planning, and plagiarism. Her theoretical work includes critical analyses of the social and pedagogical significance of the gendering of information technology, information technologies in learning and teaching, the nature of 'evidence-based' practice, the relationship between cultural capital, agency and curriculum, the significance of understanding time in higher education, and the possible future selves students project into the future.

Anna Cowan is a neuroscientist who is actively involved in educational research with a focus on the experiences of higher degree research students. She is currently the Associate Dean for Higher Degree Research in the College of Medicine, Biology and Environment and College of Physical and Mathematical Sciences at the Australian National University.

Khalid El Gaidi is a pedagogical developer at the Staff Development Centre at the Royal Institute of Technology in Stockholm, Sweden (KTH). He has worked for fifteen years with pedagogical courses for different types of teachers and is also responsible for the Research Supervision course that more than five hundred supervisors have taken. He has published in the areas of teaching and learning and supervision. His current field of interest is postgraduate supervision and the learning and teaching of mathematics in engineering education.

Terry Evans has been author and researcher in the field of doctoral studies for over twenty-five years. He is an Emeritus Professor at Deakin University where he was previously a professor and associate dean (research and doctoral studies) in the Faculty (later School) of Education. He has supervised many doctoral candidates to completion. He remains energetically concerned about the field of doctoral studies and supervises PhD candidates in Australia and overseas. He currently works as a consultant and researcher, also in Australia and overseas.

Liezel Frick is currently employed as a Senior Lecturer in Higher and Adult Education (Department of Curriculum Studies) at Stellenbosch University, where her research focuses on creativity in doctoral education. She has published various scholarly articles and book chapters related to this topic, as well as contributions on continuous professional development, assessment and recognition of prior learning, and improving students' learning outcomes. She is involved in various projects in the academic community related to student learning, continuing professional development, leadership development, and building research networks.

Barbara Grant is an Associate Professor in the Department of Critical Studies Education in the School of Education, Auckland University. Barbara's research field is higher education, in particular questions of identity, pedagogy and ethics in higher education, and she is most interested in qualitative and textual enquiries that foreground post-critical theories of education. Her main area of expertise is the supervision of graduate research students but she has researched and published in a wide range of higher education areas, including researcher identity, academic development, research methodologies and academic writing. The underlying thread connecting her enquiries is an interest in academic subjectivities/identities and ethical questions regarding the relations between academic subjects, and between them and institutions, and the higher education project at large.

Callie Grant is a senior lecturer in Education Leadership and Management (ELM) at Rhodes University. She teaches on the Honours, Masters and PhD programmes in ELM and is also involved in the research design courses. Her primary research interest has revolved around teacher leadership from a distributed leadership perspective. She is also interested in educational leadership for social justice, leadership as it relates to professionalism and the relationship of leadership to school resilience. She has an interest in the field of doctoral studies, particularly as it relates to PhDs with publications. Her most recent research is located in the field of higher education studies and stems from her own postgraduate teaching and supervision.

Ian Green is based in the Researcher Education Unit, Discipline of Higher Education, at the University of Adelaide, where he develops and delivers programmes for research degree supervisors, early career researchers and aspiring research leaders, as well as teaching in areas of educational theory and research methodology. Ian's research interests are in doctoral/researcher education frameworks and pedagogies, academic identities, and, more broadly, the culture-language-cognition nexus, with a particular focus on Australian Indigenous education issues.

Cally Guerin is Coordinator of Higher Degree by Research student programmes in the Researcher Education Unit at the University of Adelaide. Her research interests include doctoral pedagogies, academic mobility, academic integrity, researcher identities, and writing skills development for both international and local doctoral students. Her recent publications have appeared in the Journal for University Teaching and Learning (2010), Studies in Continuing Education (2012), The Journal of Further and Higher Education (2013), Innovations in Education and Teaching International (2013) and The International Journal of Doctoral Studies (2013).

Chaya Herman is Associate Professor at the Department of Education Management and Policy studies in the Faculty of Education, University of Pretoria, specializing in globalization and education policy with a focus on higher education and knowledge production at the doctorate level. In 2008 she was appointed as a senior researcher at the Academy of Science of South Africa to conduct a series of studies on doctoral education in South Africa. She is also taking part in international studies exploring the reasons for and consequences of an increase in PhD production worldwide.

Frances Kelly is a Research Fellow in Higher Education, based in the School of Critical Studies in Education, in the Faculty of Education at The University of Auckland. Frances's research is primarily in doctoral education, where she is focused on examining the idea of the PhD, or the doctorate in the cultural imagination and as it is constructed in discourse. Other areas of interest include academic identities, thesis writing and the analysis of higher education discourse. Frances is currently the Book Reviews Editor for the journal 'Higher Education Research and Development' (HERD).

Margaret Kiley's research and teaching interests for many years have been in the area of research education including: The examination of doctoral theses; experiences of international students; conceptions of research; and the introduction of coursework into the Australian PhD. Margaret completed her PhD in Higher Education at the University of Adelaide. She is now a Visiting Fellow at the Australian National University and has a conjoint position at Newcastle University, Australia. Margaret has worked in Further/Higher Education in Australia, Indonesia and the UK and has presented workshops on research supervision in Australia, New Zealand, the UK, Malaysia, Canada and the USA.

Pia Lamberti has worked for 25 years in the education field, 15 of which have been in student and staff development at the University of Johannesburg. She currently heads research capacity development in the Postgraduate Centre and teaches research writing. Her doctoral research was on written argumentation in the knowledge-focused texts of Development Studies. Her research interests cohere in the area of higher education development, and include academic literacies, curriculum development, and the scholarship of teaching, learning and supervision.

Joe Luca is the Dean of the Graduate Research School at Edith Cowan University. His research interests are focused on promoting the quality of research training, supervisory practice, online learning, graduate attributes and project management. In these fields he has written over 100 refereed journal articles, book chapters, books and conference publications. He has been recognised for his excellence in teaching and learning and awarded a national award for Teaching Excellence (Australian Awards for University Teaching) and an Australian Citation Award. He has also been awarded two Australian Government grants to help improve the quality of research training in Australia.

Sioux McKenna is the Higher Education Studies doctoral coordinator in the Centre for Higher Education Research, Teaching and Learning at Rhodes University. In this capacity she runs a vibrant PhD programme that includes academics from numerous countries and institutions. She manages various research projects including one on supervision development across South Africa. She has supervised a number of doctoral and masters studies and published in fields that include her main research interests of higher education literacies, curriculum structures and quality assurance.

Catherine Mitchell (Taranaki) is a first-generation university student undertaking doctoral research in the School of Critical Studies in Education in the Faculty of Education at The University of Auckland / Te Whare Wananga o Tamaki Makaurau. She is currently researching first-generation students' experience within doctoral education, utilising narrative methodology underpinned by post-structural theory. Catherine works part-time in learning development at Unitec Institute of Technology in Auckland.

CONTRIBUTING AUTHORS

Michelle Picard is Director of the Researcher Education Unit at the University of Adelaide and also fulfils the role of Associate Dean Learning and Teaching in the Faculty of Professions. She has worked in Australia in research education for the past seven years and previously worked in academic language and learning in the United Arab Emirates, South Africa and Oman. Michelle teaches courses in research design and communication as well pedagogy. She currently supervises six PhD students and two Masters students. Michelle publishes in higher education, particularly around research writing, academic literacies, English as an additional language and academic integrity.

Puleng Motshoane is currently employed as a Teaching and Learning consultant in the Centre for Academic Technologies (CAT) at the University of Johannesburg. She comes from a school teaching background and has an interest in the ways in which higher education is meeting the needs of a transformed South Africa. She is especially interested in the postgraduate sector and the extent to which we are building the next generation of researchers needed to ensure a stable economy. Her doctoral study focusses on how institutions support the supervision process with the aim of increasing doctoral outputs.

Susan van Schalkwyk is Deputy Director (Education) at the Centre for Health Professions Education in the Faculty of Medicine and Health Sciences, Stellenbosch University. In this role she co-ordinates capacity building activities in the faculty, serves as educational advisor on faculty-based projects and facilitates support initiatives for doctoral candidates. She is involved in teaching at master's level and doctoral supervision of students in higher education and health profession education. She has published in the field of higher education, specifically with regard to academic staff and student development, and her current research interests include doctoral education, rural medical education and medical education research.

Arnold Wentzel joined academia in 2001 after working in private business for a number of years. He is currently a Senior Lecturer in Economics in the Faculty of Economics and Financial Sciences at the University of Johannesburg, and was the recipient of a Teaching Excellence award in 2010. He has been supervising postgraduate students for fourteen years. He also teaches research writing (at both undergraduate and postgraduate levels) in other faculties at the university as well as teaching methodology to teachers of Economics and Business Studies.

CANDIDATES, SUPERVISORS AND INSTITUTIONS: PUSHING POSTGRADUATE BOUNDARIES
AN OVERVIEW

Liezel Frick, Eli Bitzer and Ruth Albertyn

Academic boundaries are in some ways similar to national boundaries – they are set up to colonise and govern, but at the same time are constantly challenged to reaffirm their authority and meaning. The postgraduate environment has been and is still colonised and governed by a variety of boundaries: inter/national, geographical, cultural, institutional, disciplinary and paradigmatic; also those of knowledge and relationships, and many more. The contributions to this book set out to explore and challenge such boundaries as they exist within the postgraduate environment.

The work of Thomas Kuhn (1962) and others on paradigms set the scene for establishing boundaries both within and between academic disciplines in terms of research. The earlier work of Becher and Trowler (2001) on academic tribes and their territories may also be useful to explain academics' search for a scholarly identity in the higher education environment. An academic tribe provides its members with an identity and a particular frame of reference. The characteristic identity of a particular academic tribe is developed from an early age – usually already at the undergraduate level, where patterns of thought are imprinted. These 'tribal' associations are often solidified at the postgraduate level.

The current academic environment, however, demands a certain degree of boundary permeability – academic tribes and their territories can no longer claim sole propriety of knowledge systems and paradigms, as the later work of Trowler, Saunders and Bamber (2012) and their co-workers attests. Various changes in higher education have contributed to a differentiated and permeable system, including changes in the internal characteristics of higher education institutions, rapid technological changes, an emphasis on market-friendly applied research, and external pressures for vocationally oriented curricula. The debates on so-called Mode 1 knowledge (based within specific disciplinary boundaries), versus Mode 2 knowledge (which refers to transdisciplinary and problem-based forms of knowledge) as espoused in the work of Gibbons (1994) and Nowotny, Scott and Gibbons (2001) have further challenged the way in which knowledge boundaries are constructed in society at large and higher education in particular. There is also the need to solve complex and large-scale problems which single disciplines or studies are unable to do. As a result, traditional knowledge systems and paradigms are challenged, as the work of Max-Neef (2005), Lather (2006) and others points out. These trends have pushed postgraduate boundaries at institutional, supervisory and candidate levels as we see the emergence of a variety of postgraduate formats, models and programmes; the practice of different forms and modes of supervision; evidence of inter-/trans-disciplinary postgraduate research; and inter/national research collaboration.

Academic institutions, postgraduate supervisors and candidates are pushed to define themselves anew amidst these moving boundaries. Barnett (2011) rightfully argues that universities currently function within the uneasy space between idea and reality, and that there is not a simple uniform idea of the university itself, or the way in which it produces knowledge. The complexity of the university, its surroundings and the diversity of its inhabitants demand a variety of approaches to establishing and supporting knowledge production through research. Understanding and implementing a strategy towards this end implies a delicate but functional relationship between higher education institutions, supervisors, and postgraduate candidates. This book provides a range of ideas on how the notion 'boundaries' (and the permeability thereof) influences institutions, supervisors and candidates at the postgraduate level. This book therefore focuses on the following (contested) boundary areas:

- knowledge boundaries;
- expansion and risk;
- doctoral writing;
- supervision strategies;
- supervising across cultures; and
- doctoral experiences and identities.

While these might not be the only boundaries that exist or are pushed within the postgraduate domain, they are key to how we understand (and challenge) the functioning of postgraduate systems.

Knowledge lies at the core of the postgraduate endeavour, and therefore it is apt to consider the role of knowledge boundaries within the changing postgraduate supervision landscape. Sue Clegg makes a convincing argument in her chapter that we need to pay greater attention to knowledge questions in doctoral education – particularly the understanding of knowledge and the need to theorise it more adequately. Bernstein's work is used as a basis to argue for the importance of theorising the differences between disciplines and for looking at the processes of regionalisation in understanding doctoral practices, as there seems to be a greater emphasis on knowledge production in the doctorate than in other areas of the curriculum. 'Knowledge questions and doctoral education' pushes knowledge boundaries in understanding doctoral education as more than simply research, but as pedagogy. This chapter does not necessarily bring new research, but it does bring new conceptual perspectives to those who research or facilitate postgraduate education. This is an important chapter for its emphasis on the role of knowledge in doctoral education and its emphasis on theorizing the role and the diversity of knowledge practices which are constitutive of doctoral education. In his chapter, Terry Evans uses contemporary research, policy and scholarship on doctoral studies, as well as the work of Kuhn and Mulkay to consider the boundary-riding and boundary-breaking work through which supervisors and candidates push knowledge boundaries. Knowledge boundaries are pushed by considering the process of undertaking a doctorate as one of working within and beyond boundaries to produce both an original contribution to knowledge (embedded in the thesis) and a new researcher in the field (the doctoral graduate). Doctoral work, therefore, works not only within a discipline's boundaries, but also within the boundaries of doctorateness.

The massification of higher education across the globe has also influenced the boundaries of postgraduate education and supervision, forcing traditional boundaries to expand. Chaya Herman's chapter focuses on the South African doctorate in the context of massive global expansion of postgraduate education which has been taking place over the last two decades. The impact this expansion has on the future of doctoral education in South Africa in terms of policy, practice and research and the role that academics and the PhD should play in knowledge creation is explored in terms of existing and expanding boundaries. Such expansion does not take place without risk. Liezel Frick, Ruth Albertyn and Eli Bitzer take up the question of risk in doctoral education with a particular focus in their chapter on how the concept of risk currently operates in doctoral education, based on a conceptualisation of risk in general and a small-scale study with experienced doctoral supervisors across disciplines at one South African university. They argue that risk is not an inevitably negative concept, but also seems to provide opportunities for increased and higher levels of scholarly performance and results. By identifying ways of containing risk, postgraduate supervisors may be better equipped to facilitate the process of student development towards an original contribution at a doctoral level, thereby being capable of dealing with the pressures of inevitable boundary expansion.

Doctoral writing fulfils a dual role – that of writing to know and knowing how to write (Aitchison 2010). This notion of doctoral writing forces us to ask whether (and if so, how) we support students' ability to contribute to the scholarly debate. James Burford reports in his chapter on doctoral writing as an affective practice which can be tied to the precarity of academic labour and what implications this may have for supervision. This position enables us to better account for the layering of affect within the lives of students, as well as its patterned distribution across doctoral education. It also helps us to unpack the complexities of doctoral writing and be(com)ing a doctoral writer. Pia Lamberti and Albert Wentzel provide insights into how authoritative disciplinary voices can be integrated into postgraduate writing. The disciplinary boundary crossing promoted by the collaboration between the two authors allows for a more nuanced and multifaceted understanding of the specific language and discursive resources required for the writing of the literature section of the dissertation or thesis. They also problematise the boundary between undergraduate and postgraduate level study, and suggest that research supervision necessarily encompasses a greater degree of explicit teaching than supervisors conventionally acknowledge.

Higher education institutions play a central role in determining the boundaries of postgraduate supervision. These institutions also provide support structures within these boundaries that aim to support postgraduate supervisors and that fit within the boundaries of the institution. However, new forms and modes of postgraduate programmes, supervision and research are emerging that may challenge the existing institutional boundaries. These challenges create the opportunity to explore how institutions relate and respond to such changes. At the same time supervisors play a key role as they negotiate boundaries between the different scholarly roles, engage in the formation and sustaining of communities of scholarly practice, conduct and reflect on forms of innovative supervision and review and revitalise existing supervisory practices. In this book, Callie Grant takes the position that the liberal notion of supervision with its traditional one-to-one relationship between student and supervisor can no longer be considered the only supervision strategy in the higher education arena in South Africa. Conceptualising supervision as being relational within a scholarly community of practice could offer beneficial alternatives and opportunities within the current diverse and complex society in terms of expanding and enriching the teaching and learning process. In a related chapter, Margaret Kiley, Joe Luca and Anna Cowan ask why coursework in Australian PhD programmes is a boundary and how it is being pushed – as different universities and disciplines have approached this supervision strategy with different concepts of coursework, its purpose, content, and placement within candidature. They examine the understandings of staff and students at two different universities on what the introduction of 'coursework' in the Australian PhD might entail – and how this might push our understanding of supervising strategies. Nonnie Botha identifies some of the ways in which cohort supervision facilitates doctoral success, by mapping Bitzer's conceptual framework for exploring doctoral success onto the outcomes of a small-scale empirical study and seeking confirmation of such indications in South African and international literature. She offers some suggestions for improving the modalities of the cohort supervision model, adding to the body of knowledge on cohort supervision as supervision strategy and thus pushing the boundaries in postgraduate supervision. In the final chapter of this section, Khalid El Gaidi uses a journeyman analogy of doctoral studies to both challenge and help us understand how the nature and communication of skills result in the development of knowledge – particularly in complex areas such as music and acquiring a native or specialised language. Due to increased numbers of candidates per supervisor, students have less time to spend with their supervisors for adequate skills transfer. Through working together with more proficient peers in research and reflecting on their experiences (such as in the journeyman's experience) PhD students are able to acquire a sense of quality in research in writing, experimenting and review. Using dialogue seminars and a pragmatic approach based on the language philosophy of Wittgenstein, Khalid El Gaidi suggests a knowledge taxonomy to analyse the specifics of skills and proposes experience-based learning to acquire such skills.

Contemporary society presents postgraduate supervisors with a diverse student body, which often demands that institutional, relational, individual and knowledge boundaries be reconsidered. Universities today are marked by increasing staff and student mobility, flexibility in programmes, multinational research partnerships, joint international appointments and publication and, most importantly, free exchange of knowledge. In order to maximise the benefits of internationalisation and ensure sustained collaboration, high levels of intercultural competence are required from all parties. Institutional, supervisory and candidate reactions to such boundary challenges may differ, therefore Michelle Picard, Cally Guerin and Ian Green propose to push the boundaries of research education through a coordinated framework for developing researchers' intercultural competency. Puleng Motshoane and Sioux McKenna focus on the integral roles that structure and culture have to play in postgraduate supervision, alongside the well-documented roles played by the supervisors themselves. They challenge policy makers and institutional management to consider the ways in which structural and cultural issues affect postgraduate supervision and how these can be fostered to improve the postgraduate supervisory process.

Postgraduate students themselves may be instrumental in pushing boundaries. Their lived experiences of supervisory practices or how they engage with boundaries as part of their postgraduate experience are valuable contributions to understanding how boundaries contribute to or hinder their ultimate success. These boundaries may relate to personal (motives for doing research, preferred learning style, confidence, past experiences, ideological perspective), social (cultural background and gender) or geographical (international students) issues. Catherine Mitchell reflects on the role of supervisors supporting first-generation students who aspire to live the academic dream. She provides a reflective account of the multifaceted nature of the supervision process from her perspective as a student. Her contribution helps us to consider what students learn from their supervisors as they imagine an academic future and how supervisors may contribute to students' movement into academia. In the penultimate chapter, Susan van Schalkwyk argues that doctoral studies represent 'complex investments' for those who embark on them. Drawing on data generated among a number of doctoral candidates who meet on a monthly basis, she sought to understand the nature of these complex investments. For such understanding she uses the work of Margaret Archer, who describes identity formation occurring through the personification of a particular role and requiring an investment or intentionality on the part of the doctoral candidate. Van Schalkwyk suggests that if supervisors hope to foster the development of a doctoral identity, then there may be a need to understand what mediates candidates' internal conversations. Such understanding may better enable them to establish nurturing spaces towards identity formation. This may require that the shroud obscuring the inner workings of the supervisory relationship is disturbed and in so doing, that the boundaries that currently define it are challenged.

REFERENCES

Aitchison C. 2010. Learning together to publish. In: C Aitchison, B Kamler & A Lee (eds). *Publishing pedagogies for the doctorate and beyond*. Oxon: Routledge. 83-100.

Barnett R. 2011. The coming of the ecological university. *Oxford Review of Education*, 37(4): 439-455.

Becher T & Trowler P. 2001. *Academic tribes and their territories: Intellectual inquiry and the culture of disciplines*. Buckingham: Society for Research into Higher Education.

Gibbons M. 1994. *The new production of knowledge: The dynamics of science and research in contemporary societies*. London: Sage.

Kuhn T. 1962. *The structure of scientific revolutions*. Chicago, IL: University of Chicago Press.

Lather P. 2006. Paradigm proliferation as a good thing to think with: Teaching research in education as a wild profusion. *International Journal of Qualitative Studies in Education,* 19(1):35-57.

Max-Neef MA. 2005. Foundations of trandisciplinarity. *Ecological Economics,* 53:5-16.

Nowotny H, Scott P & Gibbons M. 2001. *Re-thinking science: Knowledge and the public in an age of uncertainty.* Cambridge: Polity.

Trowler P, Saunders M & Bamber V (eds). 2012. *Tribes and territories in the 21st century: Rethinking the significance of disciplines in higher education.* Florence: Routledge.

PART ONE

KNOWLEDGE BOUNDARIES

KNOWLEDGE QUESTIONS AND DOCTORAL EDUCATION

Sue Clegg

INTRODUCTION

This chapter reviews some of the developments in doctoral education over the past 25 years and suggests that multiple agendas on the part of policy makers, theorists of higher education, and practitioners in the form of supervisors and other teachers have converged to produce changes in doctoral practice and understandings. This shift has occurred, in part, in response to an increasingly diverse range of research students' interests and aspirations alongside the development of newer forms of doctoral programmes. It can be broadly summarised as focusing on doctoral pedagogy (Boud & Lee 2009; Lee & Danby 2012). As a result, doctoral education has come to be understood as being about much more than the production of a thesis and a rite of passage into academia. The first part of the chapter will tease out some of these strands and argue that, while there are tensions between them, nonetheless the direction of travel towards the emphasis on pedagogy and away from conceptualisation of the doctorate as simply research is clear. The second part of the chapter will focus on knowledge questions in doctoral education and suggest that these require greater attention. In doing so I take inspiration from the Brechtian maxim that we 'should not build on the good old days, but on the bad new ones'; in other words, in taking the theme of the book of 'pushing the boundaries', I do not wish to take us back to an unreflexive view of the doctorate as an extension of research. Rather, I want to embrace the new diversity and complexity and suggest that theorising this space requires a greater attention to knowledge questions and to how knowledge is constituted. In doing so, I will make the case that the doctorate has a different relationship to discipline-as-research and indeed practice-as-research. When we examine a research degree, we are invited to evaluate not only whether the student has extended her knowledge (learning is always about knowledge making for the individual), but also whether the thesis/practice/artefact makes an 'original contribution to knowledge'. Knowledge in doctoral education is privileged in different ways than in other areas of the higher education curriculum.

It also has to be borne in mind that governments increasingly look to knowledge to transform the economy. The idea of the 'knowledge economy' has in many respects become a truism. I want to suggest, however, that what is meant by 'knowledge' in this context and its relationship to disciplinary knowledge is much less clear, and to take a critical look at the claims for knowledge-rich jobs. These are important questions in a context where concerns with social mobility and individual enhancement have become dominant discourses in framing questions about the benefits of higher education, including doctoral education, both for the individual and for nation states in what are seen to be more globally competitive times.

The intention of the chapter is not to provide firm answers. Rather, I am consciously going to stand back and paint a broad picture, as we have travelled far both in terms of developing newer practices and in researching doctoral education. I think it is timely, however, to take stock and to refocus on knowledge questions. This involves some attention to the sociology and philosophy of science as well as to curriculum and pedagogy.

THE DISTANCE TRAVELLED: THE ROUTE TO PEDAGOGY

The traditionally accepted picture of the research degree was of the apprentice scholar working with the 'master' (gender intentional) producing a piece of original research. Academics on this model treated supervising their doctoral candidates as part of their research time and as continuous with their own research activity. This model privileged a light touch notion of supervision as the coming into being of someone who was already capable of doing a doctorate (Johnson, Lee & Green 2000). Supervision here can be understood as 'looking over' – what Alison Lee and Bill Green (2009) describe as the panoptics of 'enLIGHTenment' – with vision being the dominant metaphor for knowledge and truth. Now of course this depiction is always likely to have elided multiple practices. One of the problems is that we do not have many detailed empirical studies for earlier periods of doctoral education. We do, however, have anecdotal and personal accounts of benign and sometimes not so benign neglect and we can point to the dominant and highly gendered discourse of autonomy that legitimated the supervisory model (Johnson *et al.* 2000).

The perceived wrongs of the traditional model began to trouble a number of actors and it is to these that I am going to turn. Firstly, I am going to describe how governments began to see the doctorate as not fit for purpose, using the UK as my example. Secondly, I am going to describe how concerns with quality of supervision, timeliness of completion, and the sorts of people being produced meshed into whole new regimes of governance, audit and increasingly a training model for both students and supervisors. Finally and, at least as importantly for researchers and theorists of the field, I want to argue that changes in practice were emergent from critiques by radical educators and theorists and their engagement with both students and supervisors. These contributed both to the ways the newer regimes of training were mediated into practice and to the blossoming of research into doctoral education. I am not suggesting that there is a causal sequence here, since the different temporalities of policy, practice and critique run alongside one another. Moreover, emergent tendencies and dominant concerns come to the fore at different times in different locations internationally, so while the trends I am describing are international they are always locally inflected and understood.

The concern with the quality of research degrees and their fitness for purpose has increasingly been understood in terms of post-doctoral employability. In the UK in particular, there has been ongoing anxiety over international standing and competitiveness and the ability to continue to attract financially lucrative overseas students. These concerns were articulated in a number of reports starting in 1990 with the Parnaby Report about the engineering doctorate (Parnaby 1990). This report was critical of the fitness of post-doctoral researchers for industry and proposed that the sorts of projects undertaken as part of the doctorate should be more like those in the engineering industry rather than a single in-depth study. A government White Paper, *Realising our Potential,* set the framework for science policy in 1993 and again focused on science and engineering and the needs of the economy (HMSO 1993). The government-commissioned Harris Report of 1996 also raised issues of quality and international competitiveness in doctoral education (Harris Report 1996). New quality assurance, training and other regimes followed on from these early expressions of disquiet and in particular the central concerns about the ability to exploit research and to produce employable post-doctoral researchers. So while, as Diana Leonard and Rosa Becker (2009) note, researchers have paid considerable attention to supervision in the arts and social sciences, government policy has overwhelmingly been driven by views of the economic contribution of science and engineering.

What followed has been a plethora of reforms and a bewildering number of initiatives involving a range of agencies designed to improve the efficiency and fitness for purpose of the research degree. In the UK these have included initiatives across research councils including financial penalties to reduce time to completion for full-time students; the Joint Skills Statement from all the research councils in 2001 outlining the training requirements for research students with a heavy emphasis on generic training designed to improve employability (RCUK 2001); the Roberts Report in 2002 which reiterated the focus on employability, the importance of science and engineering, and continued to drive the training agenda forward including the provision of funding to support research training (Roberts 2002); and the activities of the so-called 'Rugby Team' who produced, among other things, a report entitled *Employers' Views of Researchers' Skills* (Rugby Team 2007). The initiatives are multiple but the direction of travel and the underlying concerns are consistent: doctoral study should be more efficient and we should be equipping students with the skills necessary for employment and for the benefit of the country. In 2004, the Quality Assurance Agency produced a code of practice which covered process, environment, and the need for supervisor development opportunities, and which further increased scrutiny of university practice producing a major shift away from a focus simply on the individual supervisor towards institutional arrangements (QAA 2004). The list goes on, but the point I want to make is that both what we understand doctoral education to be and the environment in which it takes place have shifted considerably from pre-1990 understandings. This does not mean that there are not continuities at the level of practice and professional judgment but the context within which these are made has been reconfigured.

In the UK there has been a steadily increasing number of doctoral students from the late 1960s, and an increase in the diversity of students and the programmes they have followed. The increase in the number of doctoral scholars is an international phenomenon. The projected targets for increasing numbers in Malaysia, for example, is for an eight-fold increase over 15 years (Kumar 2011:25). Scale has other effects. Universities now have directors of research degrees and graduate schools and offices, and doctoral education has become a central site of performativity and risk management, as Erica McWilliam (2009) writing in the Australian context has so ably documented. So, while I have taken most of my examples from the UK, these developments are not unique.

It is also important to note that these developments have not taken place behind academics' backs. Academics have been actively engaged, although not always under terms they would have chosen because, as Karl Maton (2005) reminds us, academics have retained considerable positional autonomy. While relational autonomy has weakened, meaning that universities are responding to external imperatives not of their own making, it has been academics not outsiders who have implemented these policies. In the sphere of doctoral education, this has been for good reasons as I have already indicated. Over the period I have been describing, there have been important attempts to theorise doctoral education as pedagogy that have brought about significant advances in our understanding and in practice. Alison Lee and Susan Danby (2012), in their chapter 'Framing doctoral pedagogy as design and action', use the term 'pedagogy' to point to the relationship between learners and teachers in producing knowledge and argue that doctoral pedagogy involves not only "coming to know" but also "coming to be" (Lee & Danby 2012:4). A considerable amount of work has been done in looking at the research seminar and research lab, understanding them as sites in which "what counts as academic work is represented and authorised" (Green & Lee 1995:41). Scholars such as Liezel Frick (2012) have been doing important work on cultivating creativity in science doctorates, while others such as Claire Aitchison, Barbara Kamler and Alison Lee (2010) have analysed 'publishing pedagogies' that play an increasingly important role in doctoral education, especially under the pressure of research selectivity which has swept up doctoral scholars in its wake. For the minority of doctoral scholars who do go on to become academics, publication is now a necessity. Researchers such as Angela Brew and Tai Peseta (2009) and Barbara Grant (2003) have given us greater insight into the passions and complexities involved in supervision and into courses designed to support them. As a consequence, some of the most creative elements of support for doctoral pedagogy are now underpinned by critical inquiry and research.

My position is that what we are witnessing is a tremendously exciting period for doctoral education globally. The doctoral programme supporting higher education research at Rhodes University (2013) is an excellent example of innovation, as is Doctoralnet, an international collaboration to build a virtual graduate school (Dahlgren, Grosjean, Lee & Nyström 2012). But it is also the case that in many of its enactments, change to doctoral education is hedged about by audit and scrutiny and procedures and practices that are panoptic in their effects on both supervisor and student. Even so, the idea of doctoral *pedagogy* is now firmly enshrined.

THE VIEW FROM KNOWLEDGE

In the light of the above, the question that could be asked is why we should pay more attention to knowledge practices given that the view from pedagogy has proved so illuminating. Let me be clear: I am not suggesting that the turn to pedagogy in the research literature has totally ignored knowledge questions. As the definition by Lee and Danby (2012) suggests, pedagogy pays attention to the knowledge production of learners. In this section, however, I am going to address knowledge questions directly, including those in the policy arena, as there are important issues that are brought into sharper focus through the knowledge lens. Firstly, I am going to question the policy deployment of knowledge and in particular the seductions of science and engineering and the 'knowledge economy'. Secondly, I will take up the now commonplace idea that there have been shifts in the forms of knowledge production and interrogate rather more closely the idea of Mode 1 and 2 knowledges to suggest that this is too crude a conceptualisation. Thirdly, drawing on Bernstein (2000), I will explore the relationship between discipline-as-research and curriculum and pedagogy and the processes Bernstein describes as regionalisation, looking out from the academy and to the market. Finally, I want to conclude with some reflections on Michael Young's (2008) thesis about 'bringing knowledge back in'. I will ask whether some of the differences in pedagogical practice might be related to the different sorts of stuff we are studying and the question of natural kinds, recognising that these questions are broader than just disciplines. This is because the ways that disciplines are formed is more complex than the ontological properties of the kinds being studied.

To start with policy: As we have seen in the first part, governments (and not just the British one) are keen to stress the importance of the knowledge economy, but it is not at all clear what the relationship to 'knowledge' is. The knowledge economy is used to capture a number of things that are not straightforwardly related. One of the claims is that knowledge is now central to jobs where complex judgments are called for and that these jobs are growing in number and are central to the economic prosperity of nations. However, as Phillip Brown, Hugh Lauder and David Ashton (2011) argue in *The Global Auction: The broken promises of education, jobs and income,* the competitive logic of accumulation breaks jobs down and routinises them. So, while there is competition for global talent (and huge salaries) at the very top, the promised benefits of education for the middle class are increasingly hollow and so-called knowledge-rich jobs have become routinised and no longer guarantee large salaries nor indeed job security. It often seems that what is meant by knowledge-rich jobs simply means non-manual and, while professional jobs should embody professional discretion, in many instances these jobs have become more regulated, not less so. One of the ways of understanding the expansion of postgraduate education in general and research degrees in particular is as an attempt to secure benefits in this global world. But even research degrees do not guarantee knowledge-rich jobs.

Knowledge is also deployed by governments in relation to science and engineering and the creation of new technologies and applications. But again, the relationship between even doctoral-level work and this aspiration is not so clear. Scholars are increasingly being exhorted to define impact and utility for their work but the connection between utility and research is more complex than these exhortations suggest. Moreover, as noted by Brown *et al.* (2011), research and development is not confined to a limited group of advanced countries but is increasingly dispersed, so national governmental claims have to be read with a degree of caution. They detect a trend towards the globalisation of knowledge with even very highly skilled jobs being 'offshored' and a major shift in STEM subjects to Asia and away from the USA. At the very least then, the equation of the knowledge economy and competitive advantage looks increasingly complex and uncertain.

If knowledge is problematic in policy terms, I would suggest that some of the attempts at reformulating knowledge questions have also been somewhat simplistic. Perhaps the most popular of these formulations is by Michael Gibbons (2003) who argues that knowledge production is being cut loose from disciplinary structures. He points to the increase in research centres, institutes and think tanks although analytically these are not the same thing, nor do they share common features. The features of Mode 2 knowledge, according to Gibbons, are as follows: "1. knowledge is produced in the context of application; 2. transdisciplinarity; 3. heterogeneity and organisational diversity; 4. enhanced social accountability and reflexivity; 5. a more broadly based system of quality control" (Gibbons 2003:232). These are processes that have some face validity. However, Gibbons's account is too simplistic since it assumes that the processes he describes fit together, an assumption that is contestable. Many of the features he attributes to Mode 2 knowledge are also characteristic of developing Mode 1 disciplinary knowledge, where transdisciplinarity has been one of the distinctive ways in which disciplinary knowledge has extended itself. Moreover, many of the developments he describes are taking place within traditional universities as well as outside them. Distinguishing two separate modes is, therefore, more difficult than it appears. Gibbons also operates with a unitary notion of discipline and transdiscipline, which is unhelpful particularly in the context of doctoral education where the relationship between traditional disciplines/practices and transdisciplinary study is coming under more detailed scrutiny.

In this respect Bernstein (2000) is altogether a more useful thinker and, moreover, one whose work has been drawn on in debates about doctoral education (e.g. Scott, Brown, Lunt & Thorne 2009). So what is it that makes Bernstein good to think with? Firstly, he has a sophisticated way of thinking about disciplines and the ways they structure knowledge. Bernstein distinguishes horizontal and vertical forms of discourse and hierarchical and horizontal forms of knowledge. Vertical forms of knowledge have a strong grammar; that is, arguments that go from the concrete to the abstract, and a capacity to generate empirical correlates which allows for disciplinary progression: physics is the paradigm case. Horizontal knowledge forms have a weak capacity to generate empirical correlates and a weak grammar and their development tends to be through the proliferation of different theories and frameworks: sociology would be a good case in point. So, while universities and doctoral education have been traditionally organised around disciplines, what this means varies in terms of their knowledge practices. When we think about the doctorate as disciplinary knowledge making, therefore, we need different languages of description for different areas and we need to understand how these different disciplinary practices relate to underlying knowledge structures.

Secondly, I want to suggest that Bernstein has much to tell us about the formation of new fields and trans- or interdisciplinary fields and knowledge that look outwards towards the field of practice and the market. Bernstein describes traditional university disciplines as singulars with "their own intellectual field of texts, practices, rules of entry, examinations, license to practice, distribution of rewards and punishments" (Bernstein 2000:52). These are protected by strong boundaries and hierarchies in which the traditional doctorate plays an important role. Crucially, however, he also describes a process of regionalisation whereby new areas are created. Regions are constructed by recontextualising singulars (that is, traditional disciplines) into larger units both in the intellectual field of practice and in the field of external practice. Traditional examples of regions he gives are engineering, medicine and architecture. Contemporary regions, he suggests, are cognitive science, management, business studies, communication and media. Which disciplines enter a region depends on the recontextualising principle and its social base. What we need, therefore, particularly in the area of doctoral knowledge making, are concrete studies of the process of regionalisation because, depending on the initial structure of the singular, there will be different outcomes. Regionalisation weakens the internal classificatory principles and produces greater external dependency, including the possibilities for external regulation. This is of enormous importance when discussing newer forms of doctoral work including project- and practice-based doctorates and professional doctorates such as the EdD or EngD. David Scott and his co-authors (2009), for example, have argued that disciplines with weak horizontal structures such as education are particularly vulnerable to state intervention on the side of one of the competing positions within the discipline. They show how there are different tensions between the sites of knowledge production – research, the pedagogic, and the workplace – in different professional doctorate programmes.

The final area where I think Bernstein is helpful is in the way he distinguishes between the field of knowledge production, the field of recontextualisation (curriculum) and the field of reproduction (pedagogy). The doctorate is unique in that, unlike the rest of education, the candidate is required to work in the field of knowledge production and the recontextualising rules for the curriculum are not necessarily known in advance of the project. Some recontextualisation is already there: the new norms for research training are an example of a curriculum and a developing pedagogy. However, there is an important sense in which we can think about the doctoral curriculum as the specification of the research project itself. The curriculum is the following through of the project and the assembling of the intellectual and practical tools required to carry this out. This will mean different things in different areas depending on whether the discipline is vertical or horizontal and whether the area of study is a region looking out towards the field of practice and the market as many PhDs and professional doctorates now do. While I would not describe myself as a Bernsteinian, I would suggest that Bernstein gives us a nuanced set of concepts to work with and that we can see the different pedagogical arrangements, for example in some laboratory sciences, as related to the distinctive structures of the field of knowledge. Similarly the sorts of PhD by project explored by Allpress and Barnacle (2009) in their work on research 'through' design (not just 'about' design) relate to the distinctive knowledge field of architecture, which is a region drawing on a number of disciplines, some of which are horizontal and some vertical. Work through design is distinctive by virtue of the practices in that region and exploring this involves theorising the field of knowledge production itself, not just the recontextualisation rules.

There is additional empirical support for the idea that the form of knowledge production relates to practices from the now-classic study of *Tribes and Territories* by Tony Becher and Paul Trowler (2001), who note that the "ways in which particular groups of academics organize their professional lives are related in important ways to the intellectual tasks on which they are engaged" (Becher & Trowler 2001:23). So, for example, in some areas scientists are more gregarious (although not necessarily less competitive), reflecting the realities of lab-based work and the cumulative nature of knowledge production. The social organisation of academic work crucially involves work with doctoral scholars where, for example, the organisation of the laboratory, the development of research programmes and the nurturing of the next generation of scholars form a distinctive part of disciplinary practice. Thinking about the relationship between knowledge production practices and their social organisation is, therefore, a crucial part of doctoral pedagogy.

Other theorists have also been important in foregrounding knowledge and in breaking with a purely social constructivist understanding of knowledge. These theorists have paid particular attention to the ontological dimensions of knowing, that is that our knowing is about 'something', a something that is distinct from our knowing. Michael Young (2008), a sociologist of education, has built on Bernstein and others to argue the case for 'bringing knowledge back in' and for making a retreat from the relativism of social constructivist positions. He argues that the recognition that knowledge is socially produced (which of course it is) does not dissolve the distinctiveness of knowledge claims to be about something and about which we can make (always fallible) judgments of validity. Young (2008:28) argues:

> A social theory that seeks to link knowledge to social interests has to distinguish between two types of interests. These are 'external' or contextual interests, which may reflect wider divisions in society, and the 'internal' cognitive interests that are concerned with the conditions for the production of knowledge itself.

This argument rests on a critical realist conception of knowledge. A critical realist approach has something to say about the sorts of knowledge that we come to have of the social and natural worlds and, hence, that the practices and processes whereby we come to fallibly know the world are dependent on distinguishing between ontology and epistemology. The vertical and cumulative nature of science relates to the natural kinds that we are studying and so the practices we see in knowledge making, including in doctoral work, are distinctive. Indeed the philosopher Roy Bhaskar (1978), when arguing for the importance of ontology, starts with the beguilingly simple question of what the world must be like in order for science to be possible. He argues for a depth ontology in which structures and mechanisms, not just events, are real and he develops an account of experimental method based on a recognition that while regularity is produced through human activity the knowledge that is produced involves understanding the structures of independently existing real things.

I am not arguing here that one needs to be a critical realist to think about different knowledge practices (although I think it helps). The idea of signature pedagogies, for example, links pedagogical practices to disciplinary ways of knowing in the discipline. However, if we take the knowledge question seriously, I think it helps us think about what might be common across doctoral education but also what might be distinctive and how this distinctiveness might relate to the different sorts of stuff we are studying. The practices of the laboratory, the seminar, and the studio are material embodiments of the knowledge practices of the field and these arrangements have an ontological dimension as well as epistemological ones.

A CODA

In coming to my conclusions I have a final coda to make which relates to different sorts of knowledge and brings the body of the student back in. The people doing doctoral work are more diverse (even if, in numerical terms, traditional candidates and traditional disciplines still dominate), and knowledge-making practices are also more diverse, particularly in the newer regions. This raises the question of voice and how ideational diversity relates to knowledge. We have seen, for example, that as newer actors have come into education, new questions are asked and criticisms have been developed for example of the masculinist, colonial and post-colonial biases in knowledge production. This is a complex story that cannot be rehearsed here. Over the last decades, however, we have seen the development of powerful critiques across the social sciences and humanities and to a lesser, but significant, extent in the sciences. Women, and other minorities historically on the margins of universities, were able to attack the knowledge claims of the privileged and show them to be lacking – in effect producing newer, better knowledge claims. Doctoral studies have played an important role in the developments and some of the most exciting innovations in doctoral writing, for example, were produced by feminists. I want to suggest, therefore, that looking at new voices in doctoral education is important. It is also important to distinguish between different theorists of 'voice'. Mine is a sociology of knowledge position that does not automatically privilege particular voices (Clegg 2011). There are other positions which do. One is 'standpoint' theory, which in its strongest version in feminism claimed that women, by virtue of their distinctive experiences and through the development of a feminist stance, could have insights that others could not. Truth in this version is therefore (partially) relativised to social group and made context dependent. These arguments are of course much more fiercely contested in the social sciences and humanities because of their weak grammar and horizontal structures. The issues of standpoint and voice are likely to come to the fore in doctoral supervision and my argument is that, as well as looking at cultural diversity and recognition, there are also important knowledge questions: we should be open to the ways in which newer and better (although always fallible) knowledge claims can emerge. The birthing of these newer ideas is not always easy and there are entrenched interests including – we should recognise – our own. It is worth reminding ourselves that Brecht not only suggested we embrace the bad new days but that also, in his play *The Life of Galileo*, he forces us to confront the power struggles that not infrequently herald the adoption of new and better knowledge. If one rejects judgmental relativism (which I do) while accepting epistemic relativism, then how we judge contribution to knowledge in doctoral work has to wrestle with these issues. Voice does not foreclose the matter, it opens it up.

In summary: this chapter has encompassed a whistle-stop tour of developments in doctoral education to show there has been an important shift to a focus on pedagogy. It has also argued that knowledge questions are important and that a focus on knowledge lets us think about the research nature of the doctorate and 'the contribution to knowledge'. Knowledge, curriculum and pedagogy are related but in the research degree that relationship is closer and knowledge questions are to the fore. So, to borrow from Michael Young, I have been pushing at the boundaries to argue for the advantages of 'bringing knowledge back in' and for theorising the diversity of knowledge practices which are constitutive of doctoral education.

ACKNOWLEDGEMENTS

Peter Macauley and Margot Pearson provided useful comments on a previous version of this chapter that are incorporated into the final version.

REFERENCES

Aitchison C, Kamler B & Lee A. 2010. *Publishing pedagogies for the doctorate and beyond.* London: Routledge.

Allpress B & Barnacle R. 2009. Projecting the PhD: Architecture design research by and through projects. In: D Boud & A Lee (eds). *Changing practices of doctoral education.* London: Routledge. 126-139.

Becher T & Trowler PR. 2001. *Academic tribes and territories: Intellectual enquiry and the culture of disciplines.* Buckingham: Society for Research into Higher Education & Open University Press.

Bernstein B. 2000. *Pedagogy, symbolic control and identity: Theory, research, critique.* Revised edition. Oxford: Rowan & Littlefield.

Bhaskar R. 1978. *A realist theory of science.* Brighton: Harvester Press.

Boud D & Lee A (eds). 2009. *Changing practices of doctoral education.* London: Routledge.

Brew A & Peseta T. 2009. Supervision development and recognition in a reflexive space. In: D Boud & A Lee (eds). *Changing practices of doctoral education.* London: Routledge. 126-139.

Brown P, Lauder H & Ashton D. 2011. The Global Auction: *The broken promises of education, jobs, and incomes.* Oxford: Oxford University Press.

Clegg S. 2011. Cultural capital and agency: Connecting critique and curriculum in higher education. *British Journal of Sociology of Education*, 32(1):93-108.

Dahlgren MA, Grosjean G, Lee A & Nyström S. 2012. The graduate school in the sky: Emerging pedagogies for an international network for doctoral education and research. In: A Lee & S Danby (eds). *Reshaping doctoral education: International approaches and pedagogies.* London: Routledge. 173-186.

Frick L. 2012 Pedagogies for creativity in science doctorates. In: A Lee & S Danby (eds). *Reshaping doctoral education: International approaches and pedagogies.* London: Routledge. 113-123.

Gibbons M. 2003. A new mode of knowledge production. In: F Boekema & R Rutten (eds). *Geography of higher education: Knowledge, infrastructure and learning regions.* London: Routledge. 229-243.

Grant B. 2003. Mapping the pleasures and risks of supervision. *Discourse: Studies in the Cultural Politics of Education,* 24(2):173-188.

Green B & Lee A. 1995. Theorising postgraduate pedagogy. *Australian Universities' Review,* 2:40-45.

Harris Report. 1996. *Review of postgraduate education.* Bristol: HEFCE.HMSO (Her Majesty's Stationery Office). 1993. Realising our potential. [Accessed 8 May 2013] http://www.official-documents.gov.uk/document/cm22/2250/2250.pdf

Johnson L, Lee A & Green B. 2000. The PhD and the autonomous self: Gender, rationality and post graduate pedagogy. *Studies in Higher Education,* 25(2):135-147.

Kumar V. 2011. Supervising postgraduate students: The view from Malaysia. In: V Kumar & A Lee (eds). *Doctoral education in international context: Connection local, regional and global perspectives.* Serdang: UPM. 24-36.

Lee A & Danby S. 2012. Framing doctoral pedagogy as design and action. In: A Lee & S Danby (eds). *Reshaping doctoral education: International approaches and pedagogies.* London: Routledge. 3-11.

Lee A & Green B. 2009. Supervision as metaphor. *Studies in Higher Education,* 34(6):615-630.

Leonard D & Becker R. 2009. Enhancing the doctoral experience at the local level. In: D Boud & A Lee (eds). *Changing practices of doctoral education.* London: Routledge. 71-86.

Maton K. 2005. A question of autonomy: Bourdieu's field approach and policy in higher education. *Journal of Education Policy,* 20(6):687-704.

McWilliam E. 2009. Doctoral education in risky times. In: D Boud & A Lee (eds). *Changing practices of doctoral education.* London: Routledge. 189-199.

Parnaby J. 1990. *The engineering doctorate.* A SERC Working Party Report to the Engineering Board of the Science and Engineering Research Council. London.

QAA (Quality Assurance Agency). 2004. Information and guidance. [Accessed 8 May 2013] http://www.qaa.ac.uk/Publications/InformationAndGuidance/Documents/postgrad2004.pdf

RCUK (Research Councils UK). 2001. Research careers: Training requirements. [Accessed 8 May 2013] http://www.rcuk.ac.uk/documents/researchcareers/jsstrainingrequirements.pdf

Rhodes University. 2013. Programmes offered by CHERTL. [Accessed 8 May 2013] http://www.ru.ac.za/chertl/hestudies/phd/

Roberts G. 2002. *Roberts Report.* [Accessed 8 May 2013] http://www.hm-treasury.gov.uk/d/robertsreview_introch1.pdf

Rugby Team. 2007. Rugby-team employers' views of researchers' skills. [Accessed 8 May 2013] http://www.vitae.ac.uk/cms/files/Rugby-Team-Employers'-views-of-researchers'-skills-September-2007.pdf

Scott D, Brown A, Lunt I & Thorne L. 2009. Specialised knowledge in UK professions: Relations between the state, the university and the workplace. In: D Boud & A Lee (eds). *Changing practices of doctoral education*. London: Routledge. 143-156.

Young MFD. 2008. *Bringing knowledge back in: From social constructivism to social realism in the sociology of education*. London: Routledge.

Mulkay MJ. 1970. *The sociology of science*. London: Methuen.

Nerad M & Heggelund M (eds). 2010. *Toward a global PhD? Forms and forces of doctoral education worldwide*. Seattle, WA: University of Washington Press.

Pearson M, Cumming J, Evans TD, Macauley P & Ryland K. 2008. Exploring the extent and nature of the diversity of the doctoral population in Australia: A profile of the respondents to a 2005 national survey. Paper presented at the Quality in Postgraduate Research Conference, Adelaide, 17-18 April. [Accessed 14 March 2013] http://www.qpr.edu.au/papersdatabase.php?orderBy=author&byYear=2008

Pearson M, Cumming J, Evans TD, Macauley P & Ryland K. 2011. How shall we know them? Capturing the diversity of difference in Australian doctoral candidates and their experiences. *Studies in Higher Education*, 35(6):527-542. [Accessed 12 January 2013] http://dx.doi.org/10.1080/03075079.2011.594591

Unesco. 2008. *Trends and issues in postgraduate education: Challenges for research*. Final report of the Unesco Forum on Higher Education, Research and Knowledge. Paris.

DOCTORAL WORK AS BOUNDARY-RIDING AND BOUNDARY-BREAKING

Terry Evans

INTRODUCTION

This chapter considers the tension between candidates being 'disciplined in the discipline of the discipline' and producing significant original knowledge to earn their doctorate. That is, learning about the disciplinary boundaries within which their doctorates are conducted, and learning how to 'push' those boundaries with sufficient originality in order to be 'doctored'. For the purposes of this chapter, 'doctoral work' embraces all those forms of work and their workers that contribute to doctoral process. Supervisors (advisers) and candidates (students) are the obvious workers, but then there are those whose work it is to support doctoral work (see Edwards & Mackey 2012); in particular, administrators, counsellors, postgraduate students' associations, and those 'scholarly friends' the librarians (Macauley & Reynolds 2012).

BOUNDARIES AND DOCTORAL BOUNDARIES

We tend to think of boundaries as 'natural' physical geographic entities, but really all boundaries are socially constructed. Physical features, such as rivers and mountains, become political, cultural and geographic boundaries when we interpret and name them as such. The Limpopo River became part of the boundary between Botswana and South Africa when powerful interests decided such; it was not 'naturally' a boundary between two 'natural' entities: Botswana and South Africa. In other circumstances where the environment does not provide a notable marker for a boundary between one territory and another, people in power construct physical boundaries – such as, walls, fences – where they want the territory to be bounded. Notable examples are the (now demolished) Berlin Wall, the gated barriers between some Catholic and Protestant communities in Belfast, and the walls separating Israeli and Palestinian territories. Boundaries are surveyed, mapped and demarcated to formalise and communicate them to others, and to defend them when contested. Sometimes, certainly during earlier times of manual warfare, physical boundaries possessed inherent defensive characteristics – see Minard's graphical cartography of the losses to the French army during the Russian campaign with each river crossing (http://en.wikipedia.org/wiki/File:Minard.png).

In some respects, disciplinary boundaries are more obviously socially constructed in the sense that knowledge, even reality itself, is socially constructed (Berger & Luckmann 1967). Some may believe, however, that there are 'natural' differences between one discipline and another (mathematics and literature); others, such as Dawkins (2006), argue that in some disciplines (theology) there is no such thing and they should not exist in the academy. So, rather like the geo-political world's boundaries, there can be some marked distinctions between disciplines and some contests about them.

Universities – and the academy more broadly – demarcate disciplinaryboundaries with physical and institutional features (such as buildings, departments and journals). There is often defence of these boundaries, too, over matters such as their names, locations, facilities and budgets. Disciplinary boundaries are potentially more dynamic than geographic boundaries because the 'intellectual landscape' has to be learned by each rising generation of its scholars and teachers. The scholars' quests for new knowledge provides a dynamic imperative to each discipline so that it is reshaped and reformed by new knowledge and ideas, some of which revise and reconstruct the past. Sometimes, as Kuhn (1970) profoundly argued from the early 1960s, disciplines undergo radical revision in the form of 'scientific revolutions' or 'paradigm shifts' as successive 'anomalies' erode the foundational epistemology and methodology of the discipline. He illustrated that scientific disciplines operated with their own paradigmatic worldview that ruled the way knowledge was understood (theorised) and produced (empirically researched) in the discipline. He saw disciplinary histories as 'peaceful interludes' interrupted by 'intellectually violent' revolutions where one worldview is displaced by what becomes the new theoretical and methodological paradigm constituting. Later it will be argued that new members of the discipline, such as doctoral graduates, may be seen as likely to produce some of the anomalies that lead to the revolution or shift. Kuhn (1970:12) argued that "successive transition from one paradigm to another via revolution is the usual developmental pattern in science". In this sense, doctoral candidates may be essential to the 'usual developmental pattern' in any discipline.

Mulkay (1970) drew on Kuhn's work cited above and that of Merton (1970) in the 1930s on science and technology in 17th century England. He argued that there was a normative view of science that sees each discipline as constituted by its own rules, values and resources. Disciplines are guarded by 'gatekeepers', that is, those with powerful positions in the discipline, such as professors and journal editors. The gatekeepers guard the 'gates' of a discipline to admit only those people (for example, doctoral candidates), ideas and knowledge that conform to the discipline's interests. Mulkay argued for a broader cultural interpretation of science that took account of the social and political influences shaping its disciplines. In terms of this chapter, therefore, the disciplinary boundaries and what is bounded therein are dynamic and contestable.

Doctoral work can be seen as an activity that operates broadly within disciplinary boundaries, but which also incorporates institutional, national and global conceptualisations of doctoral work (see Nerad & Heggelund 2010), much of which might be seen as pedagogical. Arguably, there is a doctoral discipline – more in the sense of ordered training, although there is an emerging scholarly discipline – that transcends disciplinary doctoral work and gives it a common regulated form. This form is constituted by common features (such as theses and dissertations), practices (such as supervision, advising and examining) and values (such as evidence, argument and originality). Doctoral work, therefore, works not only within (at least) a discipline's boundaries, but also within the boundaries of doctorateness. This suggests that boundary crossing between disciplinary and doctoral boundaries is a fundamental feature of doctoral work.

Giroux (1992:22) was not thinking about doctoral pedagogy specifically when he theorised 'border pedagogy', but his words are apposite:

> ... students should engage knowledge as border-crossers, as people moving in and out of borders constructed around coordinates of difference and power. These are not only physical borders, they are cultural borders historically constructed and socially organized within rules and regulations that limit and enable particular identities, individual capacities, and social forms. In this case, students cross over into realms of meaning, maps of knowledge, social relations, and values that are increasingly being negotiated and rewritten as the as the codes and regulations that organize them become destabilized and reshaped.

In the case of doctoral work and the discussion of disciplinary boundaries above, it may be argued that supervisors and examiners are 'boundary riders' who teach and reinforce the boundaries, but who also aid and legitimate candidates' boundary breaking in their pursuit of significant and original contributions to knowledge. This is further explained below.

SUPERVISORS' WORK AS DISCIPLINARY BOUNDARY RIDERS

The boundaries of a discipline are not demarcated by physical phenomena such as the Limpopo River or the Berlin Wall. There are no maps with the boundaries marked to navigate their 'rides' to and along the boundaries to show their candidates where their discipline ends and foreign disciplines begin. Experienced supervisors know the boundaries and know how to teach their new candidates the scope of the territory, its major landmarks, its battlegrounds and places of safety. Before this occurs, however, prospective supervisors act like Mulkay's 'gatekeepers' and exclude potential candidates who are not well-qualified to cross the boundary into their disciplinary doctoral community. This includes ensuring that they have sufficient institutionally legitimated disciplinary knowledge (for instance, degrees) to be a potential new member (as distinct from student) of the discipline. They also deliberate on the applicant's (assumed) personal qualities for doctoral study in the discipline.

Once candidates have been accepted into their doctoral programme, their supervisors begin boundary-riding with their candidate. Historically, boundary-riders were people who rode the boundaries of large farming properties (ranches, stations etc.) on horseback to check that the boundary fences were secure and the stock was safe. Deploying this notion as a metaphor in the doctoral context when supervision commences with new candidates, supervisors are likely to establish what their candidates know of the disciplinary territory and what they need to learn about it. Perhaps most importantly, supervisors need to establish what their candidates propose to investigate, that is, to contribute as significant new knowledge to their disciplines. Thereafter the supervisors can 'shepherd' their candidate to stay within the disciplinary boundaries so that they 'graze' on 'nourishing' texts to prepare them for their research and theses. In other words, they help them produce the sort of critical literature review expected of a doctorate in their discipline.

The supervisors' boundary-riding soon ventures into teaching and reinforcing the rules and conduct of research and scholarship in the discipline. They help the candidates avoid the 'badlands' where navigation is difficult and where productive data and scholarship are hard to obtain. They help their candidates produce new knowledge that will be seen as legitimately produced by the examiner boundary riders. This means understanding and practising appropriate research methodology, research design and analyses for their discipline. Supervisors eventually help the candidates to ensure that their theses or dissertations, and any associated publications, are structured and written to conform to good disciplinary practice.

Boundary-riding doctoral work involves weaving various doctoral activities together during candidature. Figure 1 shows the percentage of candidates working on different types of doctoral work by year of candidature. This figure was produced from a national survey of doctoral candidates in Australia undertaken by Pearson, Cumming, Evans, Macauley and Ryland (2008, 2011). The data represent the percentage of candidates who, during the previous week, undertook one or more of the doctoral tasks: writing, data gathering, data analysis, research design and literature reviewing. This implies that their supervisors were boundary-riding these activities for their candidates during these times. It shows that such boundary-riding may require travelling interconnected tracks (interrelated tasks), and that tracks become more or less travelled as candidature progresses. For example, writing becomes more travelled and research design less travelled during candidature. It is noteworthy that, of the 5 935 respondents spread across a maximum of eight years of candidature – in Australia, most full-time candidates complete in four years and most part-time candidates do so in seven years – all the tracks are being traversed by some candidates irrespective of their point of candidature.

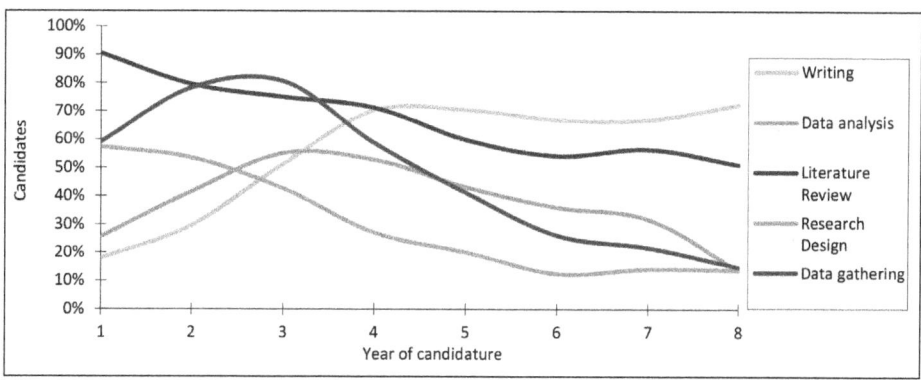

FIGURE 3.1 Percentage of candidates working on types of doctoral work by year of candidature (n=5 935)

In boundary-riding, supervisors clearly need to be responsive to candidates' 'back-tracking' and to be mindful that there are examiner boundary riders who will need to verify that the candidate has not strayed (nor been allowed to stray) from appropriate disciplinary practice tracks. In most cases, supervisors influence the selection of examiners through recommending potential examiners. (In some cases, notably in the USA, the advisers (supervisors) are also examiners.) The examiners attest to the worth (or not) of the thesis for inclusion within the disciplinary boundaries.

These supervisory and examining boundary-riding processes help to 'produce' and legitimate new scholars (doctoral graduates) for their bounded discipline. In effect, the doctoral graduates are the main source of those who become the next generation of boundary riders for the discipline. The above-mentioned boundary-riding work also includes boundary-riding in another important respect for this chapter: doctoral boundary-riding.

SUPERVISORS' WORK AS DOCTORAL BOUNDARY RIDERS

Doctoral supervision is also about riding the boundaries of doctorateness, that is, what it means to complete a research doctorate within global, national and local (institutional) rules and values about the doctorate. Arguably, disciplines are global entities whose lines of communication are deeply rooted in contemporary globalising communications technologies, but which have long histories of oral and written communications transcending national boundaries. Likewise, the emergence of the PhD, or the research doctorate, in modern universities has become a global phenomenon with some common characteristics, some national differences, and some local nuances (see, for examples, EUA 2005; Nerad & Heggelund 2008; Unesco 2008). In essence, supervisors boundary-ride their local (university's) representation of the globally understood doctorate with occasional excursions further afield, for example, to show their candidates other theses, or to find examiners or potential postdoctoral locations.

In an everyday sense, supervisors' boundary-riding includes shepherding their candidates through the procedures and obligations (such as candidature confirmation, ethics applications, progress reports, thesis submission and oral examination) as they are codified and managed at their particular university. They show candidates the doctoral boundaries: the appropriate substance and effort required for a PhD and the quality of work required, especially in the thesis, to pass examination. Supervisors and their candidates ride the doctoral boundaries together to show how far the candidates must travel and the time they need to take to earn a doctorate. Often 'journey' is used as a metaphor for the doctoral experience in publications designed to help doctoral candidates understand their 'travels' through their future studies (see, for example, Edwards & Mackey 2012). Some boundary-riding is undertaken by others in the particular university. This typically occurs in the form of, for example, workshops, seminars, writing retreats and summer schools. Online media may be used, again by the particular university, but also by others in the virtual world (see, for example, http://phdchat.pbworks.com/w/page/33280234/PhD%20Chat and thesiswhisperer.com).

Eventually candidates, by the time they complete their doctorates, are expected to 'ride the boundaries' for themselves; to become 'self-disciplined' or self-regulated in the sense that they have internalised the rules and values of the discipline and of doctoral work, and can practise them without their supervisors' boundary-riding.

The discussion in this section as well as the previous one has an important limitation that is addressed below. This limitation is that both disciplinary and doctoral boundary-riding are portrayed in rather functionalist and normalising terms. As was noted previously from Kuhn's seminal work, disciplinary life may exist like this for a period, but "successive transition from one paradigm to another via revolution is the usual developmental pattern in science" (Kuhn 1970:12). Further, one may argue that these 'revolutions' may involve shifts, not only in what occurs within the boundaries, but also in the boundaries themselves.

SHIFTING BOUNDARIES

For Kuhnian 'scientific revolutions' or 'paradigm shifts' to occur, there must those who become the 'revolutionaries' or, in the terms of this chapter, the 'boundary breakers'. Arguably, the politics of the doctoral process militate against an inductee or novice (candidate) leading a revolution, but the 'significant and original' demands of a doctorate do lead to some boundary-prodding or boundary-crossing. Supervisors, during their boundary-riding, may point to places in their disciplinary (or doctoral) boundaries that are weaker or susceptible to 'significant and original' (doctoral) breaches. Two recent studies of Australian PhD thesis records by Macauley, Evans and Pearson (2009, 2011) illustrate that there are changes within and across boundaries perpetrated by doctoral candidates. They showed that there were marked discrepancies between 1987 and 2006 in the growth of PhD theses in particular disciplines. This indicated that disciplines' research (in terms of theses produced and, consequently, their related publications) and research capacities (in terms of the graduates' embodied disciplinary research expertise) shifted considerably in relation to each other. For example, the four disciplines in Australia with the highest PhD thesis growth rates for the period 2002-2006 expressed as a percentage of their PhD theses for 1987-1991 are: Tourism 4 550%, Nursing 1 867%, Biomedicine 1 867% and Information, Computing and Communication Science 1 700% (Macauley et al. 2009:15). In contrast, the lowest growth rates for the same periods were Veterinary Science 94%, Librarianship 100%, Atomic, Molecular, Nuclear and Plasma Physics 102% and Classical Physics 102% (Macauley et al. 2009:16). It should be noted that 100% means that thesis numbers remained the same between these two periods; therefore, Librarianship maintained its numbers, but Veterinary Science declined by 6%. Furthermore, between 1987 and 2006 the numbers of PhD graduates in Australia increased by approximately 500% (Macauley et al. 2009:9) Therefore, the four lowest disciplines shrank relatively by about 80%, and the four highest disciplines increased relatively by between about 330% and 910%.

Macauley, Evans and Pearson's research in 2008 provides an indication of the actual and relative growth and decline within disciplinary boundaries for research and research capacity in Australia. It suggests that in some disciplines that there are many PhD applicants seeking entry past the disciplinary and doctoral gatekeepers or boundary riders, and in others there are relatively few. These trends may be a source of joy for some and anguish for others. In their later study Macauley et al. (2011) show, however, that these trends may be more complex. Their research in 2008 was based on PhD theses being allocated to a single discipline code, but their coding work showed that often theses spanned more than one discipline; indeed, the discipline of the research may be different from the discipline of the topic. For example, a thesis undertaken within the history discipline may be on the topic of industrial relations in a nation and/or industry. Such a thesis would have been coded as 'History' but it could also relate to the disciplines relating to Industrial Relations and the Sociology of Industry. Consequently, their 2011 work allocated one to three codes to each thesis as appropriate. Their research showed that 47.6% of PhD theses were best coded by two codes, 26.8% by one, and 25.6% by three (2011:8-9). Therefore, 73.2% of PhD theses related to more than one discipline.

The research by Macauley et al. (2008) suggests that the boundaries of disciplines may be seen to be shrinking or expanding if one accepts theses as being related to a single discipline and that these numbers indicate expansion or shrinkage. Perhaps more significantly, their later (2011) study shows that most doctoral candidates are working within two or three disciplinary boundaries and that, therefore, the supervisors (as individuals or as a team) either have to ride these boundaries, too, or accommodate them in some other way. It suggests that boundary-crossing or boundary-breaking is part of most supervisors' work.

SUPERVISING BOUNDARY-BREAKING AS MANAGING RISK

Cross/trans-disciplinary doctoral work represents forms of boundary-breaking that are both risky and potentially rewarding by being particularly and doubly/multiply significant and original. The risks are greater if the boundary rider(s) do not (seek to) know the epistemological and methodological practices of those in the other disciplinary boundaries. In many nations, universities are becoming increasingly risk aware and even risk averse; doctoral management is entrapped within universities' risk management practices (Evans, Lawson, McWilliam & Taylor 2005; McWilliam, Sanderson, Evans, Lawson & Taylor 2006). These practices often seem to deter or limit cross/trans-disciplinary work by making a particular 'home' department or school responsible for the candidature and marginalising the recognition and authority of doctoral workers in other departments and schools from whom the candidate benefits. Team supervision with the appropriate cross/trans-disciplinary expertise may well be lauded rhetorically, but it is often problematic to institutionalise fairly.

Methodological boundary-breaking is also risky, but potentially rewarding. Candidates need to understand the methodological boundaries and resolve or accommodate the epistemological anomalies between them if they are to produce a thesis that has methodological significance and originality. This may well challenge the research paradigm in the field and represent the beginning of a 'new wave' for the discipline, one that may well displace the old. Kuhn's notions of 'scientific revolution' or 'paradigm shift' occurring as a consequence of increasing anomalies arising from research and scholarship suggest that doctoral candidates may be a source of such anomalies. Kuhn (1970:151) alludes to this when he refers to Max Planck's own scientific autobiographical reflection published in 1949: "[A] new scientific truth does not triumph by convincing its opponents and making them see the light, but rather because its opponents eventually die, and a new generation grows up that is familiar (with the new truth)."

Boundary-breaking is also occurring within doctoral boundaries. Some of this concerns doctoral work that spans the academy and industry (Enders 2005). The 'professional' and 'practice-based' doctorates have created debate and change related to doctoral work (Barnacle & Dall'Alba 2011; Fell, Flint & Haines 2011). This boundary-breaking is more at the programme level rather than the individuate doctorate level. That is, it is doctoral programme leaders who are pushing the boundaries, rather than the individual candidates, although the candidates do play their part. Candidates using new representations of doctoral work for examination (and publication) constitute new boundaries for supervisors to understand and shape. These new representations arise largely from the new media and also from the new territories (e.g. professional and community) in which doctorates are undertaken. There are risks associated with candidates 'pushing the boundaries' of how they represent their work for examination, especially if examiners are unfamiliar with the media or are unreceptive to the new representations. The risky, boundary-breaking thesis, however, may satisfy examiners if the explanation (that is, the thesis as argument) is sufficient: it conforms to this doctorateness boundary in justifying its boundary-breaking form.

CONCLUSION

The ASSAf report (2010) argues that doctoral work is important for South Africa's future across a range of disciplines. Other reports have argued likewise for their national interests (Australian Government 2008; EUA 2005; Unesco 2008). This chapter has argued that doctoral work can be understood to occur within both disciplinary and doctoral boundaries that shift and change over time. Supervisors and examiners, in particular, act as boundary riders and boundary breakers for their candidates. Boundaries help to make sense of doctoral work, but sometimes they contain anomalies that frustrate this work and provoke change.

A tension exists in doctoral work: if candidates remain comfortably within the boundaries, they may limit their capacities to perform and display their significant originality. This implies that supervisors need to be prepared to teach about, and manage, the risks of boundary-breaking to ensure that their candidates graduate, and that their disciplines undergo the revolutions and paradigm shifts that sustain them into the future.

ACKNOWLEDGEMENTS

Peter Macauley and Margot Pearson provided useful comments on a previous version of this chapter that are incorporated into the final version.

REFERENCES

ASSAf (Academy of Science of South Africa). 2010. *The PhD study: An evidence-based study on how to meet the demands for high-level skills in an emerging economy*. Pretoria: Academy of Science of South Africa. [Accessed 12 January 2013] http://www.assaf.co.za/wp-content/uploads/2010/11/40696-Boldesign-PHD-small.pdf

Australian Government. 2008. *Building Australia's research capacity. Report of the House of Representatives Standing Committee on Industry, Science and Innovation*. Canberra. [Accessed 14 March 2013] http://www.aph.gov.au/house/committee/isi/research/report.htm

Barnacle R & Dall'Alba G. 2011. Research degrees as professional education. *Studies in Higher Education*, 36(4):459-470.

Berger PL & Luckmann T. 1967. *The social construction of reality: a treatise in the sociology of knowledge*. London: Penguin Books.

Dawkins R. 2006. *The God delusion*. Boston, MA: Houghton Mifflin.

Edwards B & Mackey J. 2012. Preparing for your doctoral journey. In: C Denholm & TD Evans (eds). *Doctorates Downunder: Keys to successful doctoral study in Australia and Aotearoa New Zealand*. Melbourne: ACER Press. 6-17.

Enders J. 2005. Border crossings: Research training, knowldge dissemination and the transformation of academic work. *Higher Education*, 49:119-133.

EUA (European University Association). 2005. *Doctoral programmes for the European knowledge society*. Brussels.

Evans TD, Lawson A, McWilliam E & Taylor PG. 2005. Understanding the management of doctoral studies in Australia as risk management. *Studies in Research*, 1:1-11. [Accessed 12 January 2013] http://www.newcastle.edu.au/group/sir/

Fell T, Flint K & Haines I. 2011. *Professional doctorates in the UK 2011*. Litchfield: UK Council for Graduate Education.

Giroux H. 1992. *Border crossings: Cultural workers and the politics of education*. New York: Routledge.

Kuhn TS. 1970. *The structure of scientific revolutions*. Chicago, IL: University of Chicago Press.

Macauley PD, Evans TD & Pearson M. 2008. *Classifying Australian PhD thesis records by research fields, courses and disciplines*. Report on a study for the Research Excellence Branch. Australian Research Council. [Accessed 14 March 2013] http://hdl.handle.net/10536/DRO/DU:30020658

Macauley PD, Evans TD & Pearson M. 2011. *Classifying Australian PhD thesis records by ANZSRC field of research codes*. Report on a study for the Research Excellence Branch. Australian Research Council. [Accessed 13 January 2013] http://www.deakin.edu.au/dro/view/DU:30036705

Macauley PD & Reynolds S. 2012. The librarian: The candidate's scholarly colleague. In: C Denholm & TD Evans (eds). *Doctorates Downunder: Keys to successful doctoral study in Australia and Aotearoa New Zealand*. Melbourne: ACER Press. 54-63.

McWilliam E, Sanderson D, Evans TD, Lawson A & Taylor PG. 2006. The risky business of doctoral management. *Asia Pacific Journal of Education*, 26:209-224.

Merton RK. 1970. *Science, technology and society in seventeenth-century England*. New York: Harper Row.

Mulkay MJ. 1970. *The sociology of science*. London: Methuen.

Nerad M & Heggelund M (eds). 2010. *Toward a global PhD? Forms and forces of doctoral education worldwide*. Seattle, WA: University of Washington Press.

Pearson M, Cumming J, Evans TD, Macauley P & Ryland, K. 2008. Exploring the extent and nature of the diversity of the doctoral population in Australia: A profile of the respondents to a 2005 national survey. Paper presented at the Quality in Postgraduate Research Conference, Adelaide, 17-18 April. [Accessed 14 March 2013] http://www.qpr.edu.au/papersdatabase.php?orderBy=author&byYear=2008

Pearson M, Cumming J, Evans TD, Macauley P & Ryland K. 2011. How shall we know them? Capturing the diversity of difference in Australian doctoral candidates and their experiences. *Studies in Higher Education*, 35(6):527-542. [Accessed 12 January 2013] http://dx.doi.org/10.1080/03075079.2011.594591

Unesco. 2008. *Trends and issues in postgraduate education: Challenges for research*. Final report of the Unesco Forum on Higher Education, Research and Knowledge. Paris.

PART TWO

EXPANSION AND RISK

4

THE SOUTH AFRICAN DOCTORATE

WHERE TO NOW?

Chaya Herman

INTRODUCTION

Since South Africa emerged from its isolation in 1994 it has aspired to become a player in the knowledge economy. In this context the PhD is considered to be an indicator of a country's developmental capacity and a key driver of the economy. Doctoral students are considered to be the knowledge workers who will spearhead research and development. The Department of Science and Technology (DST) envisioned a fivefold increase in the number of PhD graduates, especially in science and technology, in the span of a decade in order for the country to compete in the global arena (DST 2008).

In this chapter I take a snapshot of the South African doctorate in the context of massive global expansion of postgraduate education which has been taking place over the last two decades. I discuss the various policies that have been put in place to drive the envisaged expansion and argue that it is critical that doctoral education in South Africa continues its path of expansion. The historical data shows this trajectory and captures the particular nuances of this growth. I further argue that growth without quality defeats the purpose of the expansion; hence this chapter seeks to look at how the growth may be sustained and indeed increased while simultaneously improving the quality of doctoral education.

But before discussing the future of the doctorate, it is important to reflect on where we came from and the way the trajectory of the doctorate in South Africa has shifted and moved over time expanding race, gender and disciplinary boundaries.

PART TWO • EXPANSION AND RISK

DOCTORAL EDUCATION IN SOUTH AFRICA: HISTORICAL OVERVIEW

The doctorate has a long history in South Africa. According to the University Incorporation Amendment Act of 1896 the Council of the University of the Cape of Good Hope had the power to confer, after examination, several degrees of Doctors of Law, Doctor of Medicine, Doctor of Science and Doctor of Music.

The first LLD was awarded in 1899 to William Alison MacFadyen and the first DSc was awarded in 1907 to Charles F Juritz. PhDs were awarded since the early 1920s at the University of Cape Town. Since then South Africa has awarded about 31 000 different doctoral degrees. It is interesting to compare it with Australia, which only began to award PhDs in 1948, but has since awarded more than 100 000 various doctoral degrees with less than half of South Africa's population (Dobson 2012).

One of the main reasons for the small number of South African graduates is its traditionally elitist nature which until 1990 had privileged white men. After the 1990s, however, there was both expansion and diversification – in fact, over 60% of the total number of PhDs were awarded in South Africa (19 000) after 1990.

Between 1996 and 2012 there was a steady growth in the number of PhD graduates per annum, with the average growth being about 6% per year (Figure 4.1). It seems that South Africa has tripled the number of doctoral graduates since the transition to democracy, with a significant growth after 2007 following the initiation of the South African PhD project (NRF 2007).

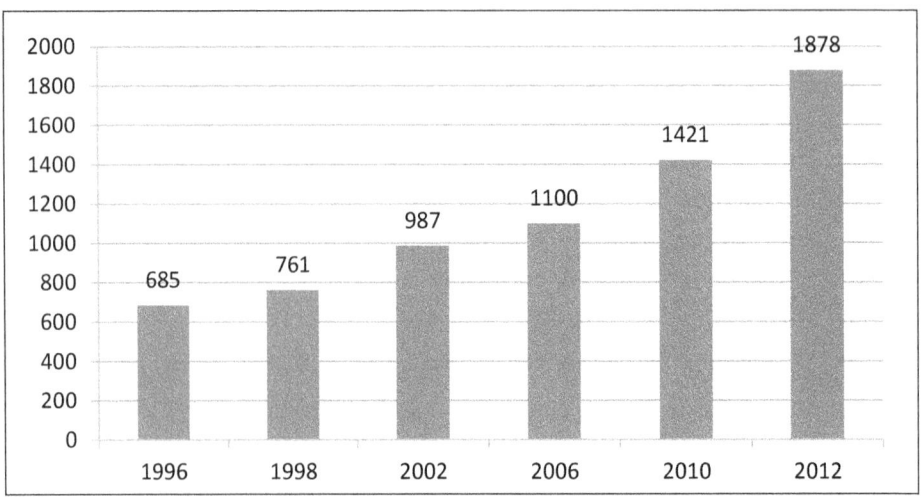

FIGURE 4.1 Doctoral graduates in South Africa per annum 1996-2012 (Source: Higher Education Management Information System (HEMIS) Tables 2 and 13 for all institutions 1996-2012)

Figure 4.2 indicates that the growth in the number of graduates is largely attributed to the recruitment of international students, which is another government policy aims at establishing South Africa as "a hub for higher education and training in the region" (NPC 2011,279) and a top destination for international students (DHET 2011, 40). International students constituted 19% of all graduates in 2000 and the percentage went up to 34% in 2010. The majority of the international students are from the Southern African Development Community (SADC) countries and the rest of Africa.

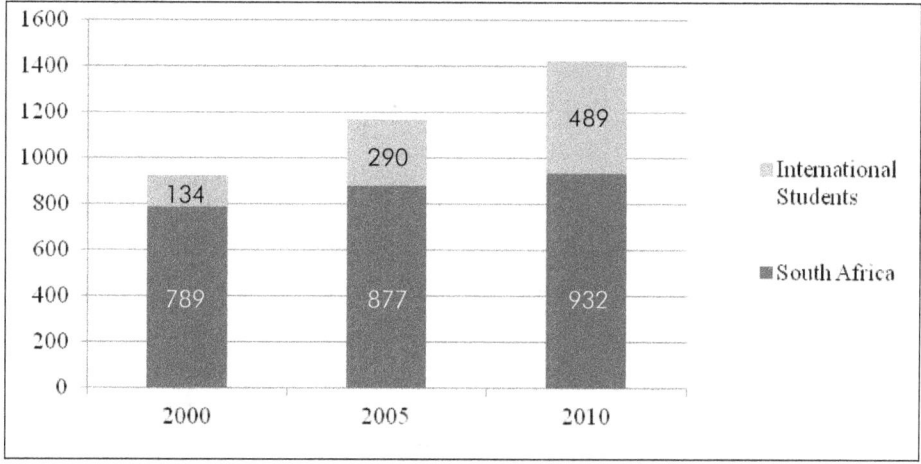

FIGURE 4.2 Doctoral graduates by nationality 2000-2010 (Source: HEMIS)

The analysis of the doctoral awards in terms of general fields of study shows that up to 2009 the highest percentage of awards was made in the field of the social sciences, while the lowest numbers came from engineering sciences, material and technologies. Since 2008 there has been a significant increase in the number of awards in the natural and agricultural sciences; and this increase may be an indication that the initiatives by the DST and NRF to increase the number of graduates in these fields are bearing fruit. However, the nearly flat line that is evident in the awarding of PhDs in Engineering Sciences remains a source of concern if South Africa wants to increase research and innovation in these fields (Figure 4.3).

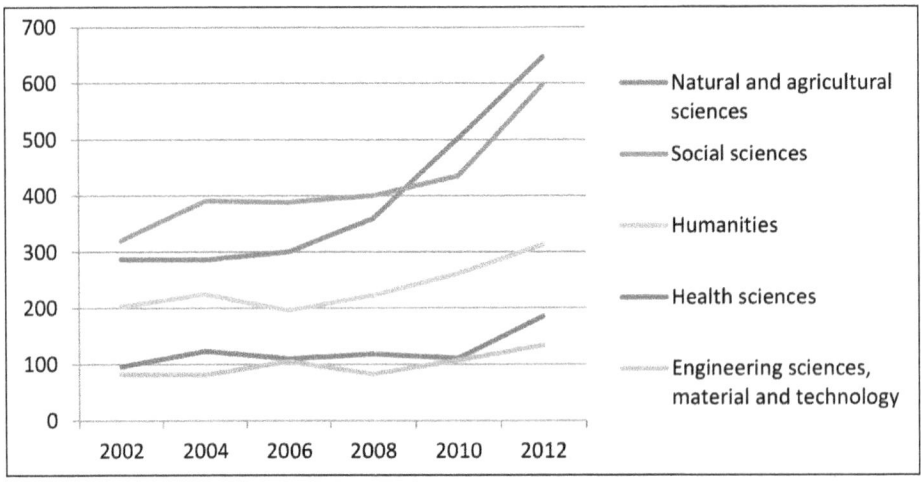

FIGURE 4.3 Doctoral graduates by field of study, 2002-2012 (Source: HEMIS)

Another policy initiative focused on increasing the number of women and black graduates. At the time of the transition to democracy, PhD graduates in South Africa were overwhelmingly white (87%) and male (65%). Fifteen years later, significant advances had been made, and in 2011 for the first time the number of African male graduates exceeded that of their white counterparts. However, the argument that the distribution of PhDs is not demographically representative is still valid (Figure 4.4). Women constituted about 42% of the total graduates in 2011.

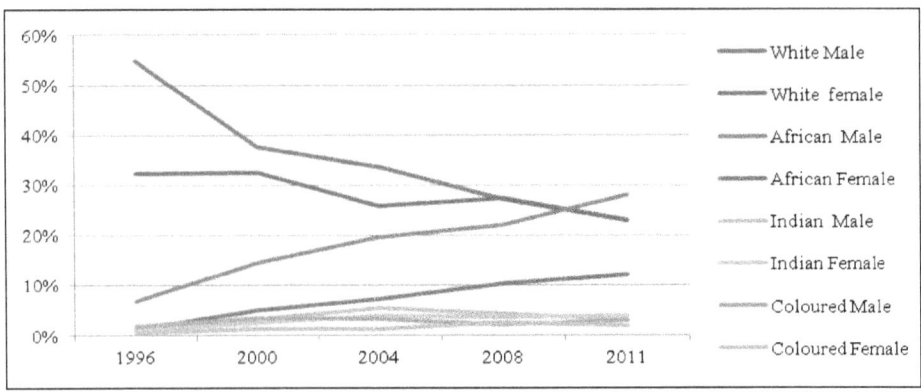

FIGURE 4.4 Doctoral graduates by race and gender 1996-2011 (Source: HEMIS)

While this improvement in racial representation is significant, it should be noted that the representation of non-South Africans is highest among black graduates. In 2011, 52% of the black graduates were non-South African, further adding to the argument about the shortage of black South African graduates (Figure 4.5).

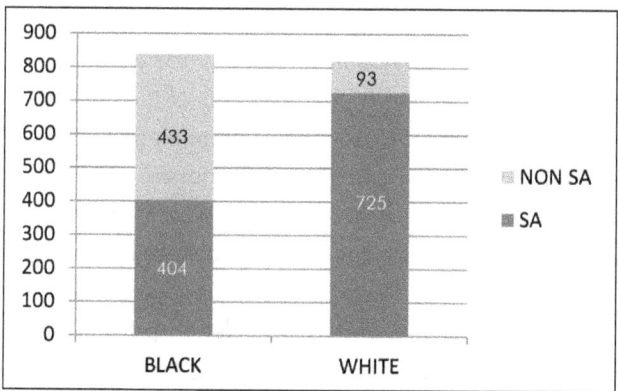

FIGURE 4.5 Doctoral graduates by nationality and race, 2011 (Source: HEMIS)

THE CURRENT STATE OF THE DOCTORATE: POLICY AND PRACTICE

With the spotlight on the doctorate as a driver for economic development, policy makers benchmarked the South African PhD in relation to other countries also identified as knowledge-driven economies. The picture was not very flattering. It appeared that in 2007 South Africa produced 27 PhDs per million of population per year while other middle-range knowledge economies produced between 100 and 250 PhDs per million of population annually (ASSAf 2010:46).

The first policy step was to set an indicator and to signpost the target in a quantitative manner, in other words, how many PhDs do we need in order to build a knowledge-based economy?

There were slight differences between documents but overall the target was set at 6 000 doctoral graduates per annum by 2018 (DST 2008) or by 2025 (NRF 2008), with 3 000 coming from the fields of science, engineering and technologies. More recently the National Development Plan's objective has been to produce more than 100 doctoral graduates per million per year by 2030, which implies an increase to 5 000 a year by 2030 (NPC 2011:66). While the common intent is a rapid and significant increase in the number of PhDs, these different goalposts could indicate the adjustment of policy to the realities.

The second step was to have a consensus report on how to meet the target. The Academy of Science of South Africa (ASSAf) commissioned a series of studies to provide evidence-based advice to policy makers on the status of the PhD and what would need to be done in order to escalate the number and quality of doctoral graduates.

Some of the studies were aimed at exploring what leaders of PhD programmes at universities as well as those working with PhD students in industry, national research facilities, centres of excellence, funding agencies or the end users of the PhDs think about the degree. The studies also investigated what models of training are used in effective PhD programmes and their purposes, strengths, weaknesses and threats. The research inquired about the barriers as well the enabling factors for students' success in these programmes, and what it would take to scale up these models. The studies followed what Elmore (1980) described as a backward mapping approach to policy development by starting with the end results in order to provide policy makers in South Africa with guidelines on what needs to be done in order to improve the quantity and quality of PhDs. The results of the various studies were published in 2010 (ASSAf 2010).

Drawing on this report the following findings are pertinent here. It was found that PhD programme leaders in South Africa tend to view the PhD as a preparation for academic career. Whether in law, humanities, science, education, mechanical engineering or the biomedical field, programme leaders appear to see the goal of the PhD as that of training lifelong scholars and thereby producing the next generation of academics. This view is underscored in the Backhouse (2009) study which identified similar attitudes. Backhouse interviewed supervisors representing pure and applied hard disciplines (mathematics and engineering) as well as pure and applied soft disciplines (English and development management). She argued that supervisors across the four disciplines tend to understand the purpose of the PhD as that of generating knowledge for undertaking research. That is Gibbons's Mode 1 type of knowledge.

Some academics who view the PhD as a preparation for academic life, were inclined to reject the view that South Africa needs more PhDs, articulating as their concern the fact that quantity means less quality and indicate their preference for a fewer PhDs with a greater impact. However, this view often raises the rebuttal that keeping the PhD elitist will perpetuate its racial inequality in the country.

Alongside this traditional understanding of the PhD as preparation for an academic career, there is also the view of the doctorate as an applied PhD, whose purpose it is to prepare students for a profession. The programmes in this mode often include some course work and cater for a large cohort of students. However, the implementation of this type of doctorate in South African universities has been highly dependent on individual or departmental entrepreneurial initiatives, sometimes with little institutional or policy support.

A third view sees the main role of the PhD as that of a service to industry. PhD programmes in the sciences are breaking disciplinary boundaries and forging different partnerships with industry, ranging from programmes which are exclusively established around the needs of an industry to those which attempt to find a comfortable balance between applied (Mode 2) and fundamental (Mode 1) research. While some supervisors feel that all knowledge should be applied, others feel that this is not the purpose of a PhD.

The ASSAf report identified a number of barriers that may stand in the way of expansion. Significantly it pointed out that the pool of potential doctoral students is too small. While some PhD programmes have to turn away students because of the lack of physical laboratory space or the lack of supervisory capacity, most programmes were struggling to find suitable students. Competition is rife for quality students and in particular for black quality students, especially (but not exclusively) in science and engineering. Some programme leaders recruit black students from SADC countries and from elsewhere in Africa in order to comply with the equity targets, as they have found that such students are generally better prepared and more dedicated than their South African counterparts and that they also have fewer family responsibilities (ASSAf 2010). Some PhD programme leaders face the challenge by beginning their recruitment efforts at undergraduate or honours levels thus 'growing their own timber'. The main reason for this practice is to ensure that the PhD students have a solid background knowledge and are capable of managing higher learning. At the same time this practice would limit the pool and the diversity of potential students. One way of escalating the number of PhDs could be to highlight this practice and to fast-track the process from honours degree to PhD. This would require an adjustment to the way universities are funded as such an innovation might mean the loss of the present university subsidy for master's degrees.

Most important, escalating the number of PhDs would also require decreasing the drop-out and repetition rates at undergraduate and postgraduate levels. CHET (2013) has undertaken detailed individual tracking analyses for cohorts of doctoral students entering the South African university system for the first time in 2001, 2002, 2003, 2004 and 2005. The average graduating rate after six years across universities in science and technology programmes was 55%, while the average graduating rate in the social sciences after six years was 51% for the 2004 and 2005 cohort.

The ASSAf report concluded that South African universities, on their own, did not have the capacity to deliver the expected target. One of the suggestions was to seek international collaboration as well as public private partnerships. Increasing the number of PhDs by forging partnerships with industry is complex. The ASSAf studies included interviews with a number of key people in major state-owned enterprises (SOEs) or public industries in South Africa, such as SASOL (South African Coal, Oil and Gas Corporation Ltd), Telkom (Telecommunication), Sappi (pulp and paper company group) and DeBeers (exploration, mining and trading of diamonds) as well as big private companies. These are the main industrial supporters of doctoral education in South Africa, whether through bursaries and subsidies or by providing training. While most industries provide financial support for the PhD as a social good, or even for the public image, answers to the question of whether the industry itself needs doctoral graduates differ greatly between those industries that have a strong focus on research and development (R&D) and those that require more operational skills (Herman 2013). So for example SASOL has a strong emphasis on R&D, and thus has a need for PhD graduates (Cele 2005). For some other industries, though, the PhD is not only unnecessary but is even seen in some cases as a luxury, with a master's degree providing sufficient skills. The low interest in the benefits of a doctoral education may therefore relate to the overall commitment to R&D in the country, which is low in relation to global benchmarks. The research conducted by Herman (2013) even detects a reluctance on the part of a number of industries to support doctoral students, a feeling strongly linked to the nature of industry in South Africa and to the perception that once they have graduated they will be lost to the companies and even to the country as part of the brain drain which is occurring from the developing to the developed countries. A great concern to the industry is the quality of the doctoral work based on the perception that universities in South Africa struggle to retain their top supervisors, despite industry initiatives which supplement the salaries of academics in key positions (Herman 2013).

A similar concern with quality and relevance was detected in a study seeking employers' perspectives on PhD graduates (CREST 2009). The study set out to survey institutions that specifically targeted graduates, such as science councils, national facilities, NGOs, other non-profit organisations and the government sector, as well as the private sector. Though the study was limited, the private sector employers felt that aside from business or financial administration, a PhD was an unnecessary degree. Employers in the fields of natural sciences and social sciences saw much value in the degree but identified a number of weaknesses with the South African PhD. These included the isolation of the graduates and their lack of exposure to international expertise and debates; the lack of quantitative and statistical grounding, a theoretical rather than a practical base, and weaknesses in conceptualisation and management of research reports and projects.

Another important barrier to the escalation agenda has to do with the supervisory capacity. Only about 36% of all lecturers at public higher education institutions have PhDs (ASSAf 2010:59). The CREST report assesses supervisory capacity as a ratio between the number of permanent academic staff with PhDs and the number of doctoral students. The norm was approximately two doctoral students to one doctoral staff member at universities and approximately 1.2 doctoral students per doctoral staff member at universities of technology. In reality, the supervision load is not shared equally among the academics with PhDs. Reputable and experienced supervisors with a good completion record may have 5-10 doctoral students, while others may have 1-2 students or even none. These ratios do not capture the full supervisory load of doctoral staff as some doctoral staff are responsible for supervising master's students (CREST 2009:13). In 2005 the ratio was 5.2 students per supervisor (CREST 2009). Furthermore, since higher education in South Africa has become teaching intensive, the burden of undergraduate teaching is high.

Other identified blockages in the system were the prevalence of the one-to-one model of supervision that may be a hindrance to escalating the number of PhDs, the bottleneck into higher postgraduate studies created by the honours degree, a lack of support for doctoral studies or recognition in the value of the award in all levels of society as well as policy that only recognised the traditional, academic PhD, while overlooking the role of the PhD as a producer of knowledge that is applicable to the workplace and the industry. The ASSAf report recommended that expanding the PhD requires a more flexible award which can facilitate innovation and collaboration.

Subsequent to the ASSAf recommendations, the NRF carried out a planning exercise in 2011, discussing what it would take to produce 6 000 PhDs per annum by 2020 (with the possibility of extending it to 2030, depending on financial constraints). This was the third step. The findings were published in a recent NRF document: *Scaling up the South African Research Enterprise 2011-2020* (NRF 2012). It suggested that the target of 6 000 PhDs in 2020 could be achieved by creating additional research chairs and centres of excellence and by supporting sandwich programmes – in other words, sending students to international partners. However, in order to do so the NRF would have to add by 2020 some R5.9 billion a year to the existing 2011 allocation level (NRF 2012). As I have mentioned, this was a planning exercise and not a commitment, but it nevertheless sends a clear message that enhancing the quality and quantity of the PhDs requires serious funding and political will.

The fourth step was to review some of the policies that relate to the PhD. This is ongoing and there are some processes and programmes in place. For example, the Department of Science and Technology (DST 2008) extended its programme to "Improve Academic Qualifications of Academic Staff and Researchers" and allocated funding to accelerate the training of doctoral students. Through this programme academic staff could take a sabbatical of between 6 and 12 months in order to complete their doctorates. The NRF also shifted its funding priorities from established researchers to new and emerging researchers.

Another policy change is the new HEQSF (DHET 2012), which attempts to develop a professional pathway as an alternative to the traditional PhD. The field descriptors of the different qualification have recently been published and the jury is still out on the impact this change will have on the practice (RSA 2013).

Professional doctorates are well established in the USA and have been so since the 1990s in Australia, New Zealand and the UK (Boud & Tennant 2006; Scott, Brown, Lunt & Thorne 2004; Servage 2009). Professional doctorates target mature students in their mid-career. They usually offer a fast-tracking doctoral research programme through the introduction of coursework, as well as the development of relevant professional knowledge. However, the system is not without its critics. There are questions about the quality and scope of the research that is carried out in such doctorates (Bitusikova 2009). It is argued that professional doctorates do not constitute a radical departure from the traditional PhD, and that the real differences lie in the target populations, in the selection criteria, and in the ability of the students to pay their fees (Neumann 2005, 2009). There is also the suggestion that the expansion in professional doctorates reflects entrepreneurial attitudes by universities, rather than a demand by the labour market for more doctorates (Servage 2009).

While introducing another type of doctorate might expand the number of PhDs it is possible that the introduction of professional doctorates to South Africa may not in itself help the country to become a knowledge economy. This is mainly because the DST/NRF vision emphasises increased PhD production in the sciences and technologies, whereas professional doctorates, with the exception of engineering, dominate the social services professions such as education, psychology, business and nursing. In other words, the professional doctorates do not serve the disciplines that are considered to be critical to the development of a knowledge economy. As a latecomer to the policy debate on doctoral education, South Africa can benefit from expertise of other countries. The trajectory and evaluation of professional doctorates in Australia, which are currently in decline (Pearson, Evans & MacAuley 2008), can serve as a case study.

THE WAY FORWARD

The backward mapping exercise indicates that there is a perception, especially among stakeolders in the industry and private providers, that some of the skills required for the knowledge economy can be provided by master's degrees, especially in engineering and technology. It shows the ambivalence toward the function of the PhD among supervisors as well as the end users, and highlights concerns about quality and capacity, all of which are serious challenges to the expansion drive.

At the same time the message was clear: we need more PhDs. Universities need more PhDs in order to keep up with the demand for higher education, especially master's degrees. Our society needs more PhDs so we can think differently about our social and political issues. We need more research and innovation. The main challenge for South Africa is how quickly the number of PhDs can be expanded while maintaining the required quality. Manuel Castells (2009), in a seminar discussing the ASSAf report, argues that there can be no compromise on the quality of the doctorate and that it is better to have a few good PhDs than many mediocre graduates. Only by building a cohort of good PhDs can we expand our supervisory capacity. Only good PhDs can change the end-user perceptions of the degree and enhance the value of the award. Similarly, Jonathan Jansen argues that we need doctoral research that will have practical, theoretical, emotional and personal significance if we want it to make any difference in the world of scholarship (Jansen 2011). Many of our doctoral students are actually in the field of academia. We need to make sure that the next generation of supervisors will have quality PhDs. Leo Rosten, a Jewish Polish teacher and academic, was quoted as saying in 1970, "First-rate people hire first-rate people, second-rate people hire third-rate people." By applying Rosten's law to doctoral education we can say, "First-rate supervisors produce first-rate graduates, second-rate supervisors produce third-rate graduates". The triumph of mediocrity means creating a chain reaction effect that will work against innovation, quality and originality.

In building the case for PhD expansion without compromising quality I suggest the following points of attention.

a)   Increasing supervisory capacity

There is an urgent need to train supervisors. A number of PhD programme leaders in South African universities stress that not enough is being done to ensure that inexperienced supervisors, such as recent PhD graduates, or unsuitable supervisors, such as those without PhDs, should not supervise doctoral students (Herman 2009). Formal training, monitoring and accountability of supervisors can counteract some of these problems. The departments or the institution can provide ongoing professional development to supervisors.

Monitoring the quality of the supervision needs to be part of a system for quality assurance in doctoral education. There is growing attention in Europe and elsewhere to issues of accountability, quality enhancement and the creation of a quality culture engaging management of doctoral education, based on both internal and external evaluation mechanisms (Byrne, Jørgensen & Loukkola 2013). Lessons learned from such systems could form a base for quality assurance processes in South Africa.

b) Introducing official part-time status

Another barrier to producing good quality PhDs is the pressure to produce more PhDs and to ensure that these should be completed in three to four years. Brenda Wingfield (2011) from the Faculty of Science and Technology at the University of Pretoria argues: "The last thing we need is 'rushed job' degrees or students who could have completed in that extra year, but have terminated their studies because of pressure to complete in a period inappropriate to them." Considering that many of our students are more mature, have families to support and are working full- or part-time, finishing the degree in 3-4 years often produces mediocre PhDs. A way forward could be an official part-time status for our PhD students, whereby completion time could be five to six years, without penalising our institutions, thus following other international examples such as Australia, the UK and Canada (Nerad & Heggelund 2008). This view is supported by Evans (2002) who maintains that having part-time enrolment can benefit those students who avoid full-time enrolment because of work, family or community commitments. At the same time, part-time enrolment can be an underlying force for the diversity of the doctoral student population and can support South Africa's expansion agenda, albeit at a slower pace.

c) A call for sustained dialogue on doctoral education in South Africa

Doctoral education in South Africa is in flux. The discourses of the global economy and government intervention are changing the way in which doctoral education is conceptualised, perceived and delivered. There is increasing diversity in the provision of the degree as well as diversity in the student population. Students are working at the boundaries of many sites and disciplines. It seems that South Africa is scoring some success in increasing the number of graduates, especially in natural and agricultural sciences, though not as quickly as it would like to. And maybe this is a good sign as we may not yet be ready to expand at a faster rate. The South African doctorate is at a crossroads between government policies, universities' histories, departments' traditions, disciplines' knowledge, the standards and ethics of supervisors, and the expectations and needs of the end users. In order to move forward we need to engage with these boundaries in a critical way and have a sustained dialogue on the role that academia and the PhD should play in knowledge creation. We need to dicuss what kind of doctorate we want our graduates to have, and how to ensure the quality of the award. We need to further explore the link between doctoral research and the country's position in the knowledge economy, and how we can graduate PhDs with the knowledge and competencies to contribute to scholarship, society and to the needs of South Africa's emerging economy.

REFERENCES

ASSAf (Academy of Science of South Africa). 2010. *The PhD study: An evidence-based study on how to meet the demands for high level skills in an emerging economy.* Consensus report. Pretoria.

Backhouse JP. 2009. Doctoral education in South Africa: Models, pedagogies and student experiences. PhD thesis. Johannesburg: School of Education, University of the Witwatersrand.

Bitusikova A. 2009. New challenges in doctoral education in Europe. In: D Boud & A Lee (eds). *Changing practices of doctoral education.* London: Routledge. 200-210.

Boud D & Tennant M. 2006. Putting doctoral education to work: Challenges to academic practice. *Higher Education Research and Development*, 25(3):293-306.

Byrne J, Jørgensen T & Loukkola T. 2013. *Quality assurance in doctoral education – results of the ARDE project.* Brussels: European University Association.

Castells M. 2009. Strengthening doctoral scholarship in the social sciences. Seminar presented at the Stellenbosch Institute for Advanced Studies (STIAS), Stellenbosch, 11 August.

Cele MG. 2005. Meeting the knowledge needs of the academy and industry: A case study of a partnership between a university and a large energy company in South Africa. *Industry & Higher Education*, 19(2):155-160.

CHET (Centre for Higher Education Transformation). 2013. *High level knowledge production: CHET data profiles of four universities.* [Accessed 8 May 2013] http://chet.org.za/files/resources/Ian%20Bunting%20Profiles%204%20Universities%205%20Feb%202013.pdf

CREST (Centre for Research on Science and Technology). 2009. *Employer study report.* Report commissioned by the ASSAf Panel on the PhD. Stellenbosch: Stellenbosch University.

DHET (Department of Higher Education and Technology). 2012. *Determination of the sub-frameworks that comprise the national qualification framework.* Notice 1040 of 2012. Pretoria.

DHET (Department of Higher Education and Technology). 2012a. *Green Paper on Post-School Education and Training.* Pretoria.

DHET (Department of Higher Education and Technology). 2014. *White Paper for Post School Education and Training, Building an Expanded, Effective and Integrated Post School System.* Pretoria.

Dobson IR. 2012. PhDs in Australia, from the beginning. *Australian Universities Review*, 54(1):94-100.

DST (Department of Science and Technology). 2008. *The 10 year plan for science and technology*. Pretoria.

Elmore RF. 1980. Backward mapping: Implementation research and policy decisions. *Political Science Quarterly*, 94(4):601-616.

Evans T. 2002. Part time research students: Are they producing knowledge where it counts? *Higher Education Research and Development*, 21(2):155-165.

Herman C. 2009. Exemplary PhD programmes in South Africa: A qualitative report of constraints and possibilities. Unpublished report commissioned by the ASSAf Panel on the PhD. Pretoria.

Herman C. 2013. Industry perceptions of industry-university partnerships related to doctoral education in South Africa. *Industry and Higher Education*, 27(3):217-225.

Jansen JD. 2011. The quality of doctoral education in South Africa: A question of significance. *Perspectives in Education*, 29(3):139-146.

Nerad M & Heggelund M. 2008. *Toward a global PhD? Forces and forms in doctoral education worldwide*. Washington: Centre for Innovation and Research in Graduate Education (CIRGE) and University of Washington Press.

Neumann R. 2005. Doctoral differences: Professional doctorates and PhDs compared. *Journal of Higher Education Policy and Management*, 27(2):173-188.

Neumann R. 2009. Policy driving change in doctoral education. In: D Boud & A Lee (eds). *Changing practices of doctoral education*. London: Routledge. 211-224.

NPC (National Planning Commission). 2011. *National Development Plan – 2030 Vision*. Pretoria.

NRF (National Research Foundation). 2007. *The South African PhD Project*. Pretoria

NRF (National Research Foundation). 2008. *NRF Vision 2015*. Pretoria.

NRF (National Research Foundation). 2012. *Scaling up the South African research enterprise 20112020*. Pretoria.

Pearson M, Evans T & MacAuley P. 2008. Growth and diversity in doctoral education: Assessing the Australian experience. *Higher Education*, 55(3):357-372.

RSA (Republic of South Africa). 2013. *Publication of the General and Further Education and Training Qualifications Sub-framework and Higher Education Qualifications Sub-framework of the National Qualifications Framework*. Pretoria.

Scott D, Brown A, Lunt I & Thorne L. 2004. *Professional doctorates: Integrating professional and academic knowledge*. Maidenhead: Open University Press.

Servage L. 2009. Alternative and professional doctoral programs: What is driving the demand? *Studies in Higher Education*, 34(7):765-779.

Wingfield B. 2011. Can we improve postgraduate degree throughput rates? *South African Journal of Science*, 107:11-12.

CONCEPTUALISING RISK IN DOCTORAL EDUCATION

NAVIGATING BOUNDARY TENSIONS

Liezel Frick, Ruth Albertyn and Eli Bitzer

INTRODUCING RISK

If you are not willing to risk the unusual, you will have to settle for the ordinary. – Jim Rohn

Risk-taking is an important form of human behaviour, but can be conceptualised in different ways (Byrnes, Miller & Schafer 1999). Some researchers in higher education point to the association between academic risk and its negative consequences (McWilliam, Lawson, Evans & Taylor 2005; McWilliam, Sanderson, Evans, Lawson & Taylor 2006; McWilliam, Singh & Taylor 2002) and therefore conceptualise risk as something that should be avoided or at least carefully managed. Others highlight risk as an opportunity for achievement (Backhouse 2009; Frick 2011, 2012; Holligan 2005). If innovation is key to the generation of new knowledge, then risk is seen to be an integral part of this process (Brown 2010). Knowledge and innovation are considered to be critical contributors to national wealth and welfare and therefore doctoral education has gained increasing significance within the context of human capital development (Bloland 2005; CHE 2009). In this context, the dynamics of balancing risk and innovation (Brown 2010; Latham & Braun 2009) may provide challenges for the supervisory relationship and the research process. Education – and more specifically doctoral education – seems to be risky given the requirement to produce original knowledge. Students need to have "the courage and confidence to take risks, to make mistakes, to invent and reinvent knowledge, and to pursue critical and lifelong inquiries in the world, with the world, and with each other" (Freire 1970, cited in Lin & Cranton 2005:458). MacKinnon (1970) agrees that the courage to take risks is an important characteristic of creative endeavours – such as doctoral studies. In this chapter we therefore take the position that risk is unavoidable within the context of doctoral education, but in order to extend the boundaries and manage risk constructively, supervisors could gain from understanding the concept of risk within this context.

This chapter takes up the question of risk in doctoral education with a particular focus on a number of ways in which the concept of risk currently operates in doctoral education. The discussion draws from a broad understanding of risk in doctoral education and the concept of risk in general, as well as a small-scale study with experienced doctoral supervisors across disciplines at one South African university. We propose that risk is not an inevitably negative concept which necessarily results in danger. Risk also seems to provide opportunities for increased and higher levels of scholarly performance and results. By identifying tensions and ways of containing risk, the boundaries of doctoral education may be challenged so that postgraduate supervisors may be better equipped to facilitate the process of student development towards an original contribution at a doctoral level. In this sense doctoral supervisors become boundary navigators.

RISK DEFINED

Risk seems to be a dichotomous concept. Byrnes *et al.* (1999) argue that risk can be either adaptive or maladaptive. In the latter case the potential hazardous consequences outweigh the potential benefits. Adaptive risk, on the other hand, does not mean avoiding all risk. Instead it refers to adapting successfully though pursuing some risks while avoiding others. Generally risk is defined in terms of risky behaviour with possible negative consequences, but it can also be defined in terms of adaptivity, rationality, and/or the importance of generic versus environmental factors in establishing human traits (Byrnes *et al.* 1999).

When defining risk in doctoral education there are four aspects that need consideration (based on the work of Byrnes *et al.* 1999). Firstly, risk is closely associated with goals, values and outcomes. It follows that if the goal is to achieve the outcome of a doctorate in the minimum allocated time, the risk of choosing a complex and less defined problem might be avoided. However, if the original contribution made though a doctoral study is valued, risk-taking may be encouraged. Secondly, risk involves interplay between an individual's subjective perception of risk and the perceptions of the larger community. What is perceived as risky within doctoral research may therefore be interpreted differently by students and their supervisors (who form part of larger institutional and disciplinary communities), and the outcome of such perceptual differences is determined by negotiation and power differences between the parties involved. Thirdly, individual skill determines to what extent actions are deemed as being risky. Thus, a research project may be less risky if the doctoral student has research and/or subject expertise. Fourthly, context is cardinal – for example, certain projects may become less risky if expert supervision and other resources are readily available in the doctoral context. It thus appears that the conceptualisation of risk reflects contradictory forces which relate to elements in the context, the relationships in the supervisory process and the outcome of doctoral education.

The context of doctoral education is pivotal as it influences both the processes and the outcomes. McWilliam et al. (2002:120) refer specifically to risk within higher education institutions as a management issue – "a system of rules, formats and technologies for communicating within and across institutions", which is intended to "shape who can take what risks and how" (Hood et al. 1992:136). Institutional emphasis on ethical conduct in research has placed the concept of risk regarding the process and outcome centre stage at higher education institutions. As such the conceptualisation of risk is primarily defined in terms of its potential negative consequences – risk-as-danger (McWilliam et al. 2005) – as is evident in the Framework Policy for the Assurance and Promotion of Ethically Accountable Research at Stellenbosch University that demands that all research be preceded by a thorough risk benefit analysis (SU 2012:2-3). Ethical risks relate primarily to the doctoral topic and project, which highlights "the danger to perform in ways that are morally and politically, as well as organizationally, acceptable" (McWilliam et al. 2005). This implies that risk is a double-edged sword which could cut both institutions and supervisors on the one hand and students on the other in scandalous ways. Thus risks in the core relationship are an added dimension. McWilliam et al. (2002) draw attention to further risks during the doctoral process ranging from co-authorship and plagiarism to 'soft' assessment, while McWilliam et al. (2005, 2006) add trivial thesis topics, suspect entry, rigour and assessment requirements, and dubious conduct and/or credentials to the list of possible risks at the doctoral level. Together with Golde (2005), these authors furthermore refer to long completion times and low completion rates (doctoral student dropout and attrition) which are a waste of resources and thus an institutional risk. Evans and Kamler (2003) and Paré (2010) point out the risks involved in doctorates via publication, where too much may be expected of students too soon. Defining risk is therefore not limited to identification of risks, but also to the calculability of risk factors and risk events which may ensue (McWilliam et al. 2006).

The institutionalisation of risk as danger is not surprising given the current worldwide emphasis on auditing and accountability within higher education. Given these definitions of risk, it is to be expected that supervisors' default conceptualisation of risk would lean towards a negative perception and thus supervision would be aimed at risk avoidance. There is a danger in what McWilliam *et al.* (2002) call a negative logic of risk, or risk avoidance (McWilliam *et al.* 2006), as it is essentially punitive in nature and may erode what Holligan (2005) refers to as scholastic autonomy and organic collegiate communities. Therefore supervisors' conceptualisation of risk is all the more important as supervisory, institutional and disciplinary constraints may impede creativity at the doctoral level and thus also the (expected) original contribution a doctoral student is able to make.

THE RISKY BUSINESS OF DOCTORAL SUPERVISION

Supervisors play a key role in doctoral students' understanding of the original contribution they are expected to create, and therefore also the extent of risk allowed in their research. Perez-Freije and Enkel (2007) noted tensions amongst team members in a creative endeavour. These authors state that balance is necessary between structured and disciplined operations and flexibility and openness in the approach, which McWilliam *et al.* (2006) refer to as risk avoidance versus risk mitigation. Delamont, Atkinson and Parry (2004:35) contend that supervision is based on the perceived tension between the need to guide and structure on the one hand, and the desire to preserve the student's autonomy on the other. Previous research (Backhouse 2009; Frick 2011, 2012; Holligan 2005) found that external factors – such as bureaucratic institutional systems, ethics and funding policies – may influence the extent to which risk-taking is possible in doctoral studies. Evans (2004) conceptualises the role of the supervisor as that of risk manager and risk mitigator, acting as an intermediary between the demands of society, the discipline(s) involved, the institution and the doctoral candidate – a position somewhat between a rock and a hard place given the pressures exerted from both sides on the supervisor(s).

Previous studies found that supervisors found it difficult to push knowledge boundaries by means of the postgraduate work they supervise, and took measures to limit risk-taking in order to ensure adequate doctoral student throughput and publication (Backhouse 2009; Frick 2011, 2012; Holligan 2005). Backhouse (2009:281) argues that through avoiding risk, supervisors may guide doctoral students away from an "exciting creative journey" towards a "series of cynical strategic choices" and "modest safe projects". By playing it safe, supervisors may actually deprive students of the opportunity to experience the real world of most research which can be messy, unpredictable and complex. Holligan (2005:270) warns that structures and guidelines offer a "mechanistic discourse of support" and may be useful to learn the rules that govern the academic game, but fail to induct novice supervisors and doctoral students into knowing how far institutional and disciplinary boundaries can be pushed. Scientific progress depends on pushing such boundaries through independent critical thought – a risky endeavour given the current emphasis on risk management and control (Pearson, Evans & MacAuley 2008). Both Backhouse (2009) and Frick (2011, 2012) argue that supervisors should support risk-taking as they guide doctoral students towards making an original contribution.

Previous studies have, however, not focused on supervisors' perceptions of risk in particular. This chapter explores whether doctoral education involves particular forms of risk for candidates and supervisors, as well as the direction and nature of the risk involved.

RESEARCHING RISK (METHODOLOGY)

A descriptive exploratory study was undertaken using qualitative data collected through conducting in-depth interviews with 11 purposively selected doctoral level postgraduate supervisors. Selection criteria for participants included context of supervision, discipline, and level of experience. Supervisors represented natural science (3), economics and management sciences (3), health and medicine (1), engineering (1), humanities (1), education (1) and theology (1) at Stellenbosch University (South Africa). In-depth interviews focused on how these supervisors conceptualised risk within doctoral education in their specific contexts. The interview schedule consisted of three guiding questions:

- How do you conceptualise risk in doctoral education?
- In what ways may risk play a role in your discipline in development of the original contribution at a doctoral level?
- How do you manage risk in your work with doctoral students?

Qualitative data analysis of transcriptions of the interviews was done with *ATLAS.ti* software. An inductive approach to qualitative content analysis was followed, according to the steps suggested by Henning, Van Rensburg and Smit (2004). This process of content analysis involved fine coding the data, categorising the codes and finally, identifying themes. Member checking was done randomly and data analysis was done by two researchers independently. The findings are reported below according to the themes we identified.

FINDING RISK: CONCEPTUALISATIONS OF EXPERIENCED SUPERVISORS

Experiences of supervisors revealed conceptualisations of risk at different stages in the research process. We report on the risks at each stage of the doctoral research process where risk was noted, including preparation and proposal stage, execution of the research plan and concluding the research. The findings relate to the risk at each of these stages and the strategies supervisors employ to support their doctoral students. Thereafter we present the conceptualisations of risk in the system and discuss how these risks influence the student and the supervisor.

Risk in the stages of the postgraduate research process: Preparation and proposal stage

The crucial preparation stage includes risks associated with conceptualising and planning which culminate in the proposal. Risks link to the type of project (more practice-based and developmental rather than scientific and research-based), unclear conceptualisation of the project, problematic topic selection (personal attachment to the topic, length and scope of the topic) and the nature of the research question.

The problem of a poorly conceptualised project is that the risks are exacerbated as the project progresses. Often students in particular fields such as education who enter the system are practitioners: "They are very able people, but they are not academics" (s7). They are students who find it hard to make the transition to research and understanding the nature of the scientific process and the depth and rigour required: "She thinks she is ready to do a doctoral study ... the subject is totally not a topic that you can use for a doctoral study" (s6). Byrnes et al. (1999) also note this type of risk due to differing perspectives. Supervisor 2 suggests that the focus needs to be on asking the student, "What is the intellectual contribution?" rather than the practical contribution of the study.

Often students want to take on complex problems. As supervisor 3 commented: "All the students that we get want to solve the world's problems." There is a risk that students read so widely initially that they battle to focus. This may be due to anxiety and insecurity in the new language of the field as well as being unsure of what constitutes a PhD study. The students may become overwhelmed by the volume of work, so guidance is needed.

Ways of overcoming risk include the prerequisite in some disciplines of having the proposal as a screening strategy to test whether the student has reached the level of clarification of concepts, context and the necessary focus: "You must first do the proposal, first get past the committee" (s6). Students also must retain the focus appropriate for their field of study.

Supervisors are expected to give strong guidance in the preparation stage to ensure that the project does not get too big (s6) and that the topic is relevant and novel so that the student can make a unique contribution (s4). Supervisors suggest that it is important not to accept students outside of their scope of expertise or interest (s10). Co-supervisors can be used where needed. Expectations of the requirements of the process, the personal cost to the student and the relationship need to be made clear at the outset. Some students have unrealistic expectations: "… the expectation that I come in here … I talk to my study leader and my study leader tells me what I should do" (s7). This dependence needs to be broken early in the postgraduate relationship as the student needs to takes ownership of the project and move to independence, especially at the doctoral level. Delamont et al. (2004:35) refer to the need to balance guidance and autonomy in supervision. Supervisor 2 asks the student, "What is the intellectual puzzle that you are proposing to research?" Sometimes this conversation about expectations with students makes them reconsider whether they are ready for the process or not. One supervisor (s2) sets as a proviso that the student read for 18 months in preparation for his or her studies.

The development of a generative relationship between the student and the supervisor was noted by supervisor 2. He "engages with the relationship between the person's identity orientation to a proposed study and moving from there to an intellectual orientation to that study that establishes the intellectual worth of the study". The essence of the support by this supervisor is intellectual grounding as well as contact and dialogue in developing scholarly depth. It may be necessary for the supervisor to find ways of supporting students in this phase when they may be feeling fearful and anxious at the newness of the field. Warhurst (2006:118) found learning to be a "painful process of becoming a different kind of person, of reconstructing identity". Clegg, McManus, Smith and Todd (2006:92) claim that the challenges linked to this level of learning are creative and hold the potential for new meaning making that should be valued. Meyer and Land (2005:375) suggest that this level of learning leads to transformed thought, to an identity transfiguration of adopting an extended discourse. A strategy to help students is through exposing them to fellow students who are at various stages in the research process and helping them to develop the language needed for the new field of study (s1). According to supervisor 3, the group setting helps students think critically as they are challenged by their peers. In the group setting the student develops critical thinking skills early in the process.

Risk in the stages of postgraduate research process: Execution of the research plan

In the execution stage there are risks related to data collection, analysis and writing up:

> The risk of the middle of course is … that people don't collect data of a sufficient quality. If you have done your data collection with the appropriate rigour, everything falls down. (s11)

> ... even though the PhD students design their own experiment and ask their own question, with input from me, there is always in the back of my mind, what happens if that does not come through? (s8)

There may be risks related to ethical issues (also noted by McWilliam et al. 2005) and access to data. Sometimes the response rate is insufficient and students may need to deviate from their original plan in their proposal. An example of this was noted by supervisor 6: "Then there was such thin superficial data that I had to say I am sorry we cannot go with this ... you need to conduct more interviews or include a focus group ... I did not allow it to go through to examination." Sometimes the response rate is so low that no conclusions can be drawn (s5). An example of risk with analysis is:

> And when I started to analyse the data, I came to totally different conclusions. And he did not do it on purpose ... it was a bona fide error ... He had actually got it wrong ... totally wrong. So, that is a risk. (s7)

Momentum is required during this phase of the project. In the data collection phase support is provided with project management skills. Regular meetings to discuss data analysis and provide help in this regard are offered by referring students to experts for assistance (co-supervisors or statisticians). Meeting with peers in colloquia also provides support as group members present sections of their work in this non-threatening environment. By being involved in dialogue, knowledge is created through "the construction and transformation of understanding through the tension between multiple perspectives and opinions" (Dysthe, Samara & Westrheim 2006:303). Colloquia encourage momentum and accountability (s5), which in turn helps with motivation (s3) and seems to be a common practice in departments. Supervisor 2 offers another strategy for maintaining momentum:

> [W]hat I am committed to, is to establish a process individually with them and ... in a collective process, so that they feed off each other ... I don't meet with them unless they give me 1-4 pages of writing ... So I establish momentum as well and I can engage with the writing much better. I establish a routine. I establish habits. (s2)

He also tries to give feedback within seven days to keep up the momentum. Supervisor 5 also emphasises the importance of momentum and notes that if students start procrastinating it is a sign that they have lost momentum. He will adopt an empowering approach and tries to engage such students and talk through the problem. If students are hesitant he will try to give direction.

In keeping the student on track and providing momentum, supervisor 8 tries to counter isolation:

> ... take a group of students to their site to help them, and that also always boosts them, so the risk there is the isolation ... because what happens in the group when one hits a low, there is another one that is on a high and they ride the wave with the one on the high, so it balances it out.
>
> ... the first-year students coming to the second-year students, passing advice on, techniques, that type of thing. It is like having each one to have ... a buffer between the student and myself, because they say a lot of the times the students are too embarrassed to come and ask me a simple question, about a simple technique.

Support is clearly vital during this stage but could be provided through group processes in addition to supervisor input.

Risk in the stages of the postgraduate research process: Concluding the research

Risk at the concluding stage includes the review process during the examination and publication process. The examination process poses risks not only to the student, who may be required to do extra work, but also to the supervisor's reputation and credibility, and to the department and the university.

> ... then a person feels that the supervisor is actually in the firing line together with the student ... so it is a great risk to get the student to the examination. (s6)

There may be hostility at this stage and there is much at stake for all parties: "... the examination process I think ... the more I see it, the more I doubt the fairness of that" (s7). The incorrect choice of examiner can influence the outcome, and problems such as selection of friends, inexperienced examiners, perspective and paradigmatic differences play an important role:

> You often don't find somebody who actually fits that bill or they are so overworked, because they get everybody's ... They need to be experts but they also need to deliver. (s10)
>
> ... although the CVs are submitted, supervisors choose their friends ... examiners look at the thesis from their own perspective ... invariably those conclusions are extremely biased. (s7)

There are risks involved prior to sending the dissertation for examination. Students may be tired of the project and want to conclude without the necessary higher conceptualisation having taken place. Students may have financial, personal or work constraints, and the supervisor may be pressurised to allow the project to go for examination to meet a deadline without having checked technical aspects or before it has reached a level of maturity and wisdom:

> ... because sometimes if you are rushing a thesis ... you might miss out on that critical kind of incubation period ... that sort of Einstein moment ... You start to see really what it is what you have found and how it connects to each other and the literature and ... then something happens. (s4)

> It can take a few months actually to really work on that ... suddenly there is a sort of you start synthesising and connecting ... then somehow there is a sort of magic that happens. (s11)

Early submission could influence the outcome and the unique contribution to knowledge required of the doctorate. This is a risk aspect also noted by Byrnes et al. (1999). At this stage the supervisor has a pronounced sense of risk and a decision needs to be made regarding whether to submit the thesis or not.

Supervisors have some suggestions which relate to intellectual development and peer review for monitoring the level of work: "It would be helpful to have an outside view as the supervisor seems to be too close to the project by the end of the process ... a round of quality control ... before the thesis is sent out for examination as they do overseas." (s9) Some supervisors encourage writing for publication as it helps students to conceptualise their work at stages along the way. Students are exposed to peer review, which also contributes to the intellectual development independent thought and integrative thinking:

> PhDs are written up in a form of a series of research papers so that the students get exposure to writing in a rigorous scientific style ... The danger there of course is writing a research paper – that is quite a tough thing to do. (s11)

> I find that if you have a thesis and you can say the following papers have already been published from this work, it sets the standard for the examiner. (s8)

The concluding stage, therefore, is a crucial risk stage which has implications for the system, the supervisor and the student.

Conceptualising risk: Risk as a reciprocal notion

There are reciprocal risks affecting the context, supervisor and student. The student is seen to be at risk if their level of preparation is unknown to the supervisors especially if students enter the system from a different university with different standards "which is a bit worrying, because you would like to take on external students, but you don't know what their background is in terms of: can they do this?" (s10). Examples of under-preparedness may be inappropriate research methodology or poor academic writing. If the student is underprepared, then the supervisor will be expected to provide more input to support the student. The risk to the supervisor is felt regarding their workload and the time it takes to do supervision. Due to the performance management system of the university, the supervisors are expected to supervise regardless of their expertise or desire to perform this task.

Lack of resources is a further risk with ramifications. Many students face financial challenges which jeopardise their progress and completion, so access to funding is vital. There is, however, tension between funded projects and motivation of students, as slotting into a funded project could influence student engagement. This debate varies across disciplines. Even though slotting into existing projects is common practice in the natural sciences, there is the risk of potential lack of engagement:

> [I]f it is primarily your interest and not the student's interest, then experience has taught me that the motivation to complete that study dries up relatively quickly … there should be enough interest to make the student excited … to complete the process. (s4)

The students' level of motivation is crucial and often the PhD product as goal is viewed as being a risk factor. "If someone walks in and says he wants to do a PhD and you ask, 'On what?' And he says, 'No, I don't know yet' … it can't work like that" (s3). Golde (2005) confirms lack of motivation as a reason for non-completion of postgraduate students. Risks for stakeholders therefore relate to preparation, support and resources.

CONCLUSION

The findings of the interviews with supervisors of doctoral students revealed that there are risks to various stakeholders (the system, student and supervisor) at the different research stages in the research process. The student enters the higher education system and the risks at this point relate to student selection and student preparation (previous research and disciplinary training) as well as resources. The student then engages with a supervisor who has certain levels of experience and expertise. The postgraduate relationship is the interface between the student and the supervisor. The stages of the research process (preparation, execution and conclusion) are conceptualised as the central core risks for these supervisors in their role in doctoral education. Supervisors report various strategies in these stages to support the students and mitigate risk. These can be summarised according to the following typology:

- **Student selection:** Clear expectations, determining and developing student capability, independence, analytical thinking skills, problem-solving skills, integrative thinking skills, creativity, and expectations

- **Conceptualising:** Wide reading, critical debate, benchmarking, time for incubation of ideas, challenging students
- **Skill development:** Academic writing, research methodological skills, incorporating expert input
- **Support:** Networking, colloquia, regular contact, communication, co-supervision; mentoring
- **Application:** Peer review, writing for publication.

Further research could explore innovative ways of balancing rather than controlling risk whilst encouraging creativity in the doctoral education process. The system where performance management is highly visible seems to predispose the supervision of students regardless of the supervisor's expertise and interest. This may lead to mechanistic supervision where control is valued to ensure throughput at an acceptable level rather than creativity which will contribute to knowledge and the expansion of science. Awareness of risk and the link to the positive component of creativity could lead supervisors to contain risk in a responsible manner. In so doing the boundaries of the conceptualising risk in doctoral education can be fruitfully navigated and even extended to ensure that a quality outcome and the original contribution to knowledge are attained in the doctoral process.

REFERENCES

Backhouse J. 2009. Creativity within limits: Does the South African PhD facilitate creativity in research? *Journal of Higher Education in Africa*, 7(1/2):265-288.

Bloland HG. 2005. Whatever happened to postmodernism in higher education? No requiem in the new millennium. *The Journal of Higher Education*, 76(2):121-150.

Brown L. 2010. Balancing risk and innovation to improve social work practice. *British Journal of Social Work*, 40:1211-1228.

Byrnes JP, Miller DC & Schafer WD. 1999. Gender differences in risk taking: A meta-analysis. *Psychological Bulletin*, 125(3):367-383.

CHE (Council for Higher Education). 2009. *Higher Education Monitor No. 7. Postgraduate studies in South Africa: A statistical profile*. Pretoria.

Clegg S, McManus M, Smith K & Todd MJ. 2006. Self-development in support of innovative pedagogies: Peer support using email. *International Journal for Academic Development*, 11(2):91-100.

Delamont S, Atkinson P & Parry O. 2004. *Supervising the doctorate*. 2nd edition. Maidenhead: Open University Press.

Dysthe O, Samara A & Westrheim K. 2006. Multivoiced supervision of master's students: A case study of alternative supervision practices in higher education. *Studies in Higher Education*, 31(3):299-318.

Evans T. 2004. Risky doctorates: Managing doctoral studies in Australia as managing risk. Paper presented at the Australian Association for Research in Education Conference, Melbourne, 28 November – 2 December 2004.

Evans T & Kamler B. 2003. Theses: For examination not publication? Paper presented at the 4th International Conference on Professional Doctorates, Brisbane, 29-30 November.

Frick BL. 2011. Demystifying the original contribution: Supervisors' conceptualisations of creativity in doctoral education. *Pertanika Journal of Social Sciences*, 19(2):495-507.

Frick BL. 2012. Pedagogies for creativity in science doctorates. In: A Lee & S Danby (eds). *Reshaping doctoral education: Programs, pedagogies, curriculum*. London: Routledge. 113-127.

Golde CM. 2005. The role of the department and discipline in doctoral student attrition: Lessons from four departments. *Journal of Higher Education*, 76(6):669-700.

Henning E, Van Rensburg W & Smit B. 2004. *Finding your way in qualitative research*. Pretoria: Van Schaik.

Holligan C. 2005. Fact and fiction: A case history of doctoral supervision. *Educational Research*, 47(3):267-278.

Hood CC, Jones DKC, Pidgeon NF, Turner BA, Gibson R & Bevan-Davies C. 1992. Risk management. In: The Royal Society (ed). *Risk: Analysis, perception and management*. London: The Royal Society. 89-134.

Latham S. & Braun M. 2009. *Closing the loop: Innovation and decline*. Academy of Management Annual Meeting, Chicago, IL. August 7-11.

Lin L & Cranton P. 2005. From scholarship student to responsible scholar: A transformative process. *Teaching in Higher Education*, 10(4):447-459.

Macauley P, Evans T & Pearson M. 2010. Australian PhDs by LIS educators, researchers and practitioners: Depicting diversity and demise. *Library and Information Science Research*, 32(4):258-264.

MacKinnon D. 1970. Creativity: A multi-faceted phenomenon. In: JD Roslansky (ed). *Creativity*. Amsterdam: North-Holland. 19-32.

McWilliam E, Lawson A, Evans T & Taylor PG. 2005. Silly, soft and otherwise suspect: Doctoral education as risky business. *Australian Journal of Education*, 49:214-227.

McWilliam E, Sanderson D, Evans T, Lawson A & Taylor PG. 2006. The risky business of doctoral management. *Asia Pacific Journal of Education*, 26(2):209-224.

McWilliam E, Singh P & Taylor PG. 2002. Doctoral education, danger and risk management. *Higher Education Research and Development*, 21(2):119-129.

Meyer JHF & Land R. 2005. Threshold concepts and troublesome knowledge (2): Epistemological considerations and a conceptual framework for teaching and learning. *Higher Education*, 49:373-388.

Paré A. 2010. Slow the presses: Concerns about premature publication. In: C Aitchison, B Kamler & A Lee (eds). *Publishing pedagogies for the doctorate and beyond*. Oxon: Routledge. 30-46.

Pearson M, Evans T & MacAuley P. 2008. Growth and diversity in doctoral education: Assessing the Australian experience. *Higher Education*, 55(3):357-372.

Perez-Freije J & Enkel E. 2007. Creative tension in the innovation process: How to support the right capabilities. *European Management Journal*, 25(1):11-24.

SU (Stellenbosch University). 2012. *Departmental Ethics Screening Committee (DESC) guidelines.* [Accessed 24 July 2012] http://www0.sun.ac.za/research/assets/files/Human_Research_(Humanities)_Ethics/DESC_Guidelines_Sept2012.pdf

Warhurst, RP. 2006. "We Really Felt Part of Something": Participatory learning among peers within a university teaching development community of practice. *International Journal for Academic Development,* 11(2):111-122.

PART THREE

DOCTORAL WRITING

DOCTORAL WRITING AS AN AFFECTIVE PRACTICE
KEEP CALM AND CARRY ON?

James Burford

INTRODUCTION

Does doctoral study feel like it used to? Judging by the tumblrs, blogs and Facebook posts I read, as well as snatches of conversation across the tearoom, it would seem that doctoral students are increasingly sore, stressed and feeling disappointed, anxious and guilty. Indeed, Roger Burrows has recently argued that the academy is threatened by a "deep, affective, somatic crisis" (2012:364). If this is indeed the case, it would seem pertinent for researchers to focus attention on the messy, ordinary and emotional lives of doctoral students, and the conditions under which they/we now study, labour and seek employment. As part of this broad project, I believe that it will be important to understand the changing role that writing and be(com)ing a writer are playing in the contemporary constitution of doctoral students. It is my contention that the permeations of managerialism, audit culture and the increasing 'metricization' (Burrows 2012) of writing is having significant impacts on the lives of not only academics, but doctoral students as well. In this time where graduates are 'without a future' (Mason 2012) and doing a PhD is a 'waste of time' given 'armies' of students competing for jobs (The Economist 2010), writing – and publication in particular – has emerged as the best known bet to secure a permanent academic position. It now seems older questions about doctoral writing may have been replaced by a growing list of them: Will I finish 'on time'? How can I maximise outputs? Which journal is most highly ranked? Is it ISI listed? What's the impact factor? And crucially, will the paper come out before I graduate so I can put it on my CV?

The boundaries I seek to exert pressure on in this chapter are those which have emerged around the study of emotion in higher education and postgraduate supervision. It is my argument that existing work could be extended by a consideration of 'affective practice' (Wetherell 2012). I believe that taking up Margaret Wetherell's work could better resource higher education researchers for the task of attending to the patterning and social circulation of affect. It might also prompt a shift from previous work, which has tended to construe the emotional as either absent or improper, in the classical Cartesian view of educating an "autonomous rational person" (Lynch 2010:59), or more latterly, a somewhat sparse palette of feelings located in the individual. In sum, I believe that taking up affective practice could invigorate the study of doctoral education, and contribute to the de-pathologisation, and de-individualisation of emotions within it.

This chapter is structured as follows: First, I briefly review the ways in which higher education researchers have understood, and worked with affect. Next, I introduce Wetherell's (2012) development of affective practice, with its linked concepts of flow, pattern, and power. Following this, I introduce my own doctoral study. I present an analysis that focuses on one case of a third-year doctoral student. Using the conceptual framework of affective practice, I explore the patterning of affect in this student's account, and discuss what such a patterning might reveal about contemporary practices of doctoral education. I conclude the article with reflections on the implications of this discussion for the practice of doctoral supervision.

AN AFFECTIVE TURN IN HIGHER EDUCATION?

In recent years there has been an 'affective turn' across the humanities and social sciences (Clough 2007). This 'turn' manifests as – and has itself manifested – a significant uptake in interest in the emotional as an object of study, as well as increasing attention to new epistemological and ontological questions that have arisen with it. It has seen the emergence of new edited books, journal special issues, conferences and scholarly journals (Davidson, Smith, Bondi & Probyn 2008). Importantly, for the purposes of this chapter, a review of recent research in higher education demonstrates a growth of articles that take up the vocabularies of this turn including 'emotion', 'passion', 'feeling' and 'affect'. Yet what seems to be missing at this stage of the conversation is an engagement with questions about how qualitative researchers might seek to trace affect, and what it might mean for the kinds of tools we take up to analyse it.

The first characterisation I would make of the field of higher education is that empirical research on the emotions remains thin on the ground. There are relatively few studies that have an explicit focus on doctoral emotions (exceptions to this include Aitchison & Mowbray 2013; Cotterall 2013; Herman 2008). At the conceptual level, however, there have been lively debates within the field about the appropriateness and potential consequences of a focus on the emotional (Ecclestone 2010; Ecclestone & Hayes 2009; Hey 2011; Leathwood & Hey 2009). Existing studies have tended to take up a defensive orientation in order to assert that the emotional is indeed a legitimate and interesting object of social inquiry. While there has been an increase in interest in the emotions and bodies of higher education subjects, in general this work has tended to construct affects as psychological states experienced by the individual. Frequently, the emotional is pathologised, with a focus on particular 'negative' and intense affects that may be diagnosed and addressed. In this chapter I am proposing an alternative approach, which might resist the individualisation and pathologisation of doctoral emotions. For example, rather than reading so-called negative affects such as depression or shame as individual maladies, I am interested in how these affective scenes might instead be described and interpreted as in social circulation, and as a consequence relational, economic and political. This requires a movement away from the restricted palette of emotions that are so often taken up in studies that use the conceptual tools of psychology. I am more interested in addressing the complexity of affective performances, scenes and events. This requires the ability to attend to more subtle emotional scenes such as *schadenfreude* (Magner 2008) or mixed ones like 'cruel optimism' (Berlant 2011) which such restricted palettes fail to observe.

A second and related issue is that a dichotomy of affects is often established – with some emotions rendered 'positive' (such as happiness, pride and relief) and others as 'negative' (such as anger, anxiety, guilt, shame, envy and disgust). Recent queer theoretical work on affect has shown the limitations of such a dichotomy, and has argued for the critical possibilities of working with 'negative' affects, rather than refusing, or seeking to transform them (Halberstam 2011; Halperin & Traub 2009; Ngai 2005). A final characterisation I would make of current studies relates to their analytic approach to affective phenomena. Many studies attempt to trace affect through first and second person speech acts (such as "I'm embarrassed" or "You're angry"). However, this has little congruence with the unannounced ways affect plays out in everyday life. What is required is a movement towards considering affective accounts through scenes, events and figures instead. Such a change in approach might also address the current tendency to focus on the dramatic, extreme and unusual rather than on more mundane and quotidian experiences, which may be characterised by more "fleeting, equivocal and muddled" affective scenes (Wetherell 2012:43). In sum, I argue that a new approach to affect in higher education is called for; one which can deal with specific affective phenomena, and trace their consequences. It is to one such promising approach that I turn next.

A NEW APPROACH: AFFECTIVE PRACTICE

The material I am mobilising to make my argument is drawn from a recent book by Margaret Wetherell called *Affect and emotion: A new social science understanding* (2012). In this work, Wetherell focuses on finding a pragmatic route for thinking about affect and emotion for social research, especially for researchers drawing on empirical material. For Wetherell, affect displays "strong pushes for pattern" (2012:13) and can be best explained and understood using the existing social science research platform of 'practice'. According to Wetherell a focus on affective practice draws attention to processes of "developmental sedimentation, routines of emotional regulation, relational patterns and 'settling' whereby multiple sources of activation and information about body states, situations, past experiences, linguistic forms, flowering thought ... become woven together" (Wetherell 2012:12). Three lines of approach are at the core of affective practice: flow, practice and power.

The first is flow. According to Wetherell, we must understand the body as a dynamic "flow immersed in other flows" (2012:31). As such, the affective activity located in our body is constantly being constituted and reconstituted. Wetherell argues that the flow of affect may become organised, or 'effloresce' with varying durations. For example, we can understand 'flow' by noticing how one affect such as panic, might emerge rapidly as we remember our looming supervision meeting; it may press upon our attention only to peter out minutes later – whereas other affective phenomena such as anxiety might be experienced as enduring background feelings, or 'atmospheres'.

The second foundational concept of affective practice concerns the patterning of affect. Wetherell argues that affectivities are practices, which may be interwoven with somatic, neural, phenomenological, discursive, relational, cultural, economic, developmental and historical patterns to form 'ruts' (Wetherell 2012). These ruts cut into the "social psychological life" of a community, becoming habit (Wetherell 2012:14). By taking affect as a practice, we can trace these patterns across a site or an institution, or widen our focus to examine the "affective citation" (Wetherell 2012:23) that subjects re-enact across a social category or historical period.

The third foundational concept of her rubric is power. Wetherell argues that global political issues, histories and identities are often refracted through "domestic, ordinary and wearing affective routines" (2012:7). This prompts her to ask questions about the regulation of affect, its uneven distribution and value. For example, who can take up what affective subject position? And, how does affective value come to be assigned to some figures and not others? A key word above is 'ordinary'.

For Wetherell, it is "ordinary demotic, affective action – which typically proceeds with little meta-commentary, self-awareness or reflexive fuss – which needs to be grasped" (2012:78). This has resonances with an archive of scholarship in cultural studies which has attended to 'ordinary' affects (Stewart 2007) and traumas (Cvetkovich 2003) or quotidian practices (Jagose 2010).

While some scholars have embraced the 'affective turn' because it offers a turn against discourse, in Wetherell's rubric the key concepts of discourse analysis remain useful. Combining aspects of discourse analysis with affective practice might encourage us to ask: what affective position or stance is this person taking up to describe events from? What broader discourses and cultural subject positions may be evident? And, what kinds of emotional characters are being formulated from moment to moment in the narratives being told? (Wetherell 2003, 2012). In the following section, I attempt to use Wetherell's rubric of affective practice to analyse two passages generated from my own doctoral study.

CATHERINE'S WRITING DIARY: 'MANAGING' TO KEEP CALM AND CARRY ON

Introducing empirical research

The empirical material I am drawing on comes from a study with 10 doctoral students in the faculties of humanities and social sciences at a research-intensive university in Aotearoa New Zealand. In generating data I have been guided by a desire to account more effectively for the affective experiences of doctoral writers, with an emphasis on producing an integrated reading of doctoral affect. Data was generated during 2013 using participant writing diaries, a residential writing retreat and semi-structured interviews. By taking up this set of methods I sought to generate material about both the domestic and ordinary affective routines of writing, as well as the sense-making that students apply to what it feels like to write and be(come) a doctoral writer. I chose to recruit students in the arts/humanities and education, as research suggests that these students experience higher rates of attrition (Cohen 2006) and are less likely to achieve standard doctoral writing outcomes, such as publication (Kamler & Thomson 2008). Rather than 'giving voice' to the stories of people as individual agents, I am using these accounts to understand the constitution of 'doctoral subjects' – that is, the series of affective positions these students inhabit.

For this chapter I have selected a single case, using just one of the methods of the larger study – the doctoral writing diary. I asked each participant to keep a diary over several months to record the actions, habits and affective textures of their writing practice. In my instructions to participants, I asked them to pay attention to the ordinary rituals and routines of their writing, what they do at various times of the day, week or month, as well as any experiences that seemed unusual. Participants were asked to record their embodied experience, where they are, and what it felt like. In selecting this particular case, I do not claim it is representative of the stories of other doctoral students. Rather, the account I present is intended to demonstrate how using affective practice as a framework combined with some tools from discourse analysis can generate distinctive understandings of affect and doctoral writing practices.

Introducing Catherine

Catherine (pseudonym) is a student in the third year of her PhD. She was the most prolific diary writer in the study, completing 14 entries over a two-month period, and generating a total of over 7 500 words. Catherine's diary entries ranged from short sketches of the shifting landscape of her emotions throughout her working day, to longer entries that explored how particular 'writerly' events such as publication or peer review felt, or how particular feelings such as rage seemed to effloresce. For this chapter I have selected passages from Catherine's second and third diary entries, which are included below.

> #### Writing journal 25-02-2013
>
> Today I managed to start writing my methodology section. I procrastinated no longer and I started writing. This process is perhaps a little more like crafting as I have three things that I have written already about my methodology. So I can recycle. This somehow makes it feel less daunting. It isn't easy to bring the three together as each have different purposes and use different analytic frames and metaphors, but somehow I feel better starting already close to my word count target of 10-12,000 words. I have set myself the target of writing 1 000 words a day, or 500 in a half day. I do this to try and motivate myself, but also to get some sense of achievement from the writing that can feel like tiny slow steps.
>
> Before I start, and in the early stages, I distract myself with some planning. I write my to do list for the week. I haven't done this since January but it now feels like I have too much to do to just rely on my intuition to manage my time. I have seven things to write, including two chapters, four papers and a workshop. That makes me feel quite scared and so I then start to break these down into numbers of words and how much I can write in a given time and this makes me feel better, it feels more manageable broken down like this. I have a nice plan for my thesis for the first time, I can add this to the increasing number of things being taped to the walls around my desk …

Writing journal 28-02-2013

… My writing has not really gone as I optimistically planned at the start of the week. I have not met my target of 500 words each half day and have even spent extra time in the evenings to try and catch up, but still not met my target. The first issue is that I end up going back over and rewriting what I have written the previous day, I can waste a lot of time honing this as it is easier than starting a new section. I need to stop this habit. I also suddenly got uncertain about some of the theory I was using and felt like I needed to go back and re-read a lot of material to clarify this. Finally I got stuck on whether I needed to make one point before I could move on to the point I really wanted to make. This is the difficulty I think with my way of writing, I don't have a rigid plan and like to let the shape and direction evolve (mutate) as I write, but sometimes this means I either write something that later is not relevant or I get stuck trying to get somewhere, I write myself off on a tangent or into a corner.

THE FIGURE OF THE RATIONAL EMOTION MANAGER

The fragments above are unlikely to be identified as 'emotional' in any common sense of the word. The text may read as relatively ordinary and mundane; a doctoral student set a writing goal, and subsequently failed to meet it. It is my argument that the banality of this material is precisely what makes it important, and so interesting to examine. I have a hunch that focusing on ordinary episodes like this might even help researchers to illuminate the consequences of similarly ordinary phenomena, such as a culture of audit and precarious labour conditions that are weaved throughout the scene of doctoral education. I will use Wetherell's work, which I introduced earlier, to help me make a preliminary analytic sketch of Catherine's two diary entries.

From a close reading of the texts I suggest that Catherine repeatedly took up the subject position of the 'writing manager'. Indeed, she used the word 'manage' three times in the first extract. To manage her writing Catherine used a number of strategies commonly called for in doctoral advice texts and writing workshops, including chapter word counts, daily word targets, to-do lists, and planning in order to 'manage' her workload. In the position of the writing manager Catherine is able to assess her own performance. While her "optimism" in setting the word count goal had not been realised, and she failed to meet her goals, and "manage" her writing, as a writing manager Catherine was able to diagnose her writing challenges. She identified "issues" and "difficulties" to address (for example. rewriting and honing) and "habits" to discontinue. There is of course a moral value attached to enacting these strategies. Catherine marked herself as a disciplined writer, even if she failed to meet her own word targets. We might read this scene as evidence of a technology of self that brings into being the self-monitoring and responsibilised 'good-student' idealised by the neoliberal university (Grant 1997).

Using Wetherell's framework, I'd like to go beyond what Catherine told us about her writing practice, to also look for affective practices in the text. We might describe the scene of Catherine's writing practice as a swirling affective soup, involving feelings of engulfment, anxiety, fear and frustration. Interestingly, Catherine repeatedly moved to not only manage her writing, but also to manage her affects, by taking up the affective subject position of the 'emotion manager'. In taking on this affective subject position, Catherine constituted herself as a student who is able to diagnose her own writing challenges, and ameliorate various negative affects. We can see her take up this affective subject position at least twice through the text. If we look at this sentence, we can see the pattern most clearly:

> <u>I have seven things to write, including two chapters, four papers and a workshop.</u> *That makes me feel quite scared* **and so I then start to break these down into numbers of words and how much I can write in a given time and** *this makes me feel better,* it feels **more manageable broken down** like this.

The underlined text at the beginning gives us clues to the context of Catherine's labour. This heavy workload suggests an affective scene of engulfment, and as Catherine noted herself, her fear of the "daunting" task of writing two chapters, four journal articles and a workshop. This amount of writing "isn't easy". But we also need to examine what Catherine did as these affects emerged. She "breaks" things down "into numbers of words" and "how much I can write in a given time". It could be argued that this breaking down is not only about numbers and words – it also appears to be a form of breaking down feelings of engulfment and fear. Indeed, Catherine "feels better" once words, numbers and feelings are dismantled in this way. This affective performance is very reminiscent of the 'Keep Calm and Carry On' meme that is so emblematic in our current cultural milieu, structured as it is by wars, austerity, and other crises. Catherine carries on, managing these affects with the strategies identified above, but also through engaging alternative affective practices of calmness, penitence and even bravery.

In examining how Catherine took up the affective subject position of the emotion manager I would like to make full use of the potential meanings of 'management'. In the first sense, Catherine appeared to 'manage' her affect by being a manager – a person in charge, a leader or commander. She is a self-manager, in the way that academics and doctoral students are now supposed to be, as autonomous and self-regulating academic workers (Gill 2009). Catherine can manage or control her writing, and also manage her affects. This meaning seems to connect to existing work produced around emotion management in the workplace which has illuminated the way in which emotion is often rendered as an oppositional narrative to the valued position of reasoned professionalism (Dougherty & Drumheller 2006). Higher education work in this vein has tended to identify the ways in which academics control and contain their emotions in culturally accepted ways given the tacit 'feeling rules' of the academy (Bloch 2002). Yet, there are other ways in which we might read Catherine's emotion management. Catherine also seemed to 'manage' her affects in an instrumental sense, by accomplishing, achieving or bringing about writing. By this I mean that writing is something that she managed to do, at least sometimes. The third meaning of management is the one I am most interested in pursuing in the remainder of this chapter. It is a meaning that is perhaps most easily conveyed through a question, such as: Will you be able to manage without it? This is managing as coping, making do, carrying on, muddling through, or surviving. This kind of management, particularly the notion of 'surviving' the PhD is a variation on a remarkably prevalent cultural and educational narrative (for example, each of these postgraduate advice texts uses the word 'survivor' in its title: Chakrabarty 2012; Hume 2005; Karp 2009; Mathiesen & Binder 2009; Murray 2009; Rittner & Trudeau 1997; Waring & Kearins 2011).

To understand this better I suggest that we need to pay close attention to the clues we have about Catherine's context. Catherine constituted herself as 'worried' and 'scared' as well as 'stuck' and 'procrastinating'. She 'beats herself up' about 'bad academic habits', which she states were highlighted in feedback received from reviewers of a journal article she had recently submitted. If we read her affective scene alongside the context of her academic labour, we remember that Catherine was not only writing her thesis, but was simultaneously working on publishing four separate papers and delivering a workshop. Catherine's affective scene may be described as one of engulfment; she appeared to be overwhelmed with writing responsibilities. Given this heavy workload, it is no wonder that the temporalities of her life were being governed by work: "[I] have even spent extra time in the evenings to try and catch up, but still not met my target." In her first diary entry on 14 February 2013, Catherine noted that so much writing hurt:

> I have had problems with my right shoulder over these past two years and so I am trying to find ways to reduce the strain on it. I use my left hand to operate the mouse now and I use speech to text when I use my laptop at home.

There is some consistency between Catherine's diary, the accounts of other participants in my cohort, and my own experience as a doctoral student. It is not just that observations about workload, and arguments about planning and discipline are often repeated; it appears there is also the repetition of a certain relation to affect. If we return to Wetherell for a moment, we could argue that Catherine's 'rational emotion management' is normatively organised as a part of socially recognised affective practices. This means that Catherine's calm and 'responsible' management of her writing and emotional performance was not random, or the result of some sort of innate biological drive toward calmness, and order – instead, its meaning is composed from the patterning of her ordinary activities.

My interpretation here is also consistent with Aitchison and Mowbray's (2013) work on the emotional management of doctoral women. As in Catherine's case, these authors found that doctoral students sought to channel their affects toward so-called productive writing behaviours. They identify the supervisor-student relationship as a site where the 'feeling rules' (Hochschild 1979) of the academy are enacted with great care. In order to maintain face when receiving feedback, students recounted attempts to act "as they imagined was expected" remaining "calm, objective and rational" and "disciplin[ing] their emotions" (Aitchison & Mowbray 2013:6). If we return to Wetherell's (2012) rubric on affect, we can begin to see how the 'affective flow' of Catherine's excerpt can be read as articulating within extensive social changes, including neoliberal transformations of higher education.

WRITING, AFFECT AND THE PRECARITY OF ACADEMIC LABOUR

To explore this further it is helpful to introduce an emerging body of research focused on the contemporary conditions of academic labour (Burrows 2012; Gill 2009; Pelias 2004; Sparkes 2007; Thatcher 2012). An increasing number of these scholars have identified 'precariousness' as one of the defining features of contemporary academic life – particularly for younger, or 'early career' academics, a claim which I, and others (Prasad 2013), have extended to doctoral students as well. Common features of precarious academic labour include an increase of temporary contact jobs, anxiety in finding and keeping work, poor pay, long hours, the muddying of boundaries between work and home, high levels of mobility, and passionate attachments to work and the identity of being an 'academic' (Gill 2010). This precarity can be clearly felt by doctoral students in Aotearoa New Zealand, with the rapid and rather brutal postgraduate education policy changes implemented by the National-led government in 2012-2013. These included the crippling of student unions through the passing of voluntary student membership legislation, and the abolition of the postgraduate student allowance, even for students partway through study.

I believe that writing is a helpful site to examine the affective consequences of precarity. As a number of scholars have noted, it appears that the performative technologies that audit and evaluate writing are associated with particular affective figurations (Burrows 2012; Gill 2009). It may be then no surprise that Catherine is feeling anxious and overwhelmed. Her institution expects her to submit her PhD thesis 'on time'. This has been clear from the first days of her enrolment. Catherine has been tracked, and is expected to meet certain 'progress' goals within a specified timescale, with the threat of a suspension of her stipend should she fail to meet or even report on these goals. The 'on-time' submission itself is not one that has been negotiated by Catherine and her supervisors, in recognition of the particular needs of her doctoral research – it is a standard timescale established by the institution and 'managed' by administrative staff, her academic supervisors, and, as I have shown here, Catherine herself. This timescale responds to the reality that The Government will not fund the institution for Catherine's enrolment past the time allotted, unless there have been exceptional circumstances during her candidature. Indeed, Catherine herself will be without the income of her doctoral stipend if her study extends beyond three and a half years. She will be expected to pay tuition fees, and her supervisors will come under increasing pressure to swiftly 'manage' her completion.

Yet, as blogs, advice texts or academic job advertisements reveal, finishing a PhD may not be enough to pursue an academic career. In order to create an employable 'CV self' Catherine is also expected to 'manage' to publish a 'reasonable' amount of peer-reviewed papers. This is an expectation felt especially by candidates seeking to enter the competitive academic employment markets of the Global North, given the ways in which publication is now used to measure both personal and institutional performance. A number of authors have argued that this fetish for publication metrics (Larsson 2009) has been internalised by academics, and emerges as a "reflexive surveillance of the self" (Lynch 2010:55). Feelings about our own sense of worth and intellectual value seem to have become coupled with the abstract performance levels implied by these measurements. Indeed, many of us may have overheard, or ourselves felt the pride and satisfaction of 'measuring up', but I suggest that this may come at the expense of other ways of feeling about writing. We might read the beginnings of this too in Catherine's account – it is accomplishing the word count itself that is reported as the 'achievement' and the 'tiny slow step', rather than other aspects of her writing development.

If academic writing has come to represent our value and worth as (future) academic workers, it is no wonder that many students feel under pressure to write. But crucially, it seems that this pressure is often experienced as individual and private. This is a result of what Gill (2010:240) refers to as the "individualising discourse" of academic labour:

> [It] devours us like a flesh-eating bacterium producing its own toxic waste – shame: I'm a fraud, I'm useless, I'm nothing. It is deeply gendered, racialised, classed, and connected to biographies that produce very different degrees of entitlement. Some may conclude that they aren't good enough, but others have already devised solutions: I must try harder, read more, understand theory better, and so on, the solution for us 'good' neoliberal subjects is simply to work even harder.

Gill asks us to think how the 'failures' of writing are viewed as moral failures which attach to the academic, or in this case, the doctoral student. This is an affective performance of disappointment in the self. We can note the self-blame that runs through Catherine's diary, and the way she draws on the language of pathology. In her three diary entries Catherine describes herself as "distracted", "procrastinating" and practising "bad habits". She addresses these bad habits with the penitence of writing at home in order to "catch up". For Gill and Pratt, her affective practices of personal responsibility, management and self-blame might best be seen as "toxic, individualised but thoroughly structural feature[s]" of the neoliberal university (2008:23). Indeed, Catherine and many other doctoral students, me included, are encouraged into these affective positions by a whole assemblage of work on writing, from advice texts, writing blogs, and writing workshops run by higher education institutions.

Altogether, these critical takes on contemporary academic labour are important for the study of doctoral emotion. By connecting particular patterns of feeling with the increasing precarity (Gill 2009) and metricization (Burrows 2012) of academic labour, these scholars open up questions of social justice. They encourage us to think against discourses which individualise emotions as the responsibility of the 'professional' scholar, and instead talk about employment conditions which lead to 'affective crisis' (Burrows 2012). In the remainder of this chapter I will advance some possible responses that supervisors might consider in their work alongside doctoral students.

WHAT MIGHT THIS MEAN FOR PRACTICES OF SUPERVISION?

In line with the arguments I have made above, doctoral supervisors might seek to perform a number of interruptions. The first could be to play their part in dismantling the idea of the 'aristocracy' of doctoral labour (Leung, De Kloet & Chow 2010). This frames scholarship as a noble vocation, and has the effect of muting discussion about financial compensation, job security and labour conditions. Another potentially profitable route may be to encourage doctoral students to form collectives. This could take shape as either *ad hoc* support groups, or more organised unions, such as the development of the Postgraduate Workers Association in the UK (Thatcher 2012). Such collectives can move to resist economic exploitation of postgraduate students, and proliferate counter discourses, which resist attempts to individualise responsibility for the problems caused by institutional and national policies and global economic forces. I am also rather fond of the technologies of resistance suggested by Leung *et al.* (2010). These include a politics of extravagant, outrageous and creative whining, an ethics of slowness, collaborative work and alternative publication strategies (Leung *et al.* 2010). Supervisors might engage important questions with their students directly such as: Why is it that any emotional burdens of writing seem to be shouldered by the individual student? Or, are the 'go-getting' feelings of passion and enthusiasm the best, or only available affective practices for 'good' doctoral writing practice?

CONCLUSION

The integrated rubric of affective practice provides researchers with helpful tools to examine the affective lives of our higher education communities. In this chapter I have paid particular attention to one affective performance by a participant – Catherine. I have argued that an important affective subject position taken up by Catherine is the rational emotion manager. I tentatively argue that the layering and re-layering of this relation to affect has solidified and become habit. And even more tentatively, I suggest that this layering might not be anchored to Catherine alone, or even the particular institutional site of my research – but it may apply more broadly to the figure of the doctoral student across a number of places. I am proposing that we can see particular kinds of emotional subjects becoming repetitively constituted in and through doctoral education. This seems to invite a number of other questions, such as: Who can take up the affective subject position evident in Catherine's excerpt? And, how might this have changed over the past decades? While it seems to be stubborn, how might it be moveable? Rather than managing to Keep Calm and Carry On, could Catherine mismanage her writing and affect in order to Raise Hell and Change the World?

In concluding I would like to advance a modest claim: considering affective practice may be helpful for future studies of doctoral supervision. Using Wetherell's ideas might enable researchers of supervision to consider why some people invest in particular affective subject positions and performances rather than others. For doctoral students, and supervisors, this could open up new pathways for appreciating our affects. Indeed, identifying the affective patterns that have congealed around our writing practices might enable us to question whether they continue to work for us, or not. We might even feel encouraged to explore affective figurations that are not yet imagined.

REFERENCES

Aitchison C & Mowbray S. 2013. Doctoral women: Managing emotions, managing doctoral studies. *Teaching in Higher Education*. doi: 10.1080/13562517.2013.827642

Berlant L. 2011. *Cruel optimism*. Durham: Duke University Press.

Bloch C. 2002. Managing the emotions of competition and recognition in academia. In: J Barbalet (ed). *Emotions and sociology*. Oxford: Blackwell. 119-131.

Burrows C. 2012. Living with the h-index? Metric assemblages in the contemporary academy. *The Sociological Review*, 60(2):355-372.

Chakrabarty P. 2012. *A guide to academia: Getting into and surviving grad school, postdocs,and a research job*. Chichester: Wiley-Blackwell.

Clough P (ed). 2007. *The affective turn: Theorizing the social*. Durham: Duke University Press.

Cohen P. 2006. The writing on the wall: Doctoral education in Texas and elsewhere. *Change:The Magazine of Higher Learning*, 38(6):42-48.

Cotterall S. 2013. More than just a brain: Emotions and the doctoral experience. *Higher Education Research and Development*, 32(2):174-187.

Cvetkovich A. 2003. *An archive of feelings: Trauma, sexuality and lesbian public cultures*. Durham: Duke University Press.

Davidson J, Smith M, Bondi L & Probyn E. 2008. Emotion, space and society: Editorial Introduction. *Emotion, Space and Society*, 1(1):1-3.

Dougherty D & Drumheller, K. 2006. Sensemaking and emotions in organizations: Accounting for emotions in a rational(ized) context. *Communication Studies*, 57(2):215-238.

Ecclestone K. 2010. Promoting emotionally vulnerable subject: The educational implications of an 'epistemology of the emotions'. *Journal of the Pacific Circle Consortium for Education*, 22:57-76.

Ecclestone K & Hayes D. 2009. *The dangerous rise of therapeutic education*. London: Routledge.

Gill R. 2009. Breaking the silence: The hidden injuries of the neoliberal university. In: R Ryan-Flood & R Gill (eds). *Secrecy and silence in the research process: Feminist reflections*. Oxon: Routledge. 228-244.

Gill R & Pratt A. 2008. In the social factory? Immaterial labour, precariousness and cultural work. *Theory, Culture & Society*, 25(7/8):1-30.

Grant B. 1997. Disciplining students: The construction of student subjectivities. *British Journal of Sociology of Education*, 18(1):101-114.

Halberstam J. 2011. *The queer art of failure.* Durham: Duke University Press.

Halperin, D & Traub, V (eds). 2009. *Gay shame.* Chicago, IL: University of Chicago Press.

Herman C. 2008. Negotiating the emotions of change: Research, restructuring and the doctoral student. *South African Journal of Higher Education,* 22(1):100-115.

Hey V. 2011. Affective asymmetries; Academics, austerity and the mis/recognition of emotion. *Contemporary Social Science: Journal of the Academy of Social Sciences,* 6(2):207-222.

Hochschild A. 1979. Emotion work, feeling rules and social structure. *American Journal of Sociology,* 85(3):551-575.

Hume K. 2005. *Surviving your academic job hunt: Advice for humanities PhDs.* New York: Palgrave Macmillan.

Jagose A. 2010. Counterfeit pleasures: Fake orgasm and queer agency. *Textual Practice,* 24(3):517-539.

Kamler B & Thomson P. 2008. The failure of dissertation advice books: Toward alternative pedagogies for doctoral writing. *Educational Researcher,* 37(8):407-514.

Karp J. 2009. *How to survive your PhD: The insider's guide to avoiding mistakes, choosing the right programme, working with professors, and just how a person actually writes a 200-page paper.* Naperville, IL: Sourcebooks.

Larsson S. 2009. An emerging economy of publications and citations. *Nordisk Pedagogik,* 29:34-52.

Leathwood C & Hey V. 2009. Gender/ed discourses and emotional sub-texts: Theorising emotion in UK higher education. *Teaching in Higher Education,* 14:429-440.

Leung H, De Kloet J & Chow Y. 2010. Towards an ethics of slowness in an era of academic corporatism. [Acessed 13 May 2013] EspacesTemps.net. Available at http://www.espacestemps.net/document8318.html

Lynch K. 2010. Carelessness: A hidden doxa of higher education. *Arts & Humanities in Higher Education,* 9(1):54-67.

Magner D. 2008. A little schadenfreude, anyone? *The Chronicle of Higher Education.* [Accessed 2 September 2013] www.chronicle.com/blogs/onhiring/a-little-schadenfreude-anyone/777

Mason P. 2012. The graduates of 2012 will survive only in the cracks of our economy. *The Guardian.* [Accessed 2 September 2013] www.theguardian.com/commentisfree.2012/jul/01/graudtae-2012-survive-in-cracks-economy

Mathiesen J & Binder M. 2009. *How to survive your doctorate: What others don't tell you.* Maidenhead: Open University Press.

Murray R. 2009. *How to survive your viva.* Maidenhead: Open University Press.

Ngai S. 2005. *Ugly feelings.* Cambridge: Harvard University Press.

Pelias R. 2004. *A methodology of the heart: Evoking academic and daily life.* Walnut Creek,CA: Altamira Press.

Prasad A. 2013. Playing the game and trying not to lose myself: A doctoral student's perspective on the institutional pressures for research output. *Organisation*. Published online, 14 June. 1-13.

Rittner B & Trudeau P. 1997. *The women's guide to surviving graduate school*. Thousand Oaks, CA: Sage.

Sparkes A. 2007. Embodiment, academics and audit culture: A story seeking consideration. *Qualitative Research*, 7(4):521-550.

Stewart K. 2007. *Ordinary affects*. Durham: Duke University Press.

Thatcher J. 2012. PhDs of the UK, unite! Your futures depend on it. *Graduate Journal of Social Science*, 9:24-39.

The Economist. 2010. The disposable academic: Why doing your PhD is often a waste of time. [Accessed 2 September 2013] www.economist.com/node/17723223

Waring M & Kearins K. 2011. *Thesis survivor stories: Practical advice on getting through your PhD or master's thesis*. Auckland: AUT Media.

Wetherell M. 2003. Paranoia, ambivalence, and discursive practices: Concepts of position and positioning in psychoanalysis and discursive psychology. In: R Harre & F Moghaddam (eds). *The self and others*. Westport: Praeger. 99-119.

Wetherell M. 2012. *Affect and emotion: A new social science understanding*. London: Sage.

INTEGRATING AUTHORITATIVE DISCIPLINARY VOICES IN POSTGRADUATE WRITING

Pia Lamberti and Arnold Wentzel

INTRODUCTION

The research on postgraduate writing reported in this chapter should be seen as a contribution to the widely-discussed ongoing debate in higher education about what is referred to as the "problem" of student writing (Lillis & Turner 2001:57; Turner 2011). The research focuses on one of the areas of greatest difficulty for novice research writers: constructing texts that incorporate multiple sources from 'the literature'. For postgraduate students, integrating the authoritative voices of the discipline into the text, without losing the integrity of the 'textual voice' (Hyland 2008), is a widely acknowledged challenge (Kamler & Thomson 2006). In this chapter, the difficulty of teaching students to use the authoritative voices in the scholarly literature they consult to develop and support their arguments in research writing is addressed, both theoretically and practically. The research reported in the chapter affirms the value of drawing on writing theory to inform postgraduate pedagogy, and of using students' texts, the textual 'products' generated in the teaching and learning process, to interrogate and extend theory about research writing. The new theoretical understanding that is developed from analysis of students' texts can be applied in teaching and supervision practices.

'Postgraduate writing', as an area of research, is interdisciplinary, as it encompasses linguistic theory, composition/writing theory and educational theory. In addition, it requires an understanding of how the knowledge structures of specific disciplines and/or knowledge domains (Bernstein 2000) affect disciplinary writing conventions. Thus, this research represents collaboration between an educational linguist (the first author), and an economics lecturer (the second author) whose writing course for underprepared aspirant postgraduate students was the catalyst for the study.

The disciplinary boundary crossing promoted by the collaboration between the two authors allows for a more nuanced and multifaceted understanding of the specific discursive resources and language required for the construction of two key types academic writing, which are closely related: the essay based on the reading of multiple sources, a ubiquitous genre (Andrews 2010:161), particularly in the humanities and social sciences, and the 'literature review' section of the dissertation or thesis. The researchers reject the "deficit" view of students that often prevails in disciplinary experts' evaluations of student writing (Lillis & Turner 2001:57). By choosing to place the focus on an entry-level course to postgraduate study, the researchers also problematise the boundary between undergraduate and postgraduate level, and suggest that more attention needs to be focused on helping students to make the transition between the levels. One implication of this perspective is that effective research supervision necessarily requires from the supervisor a greater degree of explicit knowledge about research writing than is conventionally acknowledged in the academy.

Writing researchers who work in a social paradigm argue that in order to construct effective written arguments, student writers need to use specific discursive and linguistic and resources to position themselves in relation to the authoritative disciplinary voices (Swain 2007; Tang 2009). Description of a writing course designed to help students to integrate the voices of experts into their own writing, and textual analysis of the essays that the students produced at the end of the learning process, enable the authors to demonstrate the complexity of writing that necessarily builds on the texts of authoritative sources. Consequently, the authors argue that the discursive complexity of the "knowledge-focused" texts (Bazerman 2004:60) typical in higher education calls for explicit knowledge about research writing to inform both postgraduate coursework design and supervisors' feedback on student writing. Courses such as the one that is the focus of this chapter may enable students to make the transition from being a 'course-taker' (Lovitts 2005), who *reproduces* existing knowledge, to a being a master's or doctoral student who is capable of *producing* knowledge.

THE TEACHING AND LEARNING INTERVENTION: A 'BRIDGING' COURSE TO POSTGRADUATE STUDIES

The BCom Economics Honours 'Bridging' Programme at the University of Johannesburg offers entry to BCom Economics Honours to graduates who do not automatically qualify for it. These students mainly come from two groups: (1) degree graduates who majored in economics but obtained an overall average of under

60%; and (2) diploma graduates who majored in economics. These students enter the 'bridging' programme with two main developmental needs: first, most of them have not yet adequately internalised the language and thinking of the discipline, and second, since assignments that demand the construction of extended academic writing are uncommon in undergraduate study, few students have learned to write argumentatively within the discipline.

Of the four courses in the 'bridging' programme, three aim to give students a strong foundation in the theoretical content they either missed or in which they did not perform well: microeconomics, macroeconomics and mathematical economics. The fourth course is in research and writing skills, which is especially critical since most of the students have not been required to write essays in the course of their undergraduate studies. Together, the four courses aim to prepare students for the demands of the Honours courses in economics.

In 2012, 50 students entered the semester-long research and writing course, most of them not expecting the developmental leap they would be expected to make in only 14 weeks. This was a substantial increase over 2011, when there were only 19 students. Students in the 2011 cohort regarded the course as the most demanding course in the programme. In a survey conducted by the head of the economics department, students indicated that the course was the most useful in preparing them for honours studies. One of the students from the 2011 cohort is performing very well in a master's programme, was selected as a Mandela-Rhodes scholar and is aiming to proceed to doctoral studies. Another student has been accepted for postgraduate study at a prestigious British university.

In preparation for the final assessment for the course, students worked throughout the semester on a single '"multiple-source discussion essay", on an economics topic of their choice. A "multiple-source discussion essay" is an argumentative essay requiring students to take a position on a controversial topic, using sources from the literature as support (Lamberti 2013:49). Each of the 14 lectures equipped them with a writing 'skill' that they had to apply to the essay, so that over 13 weeks of one semester, through a series of short related assignments, they progressively wrote an essay as practice. Students received formative feedback on each assignment within a week so that they could incorporate the feedback into their evolving essays. The fourteenth, and final, assignment required students to apply the skills they had learned by writing another multiple-source discussion essay independently of the lecturer for summative assessment. Students could choose to write the essay on one of two broad topics that are controversial in the discipline: (1) monetary policy, price stability and employment; or (2) economic growth, development and income distribution.

The final assignment essay was assessed by two subject content experts: the course designer/facilitator (the second author, who has taught a wide range of courses in economics and business management, as well as research writing courses) and a specialist in macroeconomics, the sub-field within which the final essay topics fell. The purpose of the second assessor was to act as another representative of the discipline and to help determine whether the students were able to engage with the subject at the level expected of novice postgraduate researchers in economics.

Prior to the course, the second author had identified specific skills the student requires if he/she is to make the transition to postgraduate level. The most important skill identified was the ability to integrate the 'voices' of the discipline (ideas or perspectives represented in the source reading) with the writer's perspective in such a way that the student's writing asserts a clear position and exhibits a consistent 'authorial voice', or 'textual voice'. As the authors prefer the term 'textual voice', it is the term used in this chapter. In order to achieve the development of a legitimate textual voice in students' multiple-source discussion essays, lectures were presented in a specific order so as to progressively develop that ability (see Figure 7.1).

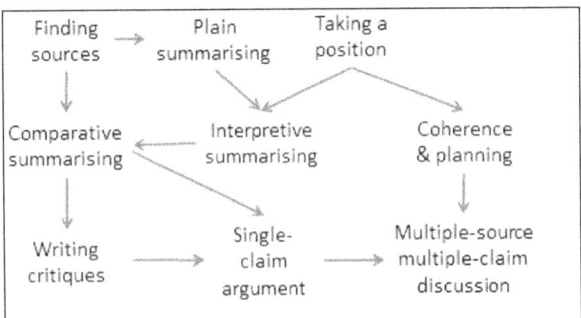

FIGURE 7.1 Sequencing of lectures

Figure 7.1 does not represent all the lectures, only those that focused on teaching the integration of authoritative sources. Within this sequence the first lecture covered finding academic sources and simple summarising of these sources. This was followed by a lecture on the importance of taking a position when writing, and expressing this as a provisional overarching 'thesis' (an assertion that is supported by evidence and reasoning). Lectures on interpretive summarising (summarising a source through the lens of a thesis) and comparative summarising (summarising two or more sources in comparison to each other) followed. Through the assignments in which students practised interpretive summarising they learned how to engage with an academic source without losing their own 'voice', while through comparative summarising they learned that new information can emerge from the way in which the author selects ideas from the sources and positions them in relation to each other. This was followed by a lecture on writing "critiques" (Swales & Feak 2004:180), which emphasised the importance of counterarguments, and this led to a lecture on making simple (single-claim) arguments. After a lecture in which students were invited to imagine a classic written academic text as a conversation (see below), they were ready to combine simple arguments into a multiple-claim discussion essay using multiple sources.

In addition to the deliberate sequencing of lectures and assignments, different metaphors relating to spoken interaction were consistently used to convey the idea of writing as embodying the integration of different 'voices'. One of the most successful metaphors was that of an issue-centred panel discussion 'talk show' in which the host integrates different voices by guiding the discussion. Students were first shown academic writing in its conventional form, for example:

> Malthus (1798) argued that population growth will eventually outstrip the rate at which food can be produced, thus leading to famines and wars over scarce resources. This pessimistic view was criticised by many economists for not anticipating the possibility of technological advances (Friedman 2002) and birth control (Thomas 1998). However, in recent times, Malthus's predictions are becoming true, especially in developing nations. Technological progress is causing more problems – such as climate change and pollution – that are harming the quality of resources required for food production. In fact, Dixon (2008) predicts that very soon major wars will be fought over increasingly scarce resources such as water.

They were then shown 'transformations' of such academic writing – in the form it would appear if a talk show discussion with source authors as participants was transcribed into a script, for example:

Student: Let's talk about whether our planet's resources can continue to support us. What is your view Reverend Malthus?

Malthus: I have been warning against this for centuries. As early as 1798 I explained that population growth will eventually outstrip the rate at which food can be produced, thus leading to famines and wars over scarce resources, because ...

Thomas: I really think that is a bit pessimistic Malthus. Come on now, there has been no ecological crisis since your published your book. In fact,

	technological advances helped to significantly and consistently raise food production …
Friedman:	And don't forget birth control which reduced population growth – something you did not anticipate at all Malthus!
Student:	But wait, just because Malthus's prediction hasn't come true yet, does not mean Bit won't happen at all. Are we not seeing this very same technological progress causing more problems now – for example pollution – which is reducing the quality of our natural resources?
Dixon:	If I may chip in here, I would like to support you in this. Good quality water is becoming increasingly scarce due to global warming and pollution. I predict that very soon major wars will be fought over increasingly scarce resources such as water – and probably other natural resources too.

The aim of such textual 'transformations' was to direct students' attention to how an author, through his/her own choices and wording, places the authors of source texts in 'conversation' with each other and uses his her representation of their ideas to move towards a conclusion. They were also made aware of changes in the direction of the argument, described as 'moves' (Swales 1990, 2004), and of the words and phrases (wordings) used to realise the moves in academic writing. As a once-off practice students wrote an argument in the format of a talk show script before changing it into a more appropriate written academic form.

While the necessarily brief overview of the research writing course provided above cannot do justice to it, it conveys the thinking behind its design and execution. The course was challenging for the students given their unfamiliarity with academic writing, and sometimes frustrating for the lecturer as, despite the provision of intensive written weekly feedback on the assignments, improvement in the students' writing was slow. However, by the end of the semester, 33 of the 50 students passed the course, and there was evidence of incremental improvement in the writing of all participants.

RESEARCHING THE TEACHING INTERVENTION

Sharing a common interest in both argumentation in academic writing and in the development of underprepared postgraduate students, the authors decided to make the research writing course described above the object of joint research. It must be pointed out that the writing course was developed and taught by the second author without the involvement of the first author, and that the collaborative research project was undertaken after the course had been completed. The two main aims of the research were: first, to establish the impact of the explicit writing pedagogy that centred on writing as conversation; and second, to build theory-based empirical knowledge about the nature of student writing in the specific context. An assumption made is that the multiple-source discussion essay task that was set as summative assessment of the course made similar linguistic demands on students as those required for the construction of acceptable argumentation in the 'literature review' of the dissertation or thesis.

Theoretical orientation

The theoretical underpinnings of the research reported in this chapter are located in social (as opposed to cognitive) theories of language and writing (Bakhtin 1981, 1986; Halliday 1978) as they have been taken up in the field of educational linguistics, specifically in the work of theorists of genre (Bazerman 1988, 2004; Martin 1997; Swales 1981, 1990, 2004) and of discourse semantics (Martin 1992, 1998, 2002). The core principles are that the making of meaning, whether in speech or writing, is essentially social (Halliday 1978) and dialogical (Bakhtin 1981, 1986).

The teaching intervention described in the section above, and the empirical research based on it, assumes that addressing 'real world' problems by framing them as research problems is an important core task students must perform in order to produce novice research. The framing of research problems requires that students participate in 'conversations' about the problems identified as worthy of consideration in the discipline. Engagement with disciplinary conversations involves the students in a recursive process of reading the texts that represent the authoritative sources and reformulating the ideas represented in the texts in texts of their own that constitute a response to the ongoing debates about the problem and which, however incrementally, contribute to knowledge about the problem.

Although comparing the decontextualised abstract writing of the disciplines in the academy to conversation may seem counter-intuitive, the metaphor of writing as conversation has been alive in American composition studies for some time (Burke 1941, 1969; Paré 1992), and has more recently become popularised in the teaching of academic writing (Graff & Birkenstein 2006). Kamler and Thomson (2006:37-38), who have definitively placed postgraduate writing on the higher education and postgraduate supervision agendas, also use a similar metaphor in comparing the choice of key authors for argumentation in the literature review to the selection of dinner guests with the dinner-table conversation in mind.

The work of Mikhail Bakhtin provides a theoretical base for the view of academic writing as fundamentally dialogical. In two of his seminal works (1981, 1986), all writing is seen as responding to previous written texts and also anticipating other written responses. Bakhtin (1981:279) emphasises that texts are oriented to what has been said before, and that all communication "in any of its forms, quotidian, rhetorical, scholarly – cannot fail to be oriented toward the 'already uttered', the 'already known', the 'common opinion'". All texts are also directed to a response: "Forming itself in an atmosphere of the already spoken, the word is at the same time determined by that which has not yet been said but which is needed and in fact anticipated by the answering word" (1981:280). The interconnectedness between texts is emphasised: "[W]hat is heard and actively understood will find its response in the subsequent speech or behaviour of the listener" (Bakhtin 1986:68-69). For any utterance, "its beginning is preceded by the utterance of others, and its end is followed by the responsive utterances of others" (Bakhtin 1986:71). A fundamental insight for researchers of research writing is that although dissertations, theses and research articles are not written in the form of dialogue, that is they are "monologic" (Bakhtin 1981:280), or one-voiced, in their structure, they are nevertheless dialogical, or multi-voiced, in that they represent the voices of the texts that have informed them and the texts that have yet to be written in response to them in the future.

Theorists who have made research writing the object of research, such as the rhetorician Charles Bazerman (1988, 2004), have used Bakhtin's ideas for a deeply enriched understanding of 'intertextuality', a term that is used to refer to the interrelatedness of texts. "[R]eading and writing are in dialogue with each other as we write in direct and indirect response to what we have read before, and we read in relation to the ideas we have articulated in our own writing" (Bazerman 2004:53). Because academic texts exist in complex relation to each other, 'intertextuality' is a key dimension of academic writing. Consequently, intertextuality needs to be a stronger focus in research on the advanced literacies required for successful postgraduate research writing. Bazerman's work highlights the challenges of intertextuality in research writing and urges a deeper understanding of the role of authoritative disciplinary sources in research by insisting that "the literature" lies at the heart of research writing:

> [A]udience and author knowledge of the subject is built on prior texts; the audience knowledge and orientation is based on their reading; and the author's authority, resources, interests, and current stance grow out of an engagement with the literature (2004:61).

> The seemingly obvious insight encapsulated in the quotation above highlights the complexity of the interrelated processes of academic reading and writing. Bazerman's recognition that academic writing is "writing about reading" (2004:59) informs our interpretation of

students' difficulties with the writing of what he refers to as "non-literary, knowledge-focused" texts (2004:60).

Building on Bazerman's foregrounding of Bakhtin's insight that texts are *necessarily* reformulations of previous texts, in this chapter research writing is viewed as multi-voiced, since it represents multiple views from authoritative sources to a greater or lesser extent. A strand of theorisation and empirical research in applied linguistics based on the understanding that texts are multi-voiced offers ways of analysing texts to track the extent to which, and in what ways, voices in authoritative source texts are acknowledged and evaluated in the texts that use them. This theory which developed from a social theory of language referred to as "systemic functional linguistics" (Halliday 1978) is known as "appraisal theory" (Martin & White 2005; White 2003). It centres on how writers use discursive resources from sub-systems known as "attitude", "engagement" and "graduation" and to effect intersubjective positioning (Martin & White 2005), in other words, it entails analysis of the ways that writers use language to position themselves in relation to their readers and to the writers of the texts they have read. The term 'discursive resources' is used in this chapter to refer to both the 'moves' that are made, the ideas that are available from authoritative source texts, and the wordings (words or phrases) that writers select to realise moves (Lamberti 2013). The term 'move' is "a defined and bounded communicative act that is designed to achieve one main communicative objective" (Swales & Feak 2000:35). As a move refers to the function that a particular wording performs in the text, one move can be as short as a "finite clause" or run over a number of paragraphs (Swales & Feak 2000:35).

Appraisal theory offers analytical concepts that the researcher can use to identify, categorise and interpret patterns in the writer's use of discursive resources, and to make observations about how these patterns affect the construction of the textual voice. The main concepts from appraisal theory that are used in this research are from the "engagement" sub-system (Martin & White 2005:35-36). This sub-system includes the discursive resources, or wordings, that writers draw on to indicate their evaluation of the ideas of others and to position their ideas in relation to those of others. These discursive resources "provide the means for the authorial voice to position itself with respect to, and hence to 'engage' with, the other voices and alternative positions construed as being in play" (Martin & White 2005:94). In appraisal theory, a distinction is made between "monoglossic" (single-voiced) and "heteroglossic" (multi-voiced) texts (Martin & White 2005:99-100). One-voiced texts silence the voices of others by making no reference to ideas from other sources. Multi-voiced texts acknowledge or invoke other voices by incorporating ideas from other sources. Research writing is multi-voiced, since research necessarily builds on the work of other theorists and researchers, and thus explicitly engages with the ideas and knowledge claims of others. This engagement is obviously inscribed in citation and referencing, but the multi-voiced nature of research texts is also embodied in the discursive resources the writer chooses to use to integrate the ideas of others into his/her own text.

Dialogical expansion and contraction

The key distinction from appraisal theory that is used in this research is between the two main categories of multi-voiced text: "dialogical expansion" and "dialogical contraction" (Martin & White 2005:102). Discursive resources from these two categories are most useful for understanding how research writers are able to manipulate language in order to integrate disciplinary sources into their own texts. Discursive resources for dialogical expansion are used to make 'space' for the voices of others (Martin & White 2005:102-116), while those for dialogical contraction are used to close down the 'space' for other voices, which allows the textual voice to emerge and stand out. Table 7.1 shows the three sub-categories of dialogical expansion that are used to acknowledge other voices, viewed in this research as moves, and provides examples of typical wordings that are used to effect each of the moves. The term "entertain" is used to refer to a move that acknowledges that diverse ideas and conflicting perspectives exist. The move highlights that knowledge claims can be contested. The term "attribute (acknowledge)" is used to refer to a move that explicitly names the source of an idea or assertion. The term "attribute (distance)" is used to refer to a move that allows the writer to distance herself/himself from the source, thus calling the source's ideas into question (Martin & White 2005:102-116).

TABLE 7.1 Typical wordings that realise dialogical expansion (based on Martin & White 2005)

Examples of linguistic resources (wordings) used	'Engagement' sub-category
it's probable/possible this may be it seems expository questions	Entertain
Kahn (2003) argues that … Hodge (2002) explains that … Epstein and Yeldan (2008) propose that … According to Svensson (1999), …	attribute (acknowledge)
Hodge claims to have shown that …	attribute (distance)

Table 7.2 shows six sub-categories of dialogical contraction identified by Martin and White, and provides examples of the wording associated with each one. The category "disclaim (deny)" refers to a move that effects the outright rejection of an idea from a source. The category of "disclaim (counter)" refers to a move that allows the writer to draw attention to conflicting ideas and to align himself with one of them in order to strengthen his/her own argument. The "proclaim (concur:affirm)" move allows the writer to represent an idea from another source as incontestable and thus to discourage opposition to the idea. The "proclaim (concur:concede)" move enables the writer to signal limited or qualified agreement with the view of a source by making a concession that functions to strengthen his/her argument. The "proclaim (pronounce)" move allows the writer to assert herself/himself as the source of an idea. The "proclaim (endorse)" move allows the writer to assert an idea from a source, simultaneously aligning himself/herself with the source and discouraging disagreement with or questioning of the idea (Martin & White 2005:117-132).

TABLE 7.2 Typical wordings that realise dialogical contraction (based on Martin & White 2005)

Examples of linguistic resources (wordings) used	'Engagement' sub-category
no; did not; never	disclaim (deny)
..., yet; ..., although; ..., but	disclaim (counter)
of course, ...; obviously, ...; ... the fact that ...	proclaim (concur: affirm)
Admittedly, ..., but/however ...; However, ... should still ...	proclaim (concur: concede)
I argue that ...	proclaim (pronounce)
As studies have shown, ...; As Blanchard and Gali (2010) show, ...	proclaim (endorse)

The effectiveness of the writer's argument depends on the discursive resources used for the construction of the textual voice, with the resources for "intersubjective positioning" (Martin & White 2005:95) being particularly important. In their writing, novice researchers are required to create an acceptable balance between acknowledging the value of ideas taken from the disciplinary sources they have used, which usually requires dialogical expansion, and asserting their own point of view, or 'voice', which requires dialogical contraction. This entails constructing a text in which the open-mindedness and critical distance that is expected in the academic context is inscribed in the textual voice. However, the text also has to exhibit a degree of authority in order to be convincing. For this reason, students who learn to balance the dialogically expansive wordings that demonstrate their engagement with the texts of the discipline with the dialogically contractive wordings that confer authority on the textual voice are better prepared for the challenges of incorporating the literature into their research writing.

Research design and methods

In order to achieve the research aims of evaluating the impact of the intensive research writing course and, more importantly, furthering our understanding of the linguistic/discursive resources students actually use in their writing so that it could inform subsequent teaching, it was decided to engage in textual analysis of the texts the students produced at the end of the course. The focus of the analysis was the construction of the textual voice in relation to the authoritative voices in the source texts that students consulted, using the concepts of dialogical expansion and contraction (Martin & White 2005). The importance of the "writer's skill at orchestrating the participation of different voices and views in the dialogic space" (Swain 2007:179) cannot be underestimated. Therefore, although all three sub-systems of appraisal theory are useful for analysing textual voice, it was decided to focus primarily on "engagement", as it has been identified as the most salient of the three sub-systems for the construction of a persuasive textual voice in the context of academic writing (Coffin 2002; Swain 2007).

Since the focus was on the student writers' construction of textual voice, it was decided to focus only on the essay introductions and conclusions, where the textual voice is less 'diluted' by the authoritative voices the students have selected to paraphrase or quote. Furthermore, since all the introductions and some of the concluding sections were too long to analyse in their entirety, it was decided that the disciplinary expert, the second author, would select for analysis only those parts of the introductions and conclusions that represent the writer's overall point of view, or argument. Only the essays on the topic of 'monetary policy, price stability and employment' were used for analysis, thus the data set consists of 23 essays. In terms of ethics, confidentiality is preserved, as students' names were removed from the texts selected as data. The essays were numbered, and are referred to by means of these numbers in the discussion of the analysis in the sub-section below. The introduction and conclusion extracts from the essays were analysed separately. Although the essays had been rated by both of the disciplinary content specialists, the marks allocated to the essays were not taken into consideration for the initial linguistic analysis of the texts. Only after all the introduction and conclusion extracts had been analysed by the first author was any reference made to the marks.

The typical linguistic markers, or wordings, associated with the sub-categories of "engagement" identified by Martin and White (2005) were used to analyse the text extracts (see Tables 7.1 and 7.2 above). In the accompanying interpretive process, the wordings used from each different category were linked to strategic 'moves'

(Swales 1981, 1990, 2004; Swales & Feak 2000) that the writer makes in order to achieve particular rhetorical effects to persuade the reader.

The use of these resources is closely linked to the point at which they are used in the overall rhetorical structure of the whole text. Typically, in academic texts such as theses and dissertations, as well as in the multiple-source discussion essays that were analysed in this research, the overall pattern is a progression over the course of the text from a high degree of dialogical expansion in the parts that constitute the 'introduction' to a comparatively higher degree of dialogical contraction in the conclusion. Also, it is generally acknowledged that the texts of disciplinary experts in a field, which have survived repeated submission to rigorous peer review, are likely to be more dialogically contractive than those of novice researchers.

When the text extracts were analysed, sections of the text exhibiting either dialogical expansion or contraction were marked using the highlighting function in Microsoft Word, with different colours used to identify each type of move, thereby making the patterns of dialogical expansion and contraction more visible to the analyst. However, it must be acknowledged that coding is subjective, and is highly dependent on the context. As acknowledgement of other voices can be more or less direct, depending on a number of factors, such as the purpose of the section of the text in relation to the whole text (Martin & White 2005:100), analysis of "engagement" in research texts is a complex process that entails interpretation that takes the context into account. The most salient aspect of context in this form of analysis is the text as a whole. Therefore, in the analysis of the conclusions, it was necessary to take into account the parts of the texts that had come before in the introduction and 'body' of the essay.

In the extracts that are used for exemplification of the analysis in this chapter, italicisation is used to indicate forms of dialogical expansion and the text that is not italicised is dialogically contractive. Bold font is used to identify the linguistic resources that are clearly identifiable as markers of dialogical contraction.

Findings and interpretation of essay introductions

A number of clear patterns were observed in the data set. Firstly, it was found that the extracts from the introductions exhibited a higher degree of dialogical expansion than was found in the conclusions. This pattern is consistent with what was expected, given the conventional academic essay structure. In the majority of the introduction extracts dialogically expansive resources were used (18 essays in the data set of 23 introductions). However, in 14 of the extracts, although dialogically expansive discursive resources are used in the first part of the extract, the latter part of the introduction extract consists of discursive resources for dialogical contraction. This observation is exemplified in the text below, in which italicisation marks out the part of the text using resources for dialogical expansion. The part of the text that is not italicised is dialogically contractive.

> *There are different perspectives to this inflation targeting and employment issue. Some individuals are of the view that the Reserve Bank promotes inflation targeting at the cost of employment ... and they feel that the Reserve Bank should abandon this monetary policy (SARB 2010). But this does the primacy of inflation targeting by the Reserve Bank imply that the Reserve Bank is not concerned about the unemployment problem?* **No** the Reserve Bank is concerned about unemployment **but** does **not** have that ability of controlling unemployment and output in the long-run **but** would rather focus on controlling what it can which is inflation. Since inflation targeting focuses on maintaining price stability in the economy, this has a high probability of reducing unemployment in the long run (extract from introduction: essay 3).

Analysis of all 14 examples referred to above shows that the dialogically contractive parts of the extracts represent the student writer's construction of a "thesis statement", which is an overall position statement in relation to a question or issue (Coffin et al. 2003:22). The finding that the majority of the essays had a thesis statement in the introduction, which is referred to as a 'front-loaded' thesis, is consistent with the way the second author taught the course. The example quoted above clearly inscribes the dialogical nature of academic writing. The lead-up to the thesis statement ends with an expository question, which the student writer answers with the dialogically contractive resource "no", which is associated with direct speech rather than academic writing. This suggests that although the writer used a dialogically contractive move that is appropriate in the assertion of a point of view, or thesis statement, in this case, what is categorised as a "disclaim (deny)" move, she/he had not yet developed full productive control of the indirect forms of the "disclaim (deny)" move that are appropriate in written academic discourse.

Another example from the data set illustrates the same pattern of moves across the introduction extract, from dialogical expansion to dialogical contraction; however, the discursive resources used to close down the dialogic space and assert the authority of the textual voice are more conventional in research writing and suggest the student is more ready for postgraduate study than the one quoted above:

> *Given the opposing views regarding the appropriate choice of monetary policy, it is therefore necessary to ask the following question: Would a monetary policy framework targeting employment be more effective than an inflation targeting framework?* The best answer provisionally is that

> a monetary policy framework that targets employment will **not** be more effective than an inflation targeting framework. This is due to **the fact that** the unemployment problem in some developing countries, South Africa in particular, is **not** fundamentally a monetary phenomenon **but** a supply side problem (Chicheke 2009). Unemployment can, therefore, **not** be solved through monetary policy, **but** by correcting structural barriers in the economy. Advocates of inflation targeting firmly maintain that it is a huge mistake to fight unemployment with monetary policy as it results in excessive inflation (extract from introduction: essay 18).

In the second part of the extract above a number of different discursive resources are used to effect dialogical contraction. The "disclaim (deny)" move that follows the expository question contributes to the construction of an authoritative textual voice. The effect of authority is strengthened by the use of resources to effect a "proclaim (concur: affirm)" move, "the fact that", which discourages contradiction of the assertion made. The repeated use of a combination of both the "deny" and "counter" resources for disclaiming used in the counter-argument simultaneously constructs an authoritative and legitimate voice, as the counter-argumentation demonstrates that the writer has engaged with ideas in the authoritative sources.

Findings and interpretation of essay conclusions

As the lecturer and assessor of the course excluded one of the conclusions because it did not make 'sense', the data set of conclusions numbered 22 extracts. Analysis of the extracts from the essay conclusions shows that extensive use was made of resources for dialogical contraction. In comparison to the extracts from the essay introductions, resources for dialogical contraction predominate in the conclusions. All 22 of the extracts from the conclusions made use of dialogical contraction. Just over half of the texts (12) made use of only "proclaim" resources for effecting dialogical contraction. The most commonly used resource was "proclaim (pronounce)". The use of this resource for closing down the dialogic space is exemplified by the two short extracts from essays 6 and 10 that follow, which are discussed below.

> The only way for South Africa to efficiently balance the trade-off between employment and inflation is if the monetary policy that works hand in hand with the fiscal policy, thus reversing the effect of past political regime and promoting growth at the same time (extract from conclusion: essay 6).

> Price level targeting is more certain about future price levels unlike inflation targeting regime. Taking into account the strategic economic direction of South Africa and the impact these two frameworks have on the economy of South Africa, price level targeting is best suited to South Africa (extract from conclusion: essay 10).

Both extracts 6 and 10 were analysed as effecting two "proclaim (pronounce)" moves. Although there are no meta-linguistic markers that explicitly mark the claims made as pronouncements, the position of the conclusion in the overall text structure, arguably, gives claims made at this point in the discussion essay the force of a statement prefaced with the phrase "I argue" or a similar equivalent. The "proclaim (pronounce)" move is strongly dialogically contractive, and therefore constructs a markedly authoritative textual voice. However, the effect of "engagement" moves depends also on other aspects of the text, resources for inscribing "graduation" (Martin & White 2005:135) and "attitude" (Martin & White 2005:42-58), which are not described in this chapter as they were not the focus of the research.

In extract 6, the linking of the phrase "only way" to the evaluative term "efficiently" inscribes an unhedged judgment, which confers a higher degree of subjectivity on the textual voice than is appropriate in a context where an objective orientation to knowledge claims is highly valued. Consequently, it can be argued that the wording that inscribes opinion suggests that the text is veering towards being single-voiced rather than effectively constructing a credible authoritative voice by means of dialogical contraction. Extract 10 also uses wording for inscribing judgment, "best suited" (categorised as "attitude" resources), but since phrases such as "more certain" and "taking into account" ("graduation resources") suggest the writer is invoking other authoritative voices, the text does not appear to be single-voiced to the extent of extract 6. Consequently, extract 10 represents a more credible authoritative voice.

In just under half of the conclusion extracts in the data set (9 of 22) dialogical contraction was effected by means of either a combination of "proclaim" and "disclaim" resources, or "disclaim" resources only. The impact on the textual voice of using resources for disclaiming is discussed below in relation to the extracts that follow directly below.

> The primacy of inflation targeting by the Reserve Bank does **not** imply that the Reserve Bank is **not** concerned about the unemployment problem in the country. **I therefore suggest that** the Reserve Bank should continue with this policy as it has a higher probability of reducing unemployment (extract from conclusion: essay 3).

> Going forward, this paper recommends that **although not** a perfect system, inflation targeting should remain the adopted monetary policy regime … as it has **proven to** [**be** the] best possible policy for price stability … Macroeconomic problems such as unemployment are mostly structural deficiencies which *can be solved in alternative approaches than through monetary policy*. **However**, policymakers should **still** consider making refinements to the inflation targeting regime, if need be (extract from conclusion: essay 18).

Dialogical contraction is effected by means of both "proclaim" and "disclaim" resources in the extract from essay 3. The first move, effected by means of negation, is categorised as "disclaim (deny)". This is followed by a "proclaim (pronounce)" move in which the authority of the textual voice is somewhat undermined by the use of the tentative reporting verb "suggest". However, given the writer's status as 'student' rather than 'novice researcher', the choice of reporting verb inscribes the writer's (understandable) lack of confidence.

In comparison, a wider range of resources for dialogical contraction are used in the concluding extract from essay 18. A combination of a "proclaim (concur: concede)" and a "disclaim (deny)" move functions to construct a strong textual voice where multiple authoritative voices are nevertheless acknowledged. A "proclaim (endorse)" move, effected by the wording "proven to [be]", is followed by a pronouncement: "Macroeconomic problems such as unemployment are mostly structural deficiencies." Since a "pronounce (proclaim)" move can make the writer sound inappropriately opinionated, the dialogically expansive claim that follows, using the word 'can', leavens the effect, inscribing an appropriate reluctance to make an unqualified assertion. The final "proclaim (concur: concede)" move, effected by the wording, "However … should still …", also contributes to the construction of an appropriate textual voice for a novice in the discipline. The two concession moves suggest a writer who has engaged with the disciplinary authorities by building on their ideas to develop a standpoint.

While the writer of essay 3 uses some of the resources required for representing in her/his writing effective engagement with the literature, and therefore shows some evidence of the ability to proceed to postgraduate level, the writer of essay 18 shows greater control of the resources for dialogical contraction, using more of the available resources more flexibly and more confidently. Linguistic analysis of the conclusion alone provides strong evidence that the writer of essay 18 is ready for the challenge of engaging with authoritative sources in order to further a research argument, and is therefore a suitable candidate for postgraduate study. Although we have chosen not to discuss the relationship between the assessors essay marks and the linguistic analysis that was subsequently conducted, it is worth noting that the marks allocated were more or less consistent with the analytical findings. For example, while essay 3 was awarded a satisfactory passing mark by both assessors, essay 18, in which a wider range of resources for effecting dialogical contraction were appropriately used, was awarded a distinction mark.

CONCLUSION AND RECOMMENDATIONS

In term of the aims of this research, we conclude that the explicit research writing pedagogy developed for the course was effective and contributed to the development of an authoritative textual voice in the students' writing. Therefore, it can be argued that the course prepared students to cross the boundary that divides undergraduates from postgraduates. The question of the value of explicit pedagogy aside, we conclude that the effectiveness of the course can be attributed primarily to the underpinning conception of academic discourse as fundamentally dialogical.

The research should also be seen as supporting four related arguments. First, that lecturers and supervisors should be more aware of how discursive resources for opening up or closing down the dialogic space are used to construct authoritative claims to knowledge. Second, that this discursive awareness should inform pedagogy at both undergraduate and postgraduate level. Third, that it may be worth exploring the use of more explicit pedagogy (Elton 2010; Stacey & Granville 2009), particularly in contexts where postgraduates are regarded as underprepared for research writing. Fourth, that greater attention needs to be paid to the *writing* of research, which should be seen as an integral aspect of the research process from the beginning, not as a final task to be completed after the research has been conducted (Badley 2009; Lee & Kamler 2008). This means that engagement with the authoritative disciplinary sources should be seen as an inextricable, and important, aspect of the research process.

In the absence of explicit pedagogy, supervision can be more frustrating than it need be. Supervisors often struggle with their students due to the knowledge gap between them. The gap is exacerbated by the tacit knowledge the supervisor has regarding the research process, which the apprentice model of supervision assumes the student will absorb. This model rarely works as well as expected since it is bedevilled by communication breakdowns, conflict and defensive behaviour. What is needed to make the supervision process more effective are ways to make supervisors more aware of their tacit knowledge and more able to communicate it to the novice researcher.

"Generative metaphor intervention" has been found to be effective in allowing constructive dialogue without accompanying dysfunctional conflict (Barrett & Cooperrider 1990:219). What this research suggests is that a generative metaphor (of research writing as dialogue) can be used as a framework to guide the interaction the supervisor has with the student even if the student has received no training in research writing. The findings suggest that the course designer's dialogical orientation to academic writing, conveyed to the students by means of the 'conversation' metaphor, facilitated acquisition of the necessary linguistic resources. Indirectly raising students' awareness of the discursive resources used in the discipline for making knowledge claims by providing regular specific feedback on students' attempts to use these resources increases the likelihood of their accessing postgraduate opportunities, increases the chances of progression to doctoral level, and increases the probability of successful completion of the doctoral thesis.

While we argue for the value of explicit pedagogy, on reflection we conclude that the meta-language (the terminology) used in this chapter to refer to the linguistic resources that were analysed in this research should not be taught because it is unnecessarily technical in nature. Rather, the insights gained from the study could be used to inform both coursework that aims to prepare postgraduates for research, and in research writing pedagogy. Course designers, lecturers and supervisors who are aware that the use of different wordings have different effects in terms of opening up or closing down the dialogic space, and thus on the construction of writers' voice and authority, will be more able to provide students with access to the discursive resources that are required for effective research writing at doctoral level.

REFERENCES

Andrews R. 2010. *Argumentation in higher education: Improving practice through theory and research*. New York & London: Routledge.

Badley G. 2009. Academic writing as shaping and re-shaping. *Teaching in Higher Education*, 14(2):209-219.

Bakhtin MM. 1981. *The dialogic imagination: Four essays*. Austin, TX: University of Texas Press.

Bakhtin MM. 1986. *Speech genres and other late essays*. Austin, TX: University of Texas Press.

Barrett FJ & Cooperrider DL. 1990. Generative metaphor intervention: A new approach for working with systems divided by conflict and caught in defensive perception. *The Journal of Applied Behavioral Science*, 26(2):219-239.

Bazerman C. 1988. *Shaping written knowledge: The genre and activity of the experimental article in science*. Madison, WI: University of Wisconsin Press.

Bazerman C. 2004. Intertextualities: Volosinov, Bakhtin, literary theory, and literacy studies. In: AF Ball & SW Freedman (eds). *Bakhtinian perspectives on language, literacy, and learning*. Cambridge: Cambridge University Press. 53-65.

Bernstein B. 2000. *Pedagogy, symbolic control and identity: Theory, research, critique*. Rev. edition. Lanham: Rowman and Littlefield.

Burke K. 1941. *The Philosophy of Literary Form: Studies in Symbolic Action*. Berkeley: University of California Press.

Burke K. 1969. *A grammar of motives*. Berkeley, CA: University of California Press.

Coffin C. 2002. The voices of history: Theorising the interpersonal semantics of historical discourses. *Text*, 22(4):503-528.

Coffin C, Curry MJ, Goodman S, Hewings A, Lillis TM & Swann J. 2003. *Teaching academic writing: A toolkit for higher education*. London: Routledge.

Elton L. 2010. Academic writing and tacit knowledge. *Teaching in Higher Education*, 15(2):151-160.

Graff G & Birkenstein C. 2006. *They say I say: The moves that matter in academic writing*. New York: Norton.

Halliday MAK. 1978. *Language as social semiotic: The social interpretation of language and meaning*. London: Edward Arnold.

Hyland K. 2008. Disciplinary voices: Interactions in research writing. *English Text Construction*, 1(1):5-22.

Kamler B & Thomson P. 2006. *Helping doctoral students write: Pedagogies for doctoral supervision*. London: Routledge.

Lamberti P. 2013. *A critical exploration of argumentation in the texts that third-year Development Studies students interpret and construct*. Unpublished doctoral thesis. University of Johannesburg.

Lee A & Kamler B. 2008. Bringing pedagogy to doctoral publishing. *Teaching in Higher Education*, 13(5):511-523.

Lillis T & Turner J. 2001. Student writing in higher education: Contemporary confusion, traditional concerns. *Teaching in Higher Education*, 6(1):57-68.

Lovitts BE. 2005 Being a good course-taker is not enough: A theoretical perspective on the transition to independent research. *Studies in Higher Education*, 30(2):137-154.

Martin JR. 1992. *English text: System and structure*. Amsterdam: John Benjamins.

Martin JR. 1997. Analysing genre: Functional parameters. In: F Christie & JR Martin (eds). *Genre and institutions: Social processes in workplace and school*. London: Continuum. 3-39.

Martin JR. 1998. Discourses of science: Recontextualisation, genesis, intertextuality and hegemony. In: JR Martin & R Veel (eds). *Reading science: Critical and functional perspectives on discourses of science*. London: Routledge. 3-14.

Martin JR. 2002. Writing history: Construing time and value in discourses of the past. In MJ Schleppegrell & MC Colombi (eds). *Developing advanced literacy in first and second languages: Meaning with power*. Mahwah, NJ: Lawrence Erlbaum. 87-118.

Martin JR & White PRR. 2005. *The language of evaluation: Appraisal in English*. London: Palgrave.

Paré A. 1992. Ushering 'audience' out: From oration to conversation. *Textual Studies in Canada*, 1:45-64. [Accessed 10 February 2013] http://www.stthomasu.ca/~hunt/audience.htm

Stacey JD & Granville S. 2009. Entering the conversation: Reaction papers in advanced academic Literacy. *Teaching in Higher Education*, 14(3):327-339.

Swain E. 2007. Constructing an effective 'voice' in academic discussion writing: An appraisal theory perspective. In: A McCabe, M O'Donnell & R Whittaker (eds). *Advances in language and education*. London: Continuum. 166-184.

Swales JM. 1981. *Aspects of article introductions*. Birmingham: Language Studies Unit, University of Aston.

Swales JM. 1990. *Genre analysis: English in academic and research settings*. Cambridge: Cambridge University Press.

Swales JM. 2004. *Research genres*. Cambridge: Cambridge University Press.

Swales JM & Feak C. 2000. *English in today's research world: A writing guide*. Ann Arbor, MI: University of Michigan Press.

Swales JM & Feak CB. 2004. *Academic writing for graduate students: Essential tasks and skills*. 2nd edition. Ann Arbor, MI: University of Michigan Press.

Tang R. 2009. A dialogic account of authority in academic writing. In: M Charles, D Pecorari & S Hunston (eds). *Academic writing: At the interface of corpus and discourse*. London: Continuum. 170-188.

Turner J. 2011. *Language in the academy: Cultural reflexivity and intercultural dynamics*. Bristol, PA: Multilingual Matters.

White PRR. 2003. Beyond modality and hedging: A dialogic view of the language of intersubjective stance. *Text, Special Edition on Appraisal*: 259-284.

PART FOUR

SUPERVISION STRATEGIES

PUSHING THE BOUNDARIES OF POSTGRADUATE SUPERVISION

THEORISING RESEARCH LEARNING IN COMMUNITY

Callie Grant

BACKGROUND AND CONTEXT

In keeping with global trends, there is a national imperative in the terrain of higher education in South Africa to increase the percentage of university students studying at the postgraduate level (RSA DHET 2012). With this comes mounting pressure to increase the throughput rates of postgraduate students in the country's universities for economic, social and political reasons, and critically in order to maintain and further what has become known as the 'knowledge project'. However, as a result of the inequities of the apartheid era, the higher education arena is faced with a complex and diverse student population (Quinn 2012) and ever-increasing student numbers (Snowball & Sayigh 2007) as it attempts to grapple with issues of epistemological access, redress and quality. To date, there is evidence to suggest that our higher education system is failing the majority of students, at both the undergraduate and the postgraduate levels (Letseka & Maile 2008; Scott, Yeld & Hendry 2007). Higher education in South Africa, therefore, must be understood to speak to both the 'knowledge project' and the issue of social justice, as without a sustained emphasis on the latter, the country will have failed in its mandate to engage in equal and equitable transformation of the higher education system.

Against this backdrop and ideological position, this chapter emerges out of my experience of teaching and supervising several cohorts of postgraduate students at the master's level in the field of Educational Leadership and Management (ELM) over a number of years. In particular, it draws on research based on three South African case studies of ELM research learning in community; the first two at the Honours' level and the third at the Masters' level. Data were drawn from course evaluations, student reflective journals, a focus group interview with students as well as official documentation such as pass rates, throughput rates, examiners' reports and supervisors' reports.

In South Africa the Master of Education (MEd) qualification is offered as either coursework/half-thesis or full thesis and, for the purposes of this chapter, the focus is on the coursework/half-thesis offering. The chapter has arisen from a concern that although many students successfully complete the coursework component of the MEd degree in the required time, the majority spends far too much time in trying to complete the half-thesis component and many do not complete at all (see also Grant 2013; Letseka & Maile 2008; Sayed, Kruss & Badat 1998 in this regard).

There may be three key reasons for this low throughput rate. Firstly, the MEd (ELM) student body is 'non-traditional' in that very few 'young' students enter the programme having followed a direct undergraduate degree, followed immediately by an Honours degree. The majority of students who enter a MEd (ELM) programme in the South African context comprise mature-aged professionals who elect to study on a part-time basis because they hold down permanent employment in schools, Department of Education offices or in education non-governmental organisations. Many of the professionals who register for these qualifications hold formal management positions in their places of work and consequently hold in balance, sometimes precariously, responsibilities related to their careers, their extended families as well as their further studies. The second reason for this low throughput rate is a consequence of South Africa's apartheid history which has resulted in students arriving at the academy with a diverse and complex array of domestic, cultural, linguistic, educational and economic capital. This range of capital inevitably presents a multitude of social and intellectual challenges in the teaching and learning processes. A final reason for this low throughput rate is that the majority of these students have little prior experience of the academic discourses in the field of ELM and neither have they been involved in research and thesis writing prior to their embarking on the MEd (ELM) qualification.

Taking the above into consideration, and holding the desire for a socially just and equitable education experience for all students as a primary goal, experience has shown that it is almost impossible for the majority of these part-time ELM students to complete the degree in the minimum number of academic study years legislated. Only in rare cases does this happen and yet, in practice, the degree remains structured as a two year offering for part-time study at the majority of higher educational institutions in our country. This sets up the unrealistic expectation that the degree ought to be completed within this period. Our responsibility as higher education professionals is therefore to challenge this discriminatory practice whilst simultaneously searching for ways to support the research learning of these students so that they ultimately reach the exit level required.

A key point of departure is to acknowledge that these MEd students are novices in the arena of research and that they require a process of induction into the academic enterprise, a view endorsed by Sayed *et al.* (1998). Our work, as legislated in the Higher Education Qualifications Framework (HEQF) is therefore to *educate and train* these novice researchers in order that they can ultimately contribute to the development of knowledge (RSA 2007:27, my emphasis). This requires a fundamental shift in our thinking about postgraduate teaching and supervision. It calls for a scholarship of teaching within the supervision process and challenges us to think creatively about the pedagogy of research learning. Research learning in this conceptualisation refers to the "domain of learning which novice researchers (such as postgraduate students) experience in the complex process of learning to become a researcher" (Jansen, Herman & Pillay 2004:79).

A strategy to strengthen the learning of research and, in so doing, push postgraduate supervision boundaries, is through the establishment of a community of practice at the MEd level with a focus on research learning. This community of practice is one in which novice researchers are supported and enabled in acquiring the knowledge and capabilities necessary for successful postgraduate study. It requires rigorous teaching within a shared, systematically organised 'pedagogical space' (Boud & Lee 2005) and inevitably stands "in contrast to the conventional focus on individual supervision relationships as the privileged if not the only acknowledged site of pedagogy" (Boud & Lee 2005:503). While there is a growing body of literature on research learning in community at the doctoral level in South Africa (see for example Jansen *et al.* 2004; Lotz-Sisitka, Ellery, Olvitt, Schudel & O'Donoghue 2010), little has been written about this approach to supervision at the master's level. Thus the purpose of this chapter is to challenge us to think differently about supervision at the master's level and, to this end, I draw on the work of Alan Fiske (1991, 1992) to reimagine the MEd pedagogical space.

REIMAGINING PEDAGOGICAL SPACE: LEARNING IN COMMUNITY

In theorising research learning and student success at postgraduate level, I take the position that the liberal notion of supervision with its traditional one-to-one relationship between student and supervisor can no longer be considered the only option in the higher education arena in South Africa. This is not to say that individual supervisor-student interaction does not still play a central role in research learning and development, only that it need no longer drive the structure and organisation of postgraduate supervision. Rather, a communal approach to postgraduate supervision is a beneficial alternative given the diverse and complex society in which we live, and the possible opportunities this diversity can provide in expanding and enriching the teaching and learning process. Thus, I believe that the supervision process can be greatly enhanced if it is conceptualised as relational within a scholarly community of practice (Wenger 1998). While Wenger's conceptualisation of community has been well critiqued (see for example Hodkinson & Hodkinson 2004; Maistry 2008), it remains important as a starting framework to the social learning processes and hence to the processes of research learning.

As ELM lecturer and supervisor, I foreground my role as teacher in the research and supervision process and consciously construct each new postgraduate group as an opportunity to support scholarly learning and knowledge generation in a community of practice. In this conceptualisation (after Wenger 1998), learning is understood as a social phenomenon where people – a diverse cohort of postgraduate students – relate to each other and participate actively in a practice through mutual engagement in the joint enterprise of research learning. Here the learning is not limited to the knowledge and technical competence required for completion of the thesis but extends beyond this to include "the emotional, social, political and cognitive experiences that together constitute such learning" (Jansen *et al*. 2004:80).

In determining how students relate to one another within this research learning community, I draw on the relational models theory of Fiske (1991, 1992). Fiske, an anthropologist working in the field of cultural psychology, argues that people across cultures are fundamentally sociable and "generally organise their social life in terms of their relations with other people" (1992:689). His theory explains social life as a process of "seeking, making, sustaining, repairing, adjusting, judging, construing, and sanctioning relationships" (Fiske 1992:689).

Fiske identifies four basic types of elementary social relationships which he believes people in all cultures use to generate most kinds of social interaction, evaluation and affect. He refers to these four relationships as communal sharing (cs), authority ranking (ar), equality matching (em) and market pricing (mp). Fiske works from the premise that people generally want "to relate to each other, feel committed to the basic types of relationships, regard themselves as obligated to abide by them, and impose them on other people (including third parties)" (1992:689). In the context of postgraduate supervision, Hugo (2012) has taken these four relationship types and applied them to the postgraduate supervision process, arguing that they help to illuminate some of the basic patterns of supervision.

Building on Hugo's (2012) ideas about the application of Fiske's relational models theory to the supervision process I have found the four relationship types pertinent to my own work around teaching and supervision within the community research learning approach. To this end, the next section of the chapter works with Fiske's four types of elementary social relationships as they apply to the community research learning approach.

APPLYING RELATIONAL MODELS THEORY TO THE COMMUNITY RESEARCH LEARNING APPROACH

Communal-sharing relationships

In relation to the postgraduate supervision process and in a conscious attempt to increase throughput rates whilst ensuring quality, each newly registered MEd (ELM) cohort is immediately set up as a structure to support novice researchers in the research learning process. The size of the cohort varies depending on supervision capacity within the faculty and success rates in the application process but, on average, a cohort of 12 MEd (ELM) students and three to four supervisors works well. The research learning community meets regularly throughout the two-year period of the MEd degree; it is guided by a clearly articulated purpose and follows a programme which includes a range of activities with a series of submission deadlines. In this conceptualisation, the coursework component of the degree is not perceived as an individual entity, disconnected from and preceding the development of the half-thesis. Instead it becomes reconceptualised as "integral to, and interwoven with, the research component and structured in ways which enable research and support the growth and development of the half thesis from the onset of the degree" (Grant 2013:1255).

Immediately after the establishment of the research learning community, 'communal sharing' relationships (Fiske 1991) are foregrounded within the group. Communal-sharing relationships, Fiske explains, "are based on a conception of some bounded group of people as equivalent and undifferentiated" (1992:690). In this type of relationship, Fiske contends, the focus is on the commonalities in the group rather than on distinct individual differences. Thus, in the initial stages of the research learning community, I consciously downplay the individual differences amongst the students and instead concentrate on making explicit the existing commonalities. These include factors such as they are all experienced educators, they have all been selected for the qualification, they are all novice researchers and they all have experience of educational leadership and management in the workplace. As a consequence of these commonalities, the students realise that they are similar in many respects and this shared experience is used to draw the group together.

I begin my teaching by intentionally encouraging the sharing of experiences and ideas in the form of everyday knowledge of educational leadership and management with which the students inevitably arrive. This everyday knowledge, sourced from the mass media or from the workplace, is a form of horizontal discourse which is "oral, local, context dependent and specific, tacit, multilayered and contradictory across but not within contexts" (Bernstein 2000:157). This tacit knowledge of leadership and management provides a useful starting point to the research learning process. Involvement of all participants is crucial in any research learning community and eliciting, sharing and opening this tacit knowledge out to interrogation is an important first stage in the induction process. Sharing of this tacit knowledge immediately draws the novice researchers into a relationship of communal sharing as does participating in the programme and committing to its purpose.

A further attempt to encourage sharing and develop communal-sharing relationships among the group is the sharing of material resources such as academic articles and books, notes, summaries as well as meals. These resources are shared according to need and, as Fiske explains, "simple membership in the group is sufficient to entitle one to the use of whatever resources the group controls, and long-run imbalance is not a violation of the relationship" (1992:693). As a bond begins to develop among members of the group, individuals begin to share their expertise which may be in the form of assistance in relation to library searches and the use of information technologies, for example. Other forms of sharing include the sharing of ideas and feedback during peer and lecturer learning processes (see Grant 2013), offered in a spirit of kindness and encouragement.

Authority-ranking relationships

'Authority ranking' is a second type of social relationship in Fiske's relational models theory. According to Fiske, authority ranking is based on a model of "asymmetry among people who are linearly ordered along some hierarchical social dimension" (1992:691). Authority ranking is a social reality and it is a dominant feature of a research learning community.

When educational professionals join the diverse community of postgraduate students in their particular degree cohort, they arrive with a lived experience of the hierarchical power relations of the schooling terrain. They are likely to assess how they stand in relation to the others in terms of their educational status (i.e. whether they are a principal, a head of department or a post level 1 teacher), their gender and age. In this regard, I deliberately adopt a range of strategies to diffuse the power differentials within the group. Within a short space of time, students realise that gender, age and professional ranking of the schooling system have little value in the research learning community where the focus is on the development of their scholar/researcher identity. Instead, what becomes important is the value each individual, regardless of gender, age or designation, contributes to the academic endeavour at any given time.

However, authority-ranking relationships do not only exist among the students. Relationships of power also exist between students and supervisors. As a consequence of institutional position and "epistemic credibility" (Fataar 2012:17) derived from field knowledge, academics command legitimate authority in a research learning community. Epistemic credibility is absolutely crucial to the teaching and supervision process and novice researchers join the academy particularly to draw on and learn from this expertise. Thus the relationship between students and supervisors is asymmetrical and, particularly in the initial stages, the relationship constitutes a relatively high power distance index (borrowing from Hofstede 1980). Within this linearly ordered relationship of power, it is the supervisor who takes on a pastoral responsibility and the students who defer to the seniority of the supervisor "in exchange for guidance and induction into how knowledge and the academic community work" (Hugo 2012:109). Over time and with increased participation in the community, the power distance between student and supervisor gradually decreases as the student begins to develop an academic voice and a researcher identity.

Equality-matching relationships

As a consequence of 'getting to know each other' and 'doing things together' in the communal-sharing relationships, educational professionals begin a trajectory inwards from the periphery of the ELM community, gradually extending their repertoire of knowing (both in relation to the knowledge field itself as well as to associated research processes) and developing their identity and agency as ELM scholars and researchers. Within this pedagogical space, turn-taking is crucial to ensure that each person gets an equal chance to contribute. As Waghid elaborates, "every person wants to be recognised as someone with the same basic moral worth as any other participant – that is, as a person who has something to say and wants to be heard" (2012:43).

In the community research learning approach, turn-taking is fundamental to teaching, learning and assessment as in, for example, the delivery of seminar presentations, the posing of scholarly questions and the giving of feedback (see Grant 2013 for more elaboration). At a more mundane level, turn-taking is also evident in the provision of communal lunches at contact sessions which take place on a rotational basis and which further build the sense of friendship and community. Turn-taking ensures what Fiske (1992) refers to as 'equality matching' relationships where each person is entitled to the same amount of time, input, feedback and resources so that equality and balance within the community is ensured. By virtue of equality-matching relationships within the community, each student becomes a visible presence with a right to turn-taking and the accompanying responsibility it involves. Each becomes bound by an unwritten contract to contribute equally to the community and this requisite involvement leaves little space for individuals to get left behind or drop out.

While equality and balance through turn-taking are important in the community research learning approach, what is even more critical is the culture of mutual respect, valuing and trust that must be created and in which the turn-taking takes place. The approach is premised on the idea that each individual in the group is competent and capable to participate in the discussions and activities. 'Respect for persons' (following Waghid 2012) is consciously taught and modelled and students are valued for their contributions made in the deliberation. They are also challenged to substantiate their claims with evidence acceptable within the traditions of the academy. Within the community, lecturers/supervisors lead a discussion in which they acknowledge that they do not know everything there is to know in the field and explain that they too are on a learning trajectory in much the same way the students are, merely a little further along in their learning.

To further build trust and respect, pedagogical spaces are created which involve the co-construction of aspects and activities of the course. Examples of this co-construction include the formulation of assignments, the setting of meeting and submission dates, the preparation of criteria for seminar assessment and the development of a protocol for generative participation in the community. In this secure environment, it is anticipated that these educational professionals will begin to develop an informed academic voice and participate equally in knowledge debates relevant to the field of ELM. My argument, following Ranson (2000:268), is that by developing their academic voice, these professionals will "find an identity and the possibility of agency in the world". Thus the community, through the equality-matching relationships, becomes one which recognises different voices and promotes genuine conversation as people learn "through dialogue to take a wider, more differentiated view, and thus acquire sensitivity, subtlety and capacity for judgement" (Ranson 2000:275). As these professionals become familiar with each other over time, they learn to respect the freedoms of others and, as Waghid (2012) rightly contends, friendships are engendered.

Market-pricing relationships

Initially, within the community research learning approach, it is the communal-sharing, authority-ranking and equality-matching relationships that drive the new learning. However, it soon becomes evident that these three relationships are insufficient on their own because students need to be individually rewarded for the value they bring to the community and the amount of work they do. This brings to the fore the relationship of 'market pricing' which, Fiske explains, is based on "a model of proportionality in social relationships; people attend to ratios and rates" (1992:692). What matters in this type of relationship, he argues, is how a person stands in relation to others. It works on variations in the relationships which adjust according to specific forces encountered.

Market-pricing relationships are crucial in the research learning community because they attribute value to individuals, at any given time, in proportion to the amount of effort they put into their work and the quality thereof. Hugo (2013:125) explains that in the context of education, market-pricing relationships capture the "continual process of professional judgement a teacher is engaged in where relative values of what students are doing change all the time, resulting in different judgements at different times based on the situation at hand".

Particularly in relation to the coursework component of the MEd (ELM) degree, professional judgments are continually being made regarding students' work. Each student is rewarded for the quality of work done in each assessment task, whether it is formative or summative. In this regard, the use of an assessment rubric typically outlines what is expected from students and offers a common measure against which the quality of each individual piece of work is judged. This form of assessment against a common measure is a commonplace example of market pricing within the higher education terrain.

However, market pricing is also evident in the social spaces of the group and may emerge spontaneously as individual students contribute something of particular value to the group. For example, a student might be approachable, warm and driven by a social justice consciousness. She might be the one to whom a struggling student turns when challenged by a difficult concept in an academic article. This student might informally mediate the learning for the other person, either during or following the contact session. In this scenario, the value this student brings to the group is high and it surpasses that of the other students. Another student might add value to the learning process because she has a lively sense of humour and an infectious laugh which contributes to a safe and relaxed pedagogical space for all in the group. Yet another student might stand out because she takes the lead at the level of the social in holding the group together. She might be responsible for developing the group identity through organising social events, designing a group t-shirt or arranging a group photo-shoot. Yet another student might add value to the group because of her exciting intellectual debates and challenging questions. She might be unrelenting in her quest to understand and be unafraid to challenge the status quo.

While market-pricing relationships are applicable among students in the community research learning approach, they also have purchase among supervisors. In a community research learning approach, it is unlikely that there will only be one lecturer/supervisor. As mentioned earlier, a number of supervisors may be involved in supporting the learning process, depending on supervisor availability and the number of students in the cohort. It is very likely that each supervisor will take on a different role within the community, determined by factors such as "her academic expertise in the student's area of study, her research and publications record, her knowledge of the relevant literature, and her knowledge and expertise in the appropriate methodological approaches" (Fataar 2012:17). Thus supervisors bring to the supervision process differing levels of experience and expertise and they are sometimes driven by different value sets. This market pricing of supervisors can become an obstacle to the community research learning approach when students fight for access to the supervisor with the highest market pricing and the most impressive lineage (after Hugo 2012) at the expense of less experienced supervisors. Thus supervision within a community research learning approach is complex and requires further deliberation beyond the scope of this chapter. Suffice to say that the mentoring of supervisors into the community approach is crucial in order to guard against uneven supervisory support. Equally important is the critique which the supervisory team brings to the research agenda and which can offer a necessary counter-voice to the lead supervisor and reduce the risks associated with lineage and potential cloning of students.

LEARNING IN COMMUNITY: MOVING CONFIDENTLY TOWARDS CENTRAL PARTICIPATION

In the chapter thus far I have used the four types of elementary social relationships associated with Fiske's (1991, 1992) relational models theory to help me describe and explain the central facets of research learning of novice researchers within a community learning approach. I have demonstrated how the four relationships of communal sharing, authority ranking, equality matching and market pricing are useful in illuminating some of the basic relationship patterns of supervision within a research learning community. However, the argument is incomplete as it stands without some discussion of how these relationships contribute to what Wenger refers to as "changing participation and identity transformation in a community of practice" (1998:11). To ensure changing participation and identity transformation, I argue that the development of confidence is a central feature of this research learning process. Here I draw on the work of Graven who asserts that "confidence is part of an individual teacher's ways of learning through experiencing, doing, being, and belonging. As such it is deeply interconnected with learning as changing, meaning, practice, identity and community" (2004:179).

Thus, through the relationships of communal sharing, authority ranking, equality matching and market pricing experienced during the interplay of learning processes (peer-, self- and lecturer-initiated) (see Grant 2013) within the research learning community, the novice researchers begin to develop confidence. This level of confidence increases over time as each student becomes progressively more proficient as both "a user of various specialist discourses and a participant within the relevant knowledge communities" (Northedge 2003:22). As the individual capacity of each student is affirmed, they grow in confidence and embark on a journey from the periphery of the research learning community "towards more central participation, identification and belonging" (Graven 2004:208). This journey in confidence culminates in the student being able to "adopt a stance, a theoretical framework, or language that they use to 'gaze' upon the world" (Bernstein 2000:164).

It stands to reason that as students develop in confidence over time, they will rely increasingly less on the support drawn from communal-sharing relationships. With increased confidence, dependence on supervisors will also decrease and the student/supervisor relationship will move towards a low power distance index (again borrowing from Hofstede 1980). Thus, as the supervisory relationship comes to term, balance is established when the student "takes on the mantle of independent researcher doing her own work in her own voice" (Hugo 2012:109). In this way, equilibrium in the student-supervisor relationship is achieved as students move towards full membership of the field.

CONCLUDING COMMENTS

The complex and diverse terrain of higher education in South Africa today demands that we think afresh about our pedagogy and supervision strategies if we are to improve the number and quality of passes as well as student throughput rates at both undergraduate and postgraduate levels. Against this backdrop, the focus of this chapter has been the MEd degree in ELM and particularly the coursework/half-thesis offering. The chapter has arisen out of a concern that many students spend far too long trying to complete the half-thesis component of the degree and some do not complete at all.

In response to this crisis, I have advocated that the traditional one-to-one supervisory relationship can no longer be considered the only option in the higher education arena in South Africa. This is primarily because the one-to-one supervision model reflects a Western preoccupation with the individual and, as such, is limited to the research learning of *one* student via *one* supervisor to the exclusion of other sources of research learning. Thus, and given the national imperative to increase the percentage of university students studying at postgraduate level, this model is fast becoming inefficient, costly and inappropriate for the South African context.

In contrast to the Western focus on the individual, South Africa's philosophical heritage hinges on the consciousness of human interconnectedness and interdependence and, as Ramphele (2008) contends, this philosophy has been imbedded in the conduct of African social relationships from time immemorial. Perhaps the time is right to bring to life this philosophy in our teaching, learning and supervision practices within the postgraduate terrain. One such way, I have argued, is to draw on social learning theory and adopt a communal approach to postgraduate supervision. This collective approach foregrounds the pedagogy of research learning, it creates the space for a diversity of views and voices to be heard and it provides structured support in an expanded and enriched teaching and learning process.

Thus the community research learning approach offers students a network of social relationships within which to learn about and do research and Fiske's (1991, 1992) work on relational models theory is pertinent here. His four types of social relationships (communal-sharing, authority-ranking, equality-matching and market-pricing) are useful in describing and explaining the relationships inherent in the various pedagogical practices as novice researchers engage in the research learning process and begin a trajectory inwards towards the centre of the practice. These four social relationships offer what Hugo (2012) refers to as an orientating device which helps one to steer a course in the complex pedagogic space of postgraduate study. But these four relationship types are insufficient on their own without some focus on the pivotal role of confidence (after Graven 2004) in our understanding of research learning in the trajectory towards more central participation, identification and belonging.

In closing, I believe that adopting a community researching learning approach in our postgraduate work has the potential to increase both the quality of student passes and student throughput rates while also offering a transformative learning experience for postgraduate students. As such, it can make a contribution to the country's social justice agenda. In this way, I argue that as we continue to theorise postgraduate supervision, the approach will push the boundaries of postgraduate work, particularly at the MEd level, beyond their current location.

ACKNOWLEDGEMENTS

This chapter would be incomplete without acknowledging two cohorts of MEd students I was fortunate to work with from 2008 to 2011. Their commitment to the academic project was a source of inspiration to me. In addition, a number of colleagues have read earlier drafts of this chapter and made valuable comments: Professors Wayne Hugo, Aslam Fataar, Chrissie Boughey, Hennie van der Mescht, Dr Carol Thomson and Ms Farhana Kajee.

REFERENCES

Bernstein B. 2000. *Pedagogy, symbolic control and identity: Theory research, critique*. Second edition. Oxford: Rowman and Littlefield.

Boud D & Lee A. 2005. 'Peer learning' as pedagogic discourse for research education. *Studies in Higher Education*, 30(5):501-516.

Fataar A. 2012. Negotiating student identity in the doctoral proposal development process: A personal reflective account. In: A Fataar (ed). *Debating thesis supervision*. Stellenbosch: SUN MeDIA. 13-35.

Fiske AP. 1991. *Structures of social life: The four elementary forms of human relations*. New York: The Free Press.

Fiske AP. 1992. The four elementary forms of sociality: Framework for a unified theory of social relations. *Psychological Review*, 99(4):689-723.

Grant C. 2013. Using assessment strategically to gestate a student thesis: Learning through community. *South African Journal of Higher Education*, 27(5):1250-1263.

Graven M. 2004. Investigating mathematics teacher learning within an in-service community of practice: The centrality of confidence. *Educational Studies in Mathematics*, 57:177-211.

Hodkinson P & Hodkinson H. 2004. A constructive critique of communities of practice: Moving beyond Lave and Wenger. Seminar paper presented at the Integrating Work and Learning – Contemporary Issues Seminar Series, University of Technology, Sydney, 11 May.

Hofstede G. 1980. Motivation, leadership and organisation: Do American theories apply abroad? *Organisational Dynamics*, 9(1):42-63.

Hugo W. 2012. Supervision response. In: A Fataar (ed). *Debating thesis supervision*. Stellenbosch: SUN MeDIA. 107-113.

Hugo W. 2013. *Cracking the code to educational analysis*. Cape Town: Pearson.

Jansen J, Herman C & Pillay V. 2004. Research learning. *Journal of Education*, 34:79-102.

Letseka M & Maile S. 2008. *High university drop-out rates: A threat to South Africa's future*. Pretoria: HSRC.

Lotz-Sisitka H, Ellery K, Olvitt L, Schudel I & O'Donoghue R. 2010. Cultivating a scholarly community of practice. *Acta Academica Supplementum*, 1:130-150.

Maistry SM. 2008. Transcending traditional boundaries for teacher professional development: Exploring a community of practice approach to CPD. *Journal of Education*, 43:127-153.

Northedge A. 2003. Rethinking teaching in the context of diversity. *Teaching in Higher Education*, 8(1):17-32.

Quinn L. 2012. Understanding resistance: An analysis of discourses in academic staff development. *Studies in Higher Education*, 37(1):69-83.

Ramphele M. 2008. *Laying ghosts to rest: Dilemmas of the transformation in South Africa*. Cape Town: Tafelberg.

Ranson S. 2000. Recognising the pedagogy of voice in a learning community. *Education Management and Administration*, 28(3):263-279.

RSA (Republic of South Africa). 2007. *The Higher Education Qualifications Framework. Government Gazette*, 5 October. Pretoria: Department of Education.

RSA DHET (Republic of South Africa. Department of Higher Education and Training). 2012. *Green Paper for Post-school Education and Training*. Pretoria. [Accessed 12 January 2013] www.info.gov.za/view/downloadFileAction?

Sayed Y, Kruss G & Badat S. 1998. Students' experience of postgraduate supervision at the University of the Western Cape. *Journal of Further and Higher Education*, 22(3):275-285.

Scott I, Yeld N & Hendry J. 2007. *Higher Education Monitor No. 6*. Pretoria: Council on Higher Education.

Snowball JD & Sayigh E. 2007. Using the tutorial system to improve the quality of feedback to students in large class teaching. *South African Journal of Higher Education*, 21(2):321-333.

Waghid Y. 2012. Education, responsibility and democratic justice: Cultivating friendship to alleviate some of the injustices on the African continent. In: A Fataar (ed). *Debating thesis supervision*. Stellenbosch: SUN PRESS. 37-55.

Wenger E. 1998. *Communities of practice: Learning, meaning and identity*. Cambridge: Cambridge University Press.

COURSEWORK IN AUSTRALIAN PHD PROGRAMMES

WHY IS THIS A BOUNDARY AND HOW IS IT BEING PUSHED?

Margaret Kiley, Joe Luca and Anna Cowan

BACKGROUND

Other than in a few isolated instances, the Australian PhD has been almost exclusively through 'experiential research learning'. In other words candidates work with a supervisor or supervisory panel who guides their learning of, and about, research through undertaking a research project. To support candidates and supervisors universities generally offer a broad range of workshops, seminars, and other learning activities (Cumming & Kiley 2009) but until very recently, formal coursework has not been a standard part of the Australian PhD although it is part of the Professional Doctorate.

Within this context, it is of note that over the past 12 to 18 months the introduction of coursework into the Australian PhD is a development that is quickly gaining interest, although with varying levels of support from candidates and supervisors. One of the major areas of discussion relates to whether the coursework is related to research processes e.g. research methods, or whether it is more of a disciplinary nature, or whether it should be more closely related to employment capability.

This paper reports the findings from a research project currently being undertaken in Australia and includes the various negatives and positives that candidates and staff have expressed regarding the introduction of formal coursework, and the models being developed. It notes the boundaries between coursework and research degrees and the hurdles they present to students, supervisors and institutions.

It is of interest that the development of coursework in the Australian PhD is occurring at the same time as the implementation of the new Australian Qualifications Framework (AQF) and the introduction of the Tertiary Education Quality Standards Agency (TEQSA). These two separate but linked developments have caused all universities to examine and more closely define curriculum, course articulation, and pedagogical implications at the postgraduate coursework and research levels. Given that Australia is one of the few countries that does not offer formal coursework in the PhD it is worth looking at those systems that do. For example in North America the doctorate involves a combination of research and coursework with increasing specialisation and intensity. The provision of coursework in PhD programmes is commonplace in North America and Europe and it is of interest to note that when a phrase such as 'coursework in the PhD' is mentioned in Australia the most common response is 'Oh, you are talking about the US model'. Certainly the doctoral degree in North America involves a combination of research and coursework. Furthermore, the doctorate across Europe includes coursework and in the UK it is noteworthy that the inclusion of coursework in the doctorate is becoming increasingly common (see for example http://www.esrc.ac.uk). Having said that, in Australia the professional doctorate has included coursework, however, despite a surge in popularity in the 1990s, the number of professional doctorate programmes in Australia accounts for a very small percentage of the total doctoral enrolment.

Therefore, while we can learn from other systems and models, the adoption of programmes from elsewhere is clearly not appropriate given the particular qualities of the Australian PhD programme. One of these qualities is the funding model in Australia which leads some Australian Deans to consider the addition of coursework to be out of the question. One of the main reasons for this view is that funding for PhD candidates through the Research Training Scheme (RTS) is for a maximum of 4 years (FTE) and there is some concern that coursework will increase the time to completion. Given that Government funding is only for the four years of funding provided by the RTS, it is not surprising that many university Deans of Graduate Research are concerned that if there is additional time required for coursework then from where will the funding come? Additionally, where do universities find the funding to cover the costs of additional coursework teaching? These are just some of the issues related to the possible introduction of coursework in the PhD. Despite these issues, an informal survey of Australian universities conducted early in 2013 found that 55 per cent reported that they have been actively discussing and implementing some form of doctoral coursework into their PhD and another 20% considering this action in the near future.

In curriculum terms, a basic question that needs to be answered is: Should coursework in the doctorate be provided to address a perceived deficit in the candidate's prior research learning, or is coursework a means of 'value-adding' to a learning experience. Or maybe coursework should relate to broader skills such as leadership. For example, McAlpine and Asghar (2010) suggest institutions could offer candidates leadership that incorporates the broad skills of "teamwork, communication and collaboration". An issue impacting on this question relates to the increasing variation in 'the Australian PhD'. While an obvious variation might be claimed to be the Professional Doctorate and the PhD, recent research suggests that there is substantial variation within the programme generally termed 'the PhD' (Group of Eight 2013) as well as the pathways into a doctoral programme (Kiley 2011). With an average commencing age of 33 for PhD candidates across all disciplines (Department of Innovation 2011) it is clear that many candidates have had substantial work experience prior to commencing their doctoral studies, particularly in the social sciences. Furthermore, the percentage of international students undertaking doctoral studies has increased considerably for example "total research student numbers from 2001 to 2010 increased by 29%, principally due to overseas student growth with the proportion of domestic students decreasing from 86 per cent to 73 per cent" (Larkins 2012:2).

Workforce issues are significant issues in Australia and the employability of doctoral graduates has come under considerable scrutiny (Neumann & Tan 2011; Department of Industry 2012). However, this discussion is not confined to Australia. For example, Kyvik and Olsen (2012) undertook a study in Norway which addressed graduates' views on the relevance of doctoral coursework to three types of employment, academia, applied research institutes and industrial laboratories, and non-research workplaces. They found that while the coursework was considered less helpful than the knowledge they had gained from their research, for those working in non-research environments, the various generic skills they had developed were considered more helpful than in other employment areas.

A further issue related to coursework relates to pedagogy, that is, how are the various learning experiences provided for candidates? From studies undertaken by Cumming and Kiley (2009) and McAlpine and Asghar (2010:168) to name just two, many of the positive experiences reported by candidates were of a collaborative, candidate-centred nature. These include experience such a reading and writing groups, involvement in professional associations, and work experience.

This chapter addresses some of these above issues through a study undertaken with two Australian universities. The study reported here was part of a larger study undertaken across a range of Australian universities but these two universities undertook specific, in-depth studies with a view to introducing some form of coursework into their existing programmes.

PART FOUR • SUPERVISION STRATEGIES

RESEARCH DESIGN

The two universities involved in the study were quite different from one another. University A is a new generation university with a strong focus on the professions and, on the whole, a mature-age student cohort. This university has a very active Graduate Centre that initiates policy development and its implementation across the institution as well as support and development for all candidates and supervisors. This institution had discussed the idea of introducing coursework, but this had not been formalised at the time of the research. For University A, supervisors and candidates across a range of Humanities and Social Sciences (HASS) and Science, Technology, Engineering and Mathematics (STEM) disciplines were involved in the research. University B, on the other hand, is a research-intensive university and only the Science supervisors and candidates were involved. The focus on Sciences was for a number of reasons, with one of the main ones being that the Social Sciences at that university had already introduced coursework and the study was aimed at working with groups considering the introduction of coursework. This university has a decentralised approach to policy development and implementation. This is evidenced by different parts of the university having quite different policies and practices related to coursework in the PhD. For example, one faculty has had required PhD coursework for almost 30 years, another had introduced quite different forms of coursework a few years ago, and some faculties have no requirements regarding coursework at all. The faculty in the study was at the stage of considering the introduction of coursework.

Given the structures and approaches of these two institutions, and that they were in quite different parts of the country and representing quite different types of institutions, they were regarded as excellent choices to demonstrate variation as well as any possible similarity in the research.

Data were collected from both universities using two different methods. The first was from workshops and focus groups with staff and candidates. The second was from an online survey to candidates.

The aim of the workshops and focus groups was to facilitate participants in their discussions of the various issues related to why they might want to introduce coursework, how they might do that and what the content might address. Overall, 70 candidates and supervisors took part in the workshops/focus groups (31 at University A and 39 at University B). The second form of data came from an online survey administered to candidates from each of the universities. The survey asked candidates about their views and experiences of coursework, their expectations of employment after their doctorate; and various kinds of demographic information related to study and employment. Responses to the survey varied with 132 from University A and 185 participating from University B (response rates of 19 per cent and 23 per cent respectively).

FINDINGS

Focus groups of supervisors and candidates

With each focus/discussion group with staff and candidates the most common responses early in discussion were negative, for example:

- If students were 'off doing coursework' that would take time away from their 'research' requiring additional candidature time but there was no additional funding
- Coursework implied a lack of individual learning and development opportunities if candidates were all required to undertake the same coursework
- When should coursework be offered, should it be at the beginning, at the end or throughout candidature?
- How could the disciplinary nature of research degrees be addressed if there was some form of faculty of university required coursework?
- Who would teach these courses when staff already had full teaching loads and would they have the expertise and who would handle the additional administrative loads?

However, after some discussion several perceived benefits of formal coursework emerged as follows:

- The development of peer networks through being in courses thereby alleviating isolation, particularly in the Humanities and Social Sciences.
- Opportunities for candidates to work across disciplinary and epistemological boundaries.
- Assistance to supervisors in that they did not have to work with each candidate on the same issues, i.e. levels of efficiency.
- The possibility of a more equitable education for candidates with less reliance on the quality of individual supervisors.
- Opportunities to address particular values and directions of the university.
- Greater opportunities to address employability and generic skills.

Given the diversity of candidates which include increases in international enrolments, part-time (almost 50 per cent for domestic candidates have some periods of part-time enrolment), females (now 50 per cent) and age as noted above it is not surprising that an issue that arose strongly in any workshops with research supervisors and candidates was the passion with which those involved addressed the importance of recognizing and accommodating the individual needs of candidates, as well as the school and disciplinary idiosyncrasies which shape the candidate's experience. In several cases, in initial discussions, staff can see no way in which candidates could engage in some form of faculty, let alone university-wide programme. Academics and candidates argued that there needed to be greater flexibility, as well as being much more alert to what is needed and how and when it is provided or delivered. Much of this thinking accounts for suggestions such as Individual Learning Plans for candidates. Similarly, it was suggested that many candidates needed to be more proactive in terms of determining their own learning needs and required training and development.

Once some of the major issues had been discussed, the groups began to discuss content, including aims and learning outcomes. From the discussion it was possible to identify three main kinds of courses, namely enabling, enriching and articulating courses:

- Enabling courses aim to assist candidates in 'getting off to a good start' and/or to accommodate candidates who are underprepared in research. These courses might have a focus on research processes which are front-ended into the first six to nine months of candidature or advanced level disciplinary knowledge in the first 12 months. Such courses are often considered as providing exit qualifications e.g. Graduate Certificate or Diploma, for candidates who do not complete the PhD award.
- Enriching or value-adding, the second view, is where a university provides specific experiences for candidates that are beyond the standard 'completion of a PhD'. These experiences might relate to the nature of the university, for example the values of social justice or ensuring that one's research contributes to the region. Or, they might be designed to enable candidates to gain experiences by studying in another country or institution for part of their candidature.
- Articulating, the third view, relates to skill development to meet the perceived criticisms of employers. These courses are generally made available later in candidature or on completion of the degree and might include experiences such as teaching, project and financial management or six-months industrial/commercial setting that provides assessable skill development in an authentic setting beyond the academy.

Decisions as to the type of approach have been motivated by a number of factors including: the size of candidate cohort; the characteristics of the 'typical' candidate: and the characteristics of the discipline and university.

Survey results from candidate survey

The survey results are presented in two main parts: a) the demographic differences and b) comments related to coursework with comments related to demographic differences where relevant.

Demographic differences

The respondents from the two universities were both very similar with regard to the split between domestic (just on 70 per cent) and international (30 per cent) each. Also, the respondents were very similar in their stage of candidature at the time of completing the survey with approximately 28 per cent in the first third of candidature, 26 per cent in the middle 46 per cent in the final third. Table 9.1 outlines some of the demographic details of the respondents including sex, age, enrolment type and employment prior to candidature.

TABLE 9.1 Respondent demographics sex, age, enrolment status, programme and employment

	University A %	University B %
Female	69	61
Male	31	39
Age:		
• 20-29	7	53
• 30-39	35	26
• 40-49	24	14
• 50-59	29	5
• 60+	5	2
Full-time	64	80
Part-time	36	20
Enrolled in:		
• PhD	95	98
• Professional Doctorate	4	1
• Other	1	1
Employment prior to candidature:		
• Full-time	55	49
• Part-time/casual	36	34
• Not at all	9	17

The data regarding age accord with recent Australian Government data that suggests that while the median age at commencement of all candidates in Australia across all disciplines is 33, in the Chemical Sciences, for example, the median age is 22 and in areas such as Education it is closer to 45 years (Department of Innovation 2011).

Of all respondents employed prior to enrolment, 49 per cent in University A had been employed in the Education field, followed by 20 per cent in government and in University B 47 per cent had been employed education, followed by government with 21 per cent. Education was also the most popular field for both cohorts with regard to anticipated employment after graduation with remarkable similarity between the two cohorts of 67 per cent from University A and 68 per cent from University B with over 80 per cent from both groups expecting their employment to be in the university sector rather than schools or the technical and vocational education sectors.

Views on coursework

Following the details regarding the demographic data of respondents, we now move on to respondents' experiences and views on coursework in the PhD. Given that formal coursework had not yet been introduced into the two cohorts, it is not surprising that only quite small percentages of respondents had undertaken coursework as part of their doctoral programme: in University A 15 per cent and University B only 10 per cent had been undertaking formal coursework. With such a small number it is difficult to draw any conclusions from the following, however, as a matter of interest all agreed that the courses were relevant to their doctoral programme and the main benefits of the coursework included:

- Providing background knowledge for doctoral research
- Increasing knowledge about the discipline field
- Helping solve problems in the field of study.

However, when all respondents were asked if they thought coursework should be required 55 per cent and 52 per cent respectively suggested that approximately one third of their doctoral programme should be coursework with the majority suggesting it should be in the first year of candidature.

DISCUSSION

From the research two specific examples serve to demonstrate the variation of institution, curriculum and purposes for introducing coursework into the PhD.

The first example is from University A, the new generation university with a strong focus on the professions. At this university, using the Australian Qualifications Framework (AQF) as a model, staff and candidates started by developing a matrix of learning outcomes that they believed candidates should be able to demonstrate at the completion of their doctoral programme. With this matrix the university is now developing individualised skills audits and learning plans. These will be provided to enable candidates to work with their supervisory team to identify the areas in which they have strengths and where there are areas that need addressing. From there each candidate will develop a learning plan to assist them in meeting the university's milestones for candidature. This outcome has been particularly important to staff at that institution because it explicitly addresses the strong focus on the individual candidate and supervisory team that had been made so clear in early discussions.

The second example comes from one discipline in the Sciences at University B. This discipline generally takes younger students, i.e. early or mid-twenties from a variety of undergraduate disciplinary backgrounds, and so staff are very keen to introduce one year of coursework at the beginning of doctoral candidature which is disciplinary in nature. This, they argue will ensure that all PhD candidates are 'on the same page' when they commence their research given the variation in their previous disciplinary experience.

Other examples identified from the broader research project include:

- Four formal research-processes courses in which candidate enrol and must successfully complete in their first 12 months.
- Two courses related to approaches to research and ethics which are conducted across the whole university for all new candidates in their first year. This approach is designed to provide new candidates with a broad overview of the different type of research being undertaken across the institution and the related research methods.

As this chapter has attempted to demonstrate, suggesting something seemingly as simple as 'introducing coursework into the PhD' is anything but simple. Variations are evident depending on university type, candidate cohort, and discipline. As various models emerge, and as staff and candidates become more used to the idea of coursework in the PhD, it is anticipated that institutions will learn and 'borrow' from one another but for the moment the strong variation provides an exciting opportunity for curriculum developments in Australian research education.

ACKNOWLEDGEMENT

Support for this project has been provided by the Australian Government Office for Learning and Teaching. The views in this project do not necessarily reflect the views of the Australian Government Office for Learning and Teaching.

REFERENCES

Cumming J. & Kiley M. 2009. *Research Graduate Skills Project*. Canberra, Australian National University.

Department of Industry, Innovation Science, Research and Tertiary Education. 2012. *Australian Small Business: Key statistics and analysis*. Canberra: Department of Industry, Innovation Science, Research and Tertiary Education.

Department of Innovation Industry Science and Research. 2011. *Research skills for an innovative future: A research workforce strategy to cover the decade to 2020 and beyond*. Canberra: Department of Innovation, Industry, Science and Research (DIISR).

Department of Innovation Industry Science and Research. 2011. *Research workforce strategy: Discipline case studies*. Canberra: DIISR.

Group of Eight. 2013. *The changing PhD: Discussion paper*. Canberra: Group of Eight.

Kiley M. 2011. *Where are out doctoral candidates coming from and why?* Canberra: The Australian National University.

Kyvik S. & Olsen T. 2012. The relevance of doctoral training in different labour markets. *Journal of Education and Work* 25(2):205-224.

Larkins F. 2012. *Australian Higher Education Policy Analysis: Gender, citizenship and discipline in Australian Higher Education Research Training*. Melbourne: L.H. Martin Institute.

McAlpine L. & Asghar A. 2010. Enhancing academic climate: Doctoral students as their own developers. *International Journal for Academic Development* 15(2):167-178.

Neumann R. & Tan T. 2011. From PhD to initial employment: The doctorate in a knowledge economy. *Studies in Higher Education* 36(5):601-614.

10 THE COHORT SUPERVISION MODEL
TO WHAT EXTENT DOES IT FACILITATE DOCTORAL SUCCESS?

Nonnie Botha

INTRODUCTION AND BACKGROUND

The cohort supervision model for master's and doctoral students is employed in various permutations in many different countries in the world. This is reflected in some of the recent literature that refers to cohort supervision occurring in Australia (Carson 2012), New Zealand (McDonald & Kēpa 2012), Norway (Dysthe, Samara & Westrheim 2006; Samara 2006), South Africa (De Lange, Pillay & Chikoko 2011; Samuel & Vithal 2011), the UK (Fenge 2012; Wisker, Robinson & Schacham 2007) and the USA (Holloway & Alexandre 2012; Santicola 2013; Tuckwiller & Childress 2012). Undoubtedly, this supervision model is probably applied in many more countries and is reported on in literature that was not consulted.

Research on the cohort supervision model, as reported in the literature, covers a number of aspects and makes some significant recommendations. Some studies highlight the challenges related to this supervision model, which include finding time to participate (De Lange et al. 2011:27; Dysthe et al. 2006:300), being committed to the model (De Lange et al. 2011:27; Dysthe et al. 2006:300), the quality of supervisors' participation (De Lange et al. 2011:27), finding the ideal size (De Lange et al. 2011:27) and the ideal programme for a particular group (Tuckwiller & Childress 2012:51). These are seen to be challenges since they might differ from one cohort to the next, dealing with conflicting ideas (De Lange et al. 2011:27) and exposing cohort students to academic opinions from outside the particular cohort (Tuckwiller & Childress 2012:51). The advantages of this supervision model are indicated in some studies, these including that it offers an opportunity for scholarly development for both students and supervisors (De Lange et al. 2011:27; Dysthe et al. 2006:300; Samara 2006:115), provides sustained support (De Lange et al. 2011:27; Wisker *et al.* 2007:309), promotes increased completion rates (De Lange *et al.* 2011:27), develops a community of practice (COP) (De Lange *et al.* 2011:27; Wisker *et al.* 2007:309), is regarded as convenient (Tuckwiller & Childress 2012:51) and provides a plan of progress in advance (Tuckwiller & Childress 2012). The objectives of such groups are described as to improve students' academic writing, to provide support to students throughout all the stages of their research and to promote timely completion (Dysthe *et al.* 2006:300). Some authors argue that timely completion is probably due to the relationships that develop over time in this supervision model (Tuckwiller & Childress 2012). Other objectives are to "support intellectual development and knowledge production" through a community of practice, to provide "a safe and critical space for learning to work together" and to promote the renewal of research (De Lange *et al.* 2011:17). The value of peer learning is the focus of the study reported on by Fenge (2012:401) while Holloway and Alexandre (2012:88) report on an investigation into relational structures in cohort supervision. The characteristics of graduates from a doctoral cohort programme emerged from a study by Santicola (2013:260-262), namely they are all committed and disciplined, they prioritise the doctorate, they prefer to work alone and independently and they are usually employed full time.

Although the cohort model of postgraduate supervision is used widely internationally and research has been conducted on its objectives, advantages and challenges as well as on how to improve specific cohort programmes, the ways in which it facilitates doctoral success in particular have not yet been investigated. This chapter aims at filling this gap in the research spectrum by identifying the ways in which cohort supervision may facilitate doctoral success. Examining what doctoral success exactly entails and how it can be measured, falls outside the scope of this chapter; instead it will focus on applying Bitzer's conceptual framework for exploring doctoral success through a small-scale empirical study as well as exploring some literature. While the empirical research provides data from two South African universities, thus supplementing the South African-based literature, most of the literature reports on an international perspective on this matter. The potential significance of my small contribution lies in some emerging pointers towards a supervision pedagogy that may better enhance doctoral success.

In the context of this chapter it is worthwhile to note the various forms of supervision that include more than one student and/or more than one supervisor, therefore a brief overview is presented below of such supervision forms as described in selected literature. This is followed by an exposition of Bitzer's conceptual framework for exploring doctoral success, which is subsequently mapped onto the outcomes of a small-scale empirical study, thus identifying ways in which cohort supervision facilitates doctoral success. Confirmation and expansion of the mapping outcomes are sought in the literature, hereby providing insights into the South African as well as the international context of cohort supervision. Finally, the chapter is concluded by presenting some suggestions for improving the cohort supervision model in the form of emerging pointers towards a supervision pedagogy that enhances doctoral success, nationally and internationally.

FORMS OF SUPERVISION WHERE MORE THAN ONE STUDENT AND/OR SUPERVISOR IS INVOLVED

As mentioned above, it could be useful to take cognisance of ways in which the traditional one-to-one supervision model has been supplemented or replaced by other forms of supervision, mainly to improve the quality of the supervision and thus the student experience and development towards doctorateness. One of these attempts at improving quality is to add additional supervisors to support student development. Zhao (2003:191) refers to new supervisory practices that include joint supervision of one student by two or more supervisors and "committee supervision, which provides complementary expertise that students can call upon". Watts (2010:335) worked on team supervision where supervision teams of two, three and four members are not uncommon, while Manathunga (2012) reported on team supervision in connection with supervisor support and development. Wisker et al. refer to guardian supervisors, who are expected to "encourage the work of the student group and of the individual students with their research and supervisor" (2007:309).

Creating contexts where students can draw on each other's inputs, sometimes with supervisor guidance, is one of the quality additions in the supervisory spectrum referred to in the literature. Chisin and M'Rithaa report on the Design Research Activities Workgroup (DRAW) that was initiated at the Central University of Technology in South Africa "to support postgraduate students within the design departments and to improve supervision capacity" and which is based on a collective learning approach "while critically re-interpreting the interaction between supervisors and postgraduate students" (2012:88). Collaborative study groups (Abbey 1997, cited in Conrad 2003), research writing groups (Maher 2008, cited in Fenge 2012) and supervisory groups that involve "students in their own and other's supervision" (Zhao 2003:192) are other variations of this form of support. Closely related to these is the workshop approach as mentioned by Zuber-Skerritt and Knight (1986, cited in Conrad 2003), Topping (2000, cited in Conrad 2003), Juniper and Cooper (2002, cited in Conrad 2003) and Burnett (1999, cited in Zhao 2003:192). Dysthe et al.

(2006) explored alternative supervision practices, including student colloquia, which are also close to the workshop approach.

The above-mentioned supervision practices all involve either more than one student or more than one supervisor or both. For the purpose of this chapter the term cohort supervision will refer to those alternatives to the one-to-one supervision model that combines the inputs from student peers as well as supervisor peers, thus doubly enriching the student (and supervisor) experience and usually involving students that are in the same phase of their studies. Although the number of research publications on the cohort model is rather limited, there are some references to it in the literature. Work that focused on the cohort model of supervision was done by Teitel (1997), who 'took stock' of a doctoral cohort programme with the purpose of improving it and Zhao (2003:192) who identified various models of supervision, including a collaborative cohort model. Conrad reports on work done to identify "especially effective supervision and support by the department and faculty" (2003:2) and mentions a number of studies that highlight efforts to overcome isolation, usually by providing space for community; these studies refer to, inter alia, cohort supervision (Phillips 1989, cited in Conrad 2003; Witte & James 1998, cited in Conrad 2003). Dysthe et al. (2006) explored alternative supervision practices, including when there are two supervisors and their students, which can be regarded as a rudimentary form of cohort supervision. Wisker et al. (2007), who built their work about supervisory relationships around the theoretical framework of communities of practice, refer specifically to cohorts of postgraduate students in this context. De Lange et al. (2011:15) report on cohort supervision as having "great value in developing scholarship and reflective practice in candidates, in providing support and supervision, and in sustaining students towards the completion of their doctorates". Samuel and Vithal (2011:76) explore the cohort model as a context that promotes "multi- and interdisciplinary notions of responsiveness to knowledge production in community". Fenge (2012:403) highlights that some form of group supervision is likely to be of special importance in professional doctorates, as such students need to connect their research to their practice, specifically mentioning the cohort model. Other recent studies on cohort supervision include that by Holloway and Alexandre (2012) who explored relational learning and boundary crossing in cohort communities, McDonald and Kēpa (2012:1) who reported on a cohort study that "realises the potential of the Maori PhD candidate in the project", Tuckwiller and Childress (2012) who assessed a doctoral cohort programme with recommendations for improvement and Santicola (2013) who investigated student characteristics that contributed to persistence in a doctoral cohort programme. The above-mentioned conceptions of cohort supervision are all perceived in the literature to have distinct advantages more so than disadvantages, thus making efforts to improve and re-vision the various models worthwhile for students, supervisors and universities.

BITZER'S CONCEPTUAL FRAMEWORK FOR EXPLORING DOCTORAL SUCCESS

Bitzer developed his "preliminary theoretical or conceptual framework that might be useful for further investigating the phenomenon of doctoral study success associated with quality" (2011:425), by exploring factors that could possibly limit or promote success and quality in doctoral studies. These factors are categorised as the doctoral candidate's personal context, support context, programme context and institutional context. The framework is shown below in Figure 10.1.

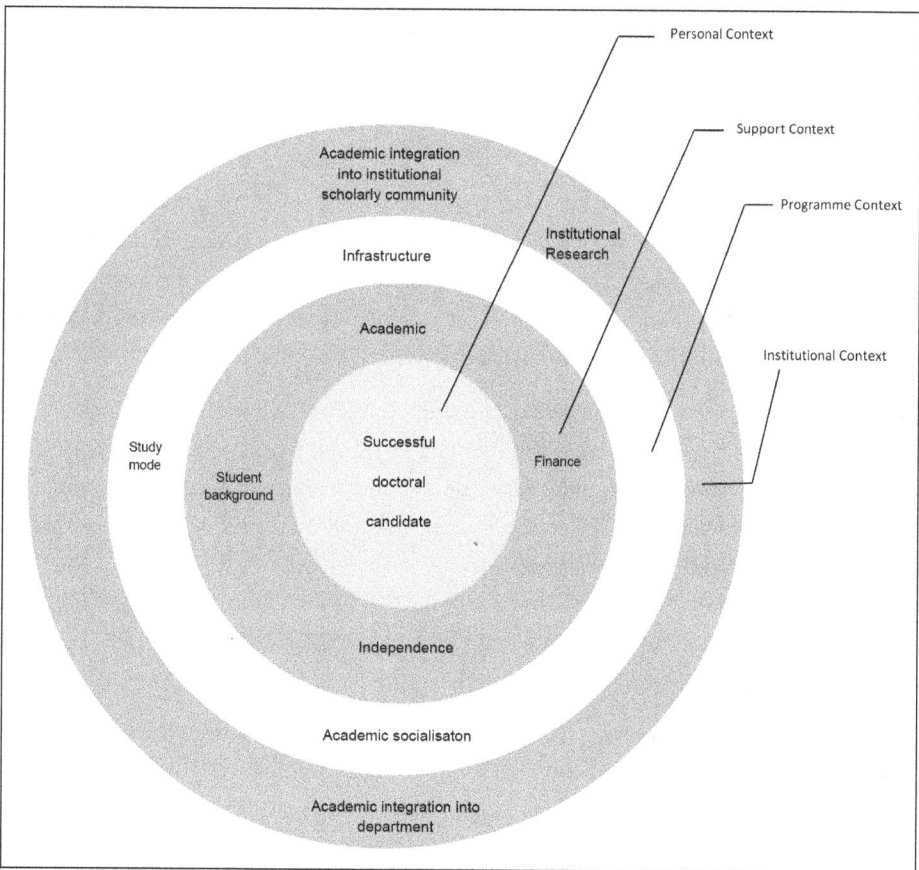

FIGURE 10.1 Bitzer's conceptual framework for exploring doctoral success (Bitzer 2011:438)

The doctoral candidate him-/herself is at the core of doctoral success. Thus the personal environment and the qualities of the doctoral student are crucial for attaining success in doctoral studies (Bitzer 2011:438).

The successful doctoral candidate is situated within the support or social context. Critical factors in this context are potential academic isolation, independence, student background (diversity) and financial support. It is important to note that none of these factors on its own is likely to explain doctoral success, but that how they relate to each other and the dominance (or not) of any one or more of the factors need to be taken into account (Bitzer 2011:438-439).

The third factor represents the programme context. The mode of study (examples of this include whether it is part-time (PT) or full-time (FT) study; research only, structured coursework only or a combination of the two) is a critical factor in this context. Other crucial factors in this context are the infrastructure offered to the candidate by the department or institution, the monitoring of the study and the extent of academic socialisation of the candidate (Bitzer 2011:439).

The widest environment that influences doctoral success in this framework is the institutional context. The doctoral candidate's integration into and participation in the institutional scholarly community is seen as critical to doctoral success (Bitzer 2011:439). It seems clear that all factors in this theoretical framework overlap with each other and that they are interdependent.

The above-mentioned four contexts of the doctoral candidate are now mapped onto the cohort supervision environment as it emerged from the outcomes of a small-scale research project, in order to determine the extent to which this kind of supervision facilitates doctoral success. The mapping is also confirmed and supplemented from selected literature on cohort supervision.

MAPPING THE CONTEXTS OF THE DOCTORAL CANDIDATE ONTO THE COHORT SUPERVISION ENVIRONMENT

The cohort supervision environment has been reported on in the literature; however, very little has been published on the South African context and although slightly more appears on the international context, the latter is also quite limited. To gain additional insights about the South African context, a small-scale empirical research project was conducted.

Small-scale empirical research

The empirical study was conducted to determine the extent to which the cohort supervision model, as it occurs at the specific site, facilitates doctoral success according to Bitzer's conceptual framework. A case study design was employed, contextualised in one faculty at a South African university with additional enrichment from the context of a second South African university. In the former faculty, the cohort supervision model is used for master's and doctoral students who prefer to participate in the group sessions, additional to the one-to-one supervision they receive from their respective supervisors. As the cohort supervision model has been initiated only very recently for the doctoral group in this faculty, they did not participate in the research and data was generated only from the faculty's master's group, for which programme cohort supervision has been conducted since 2007. Although Bitzer's theoretical framework focuses on doctoral success, it could be argued that much of the work done by master's students towards their dissertations is similar in nature to that done by doctoral students, with the main difference being in the level and originality of the work, thus justifying the inclusion of a master's group in the research.

Data was generated through questionnaires and individual interviews. Questionnaires were sent to all eight master's students and their supervisors who participated in the cohort supervision model in 2012. A relatively low response rate of almost 36% occurred, but due to the interpretive nature of data analysis, this could be regarded as an acceptable response rate. Individual interviews were also conducted with two cohort supervision coordinators, one coordinating the master's cohort at one university and the other previously coordinating the doctoral cohort at another university. The interviews were recorded, transcribed and analysed within the pre-imposed categories and sub-categories of the selected conceptual framework. The analysis also aimed at identifying categories and sub-categories additional to the pre-imposed ones.

Both the questionnaires and the interview schedules were developed from Bitzer's conceptual framework for exploring doctoral success (2011), as described above. The questionnaire consisted of four open-ended questions, each one addressing one of the four factors in the conceptual framework, namely the doctoral candidate's personal context, support context, programme context and institutional context. Table 10.1 shows the gist of the questionnaire questions; the interview questions were similar.

TABLE 10.1 Questions in questionnaire

Question 1
Please indicate how you experienced the cohort group supervision model, as relevant to students' personal context, referring to student personality; student thinking style(s); students' knowledge of research and studies at this level; students' ability to cope with the level of work; students' motivation.
Also indicate challenges you experienced and how you believe the cohort supervision model could be improved, relevant to the students' personal context.
Question 2
Please indicate how you experienced the cohort group supervision model, as relevant to students' support context, referring to academic isolation (or not); financial support; independence; benefit (or not) from interaction with other students and supervisors.
Also indicate challenges you experienced and how you believe the cohort supervision model could be improved, relevant to the students' support context.
Question 3
Please indicate how you experienced the cohort group supervision model, as relevant to students' programme context, referring to study mode (full-time/part-time studies); academic socialisation ('becoming an academic'); available infrastructure (internet, working space, statistical and language support, etc.); monitoring and progress.
Also indicate challenges you experienced and how you believe the cohort supervision model could be improved, relevant to the students' programme context.
Question 4
Please indicate how you experienced the cohort group supervision model, as relevant to students' institutional context, referring to students' academic integration into the department/faculty; students' academic integration into the institution's scholarly community.
Also indicate challenges you experienced and how you believe the cohort supervision model could be improved, relevant to the students' institutional context.

Permission was sought from the relevant university structures to conduct the research and the study was given ethical clearance after due procedure was followed. Ethical considerations were adhered to through anonymity, confidentiality, voluntary participation and by seeking prior permission from participants to use the information they provided through questionnaires and interviews, in the research.

The outcomes of the empirical study provided insights about cohort supervision (CS) and these are mapped below against Bitzer's framework to reflect the ways in which the cohort supervision model enhances doctoral success.

Mapping the outcomes of the empirical research onto the four aspects of Bitzer's framework and the international literature

The data analysis process included the matching of data from the interviews and questionnaires with the four factors, and their sub-factors, from the chosen conceptual framework. In many cases the data from the separate questionnaires and interviews confirmed and re-confirmed each other, therefore the data interpretation process involved grouping the confirmations together and summarising these per sub-factor. The summarised interpretation of the participants' experiences is discussed below. The links between the interpretation and the empirical evidence are not provided in each case below, as this would result in continuous duplication, therefore some examples of such links are provided to illustrate the points under discussion.

FACTOR 1: THE PERSONAL ENVIRONMENT AND QUALITIES OF THE DOCTORAL CANDIDATE

Personality

From the interviews and questionnaire responses it was clear that both the supervisors and the students were of the opinion that students would benefit optimally from cohort supervision (CS) if they prefer working in a group, are outspoken, willing to take risks, need guidance and are open to receive it, and if they are open-minded and happy to accept and share ideas. Students would benefit less if they are reluctant to expose themselves, less secure about their own academic performance and more reserved. Such students need special support and reassurance. Those who prefer to work individually might drop out. One of the interviewees said that "student personalities are actually the driving force behind the model". The international literature also shows that CS lends itself strongly to participatory learning (Fenge 2012:409).

Thinking style

Supervisors were of the opinion that a variety of thinking styles is accommodated in CS through offering a variety of activities (work in plenary, smaller groups, presentations and e-mail communications), exposure to a variety of academic perspectives and thinking styles and by offering a safe environment.

Research knowledge and level

One interviewee stated that "students come in again with a whole variance of what they know and what they don't know" and that they "develop over time". Supervisors agreed that students are often very diverse in terms of research knowledge and level of academic abilities. They believe that CS supports students who need more time to develop or are underprepared; enriches academic discourses and knowledge of research methodologies; expects wide reading and advance preparation; promotes quality work through constant sharing; develops reflective assessment skills; enhances ability to develop an academic argument and supports academic writing skills.

Ability to cope with level of work

The data clearly reflected that this ability is mainly a function of what students know and how they benefit from CS (come prepared, are motivated and use opportunities to grow). Unfortunately, according to a supervisor, some students "struggle to breach the gap between the requirements of working towards a master's degree and completing an assignment" and they have difficulty in coping with the level of academic work. Supervisors and students agreed that CS facilitates improved coping through offering benchmarking against peers, a variety of perspectives and interrogation angles, diverse audiences, experiences in academic discourse and debates as well as the potential for support groups outside the CS meetings.

Motivation

The data indicated that motivation seems to be driven by the demands placed on students in the CS, which have a constant rhythm of prepare-present-discuss; this in itself it constitutes a self-reward. CS is also driven by the set milestones, the idea of the collective and accountability for own progress. The international literature indicates that the doctoral student who participates in a CS model usually shows commitment and discipline (Santicola 2013:257-258), which could be linked to the qualities of the doctoral candidate.

FACTOR 2: THE STUDENT'S SUPPORT OR SOCIAL CONTEXT

Academic isolation

Participants in the case study were of the opinion that CS complements one-to-one supervision and thus counteracts academic isolation, as illustrated by the statement that both students and supervisors "feel part of a group who share their concerns". Wenger's communities of practice (COPs) could be used as the underpinning binding theory. The data in the case study also shows that CS provides a sense of community and emotional support. COP with peers could be extended beyond scheduled group sessions. CS is very good in counteracting academic isolation, as it breaks down isolation and promotes academic cohesion. The literature confirms this, as the outcomes of a study reported on by Teitel show that CS promotes increased connections, support and networking among students (1997:77-79).

Independence

A supervisor indicated that "students who have completed group supervision sessions successfully are much less dependent on supervisors afterwards" and it allows students to find their own voices and own independent spaces. The data also shows that students are expected to collaborate and interact during group sessions, but then to work independently in between; they become initiated in the rhythm of academic work at this level.

Diverse student background

A student has access to a team of experts as well as peer input, which can be used as a sounding board and helps to "shift my thinking", as indicated by one student. Students learn from each other; they learn to listen, engage, critique and offer thoughtful response. "In explaining I clarify my own decisions", one student explained. In one-to-one supervision all of this does not necessarily happen (the supervisor talks more, the student gets less opportunity to respond and articulate). CS has the potential for deep teaching and learning if participants are willing to share. Having a supervisory team is the norm in some countries, which has some of the benefits of CS, but not all of them.

Financial support

The case study showed that funding is not available via CS; however, CS facilitates improved throughput rate, thus decreasing the study period and financial obligation to studies. The possibility of outside funders for cohorts could be explored.

The literature confirms the above interpretation of the empirical research regarding the link of CS with support or social context: De Lange et al. (2011:27) found that CS provides support and supervision; CS offers a community of practice that supports learning, a place of safety, and an opportunity to compare oneself with others (Fenge 2012:408) and it also "facilitates gaining positively from power relationships through peer support" (McDonald & Kēpa 2012:154). The CS model is also shown in the literature to sustain "students towards the completion of their doctorates" (De Lange et al. 2011:27) and students eventually prefer to work independently (Santicola 2013:258, 259). Having a diversity of people together in the CS meetings is regarded as advantageous in the literature, as it promotes the cross-pollination of ideas (Fenge 2012:409) and "drawing from the pool of collective expertise" (McDonald & Kēpa 2012:154).

FACTOR 3: THE STUDENT'S PROGRAMME CONTEXT

Mode (Part-time, PT/ Full time, FT)

The data analysis clearly indicated that CS could be planned to suit both PT and FT students. One may ask whether these should be combined or remain separate in CS. The participants believe that it is important to consider student and supervisor needs when scheduling days and times for PT and FT. PT students are sometimes "a bit frazzled", said one coordinator, and it is believed that FT students benefit optimally from CS.

Infrastructure (department or institution)

An interviewee indicated that CS space is usually available only in non-peak lecture times; it would be beneficial to educate authorities about the idea of officially scheduling time and space for master's and doctoral meetings. Another interviewee felt that the ideal is to have a postgraduate lounge and secure, private work stations, but funding is often an issue. Supervisors indicated that students often need support with language and computer skills; these are essential for quality work.

Monitoring of study

The data from the case study showed that CS promotes improved progress through scheduled expectations. Scheduling space for inputs from students and supervisors about their needs at the end of each session promotes better monitoring and progress. Joint reflection in the group after each session about what worked and what did not work enhances the benefits of future sessions as indicated by an interviewee: "… trying to make sense that what we offered was meaningful; what were the shortcomings and what were the strengths and how to build on the strengths". It is not always clear to the participants in the case study research who has the responsibility for monitoring progress: the supervisor or the CS coordinator? Slower students could continue to benefit if they stay in the CS group, while faster students could become frustrated, benefit less and eventually drop out ("wasting our time", as one student indicated). Applying policy when progress is poor is essential for enhancing success.

Academic socialisation

Some participants in the case study were of the opinion that CS facilitates student induction into academia, including 'operating' in an academic environment and becoming more comfortable with academic engagement. One of them said that "the sessions help students to collaborate with other academics." Interaction with others and diversity promotes academic socialisation, especially in discussions and through the various discourses. The literature on the CS model reports on aspects that are relevant to programme context, as emerged from the empirical research. One example is that CS is appropriate for students who are in full-time employment (Santicola 2013:259). CS is also regarded as especially promoting academic socialisation as it is thought to have "great value in developing scholarship and reflective practice in candidates" (De Lange *et al.* 2011:27) and is "depicted as having a key role to play on the doctoral journey on both individual and group levels" (Fenge 2012:407).

FACTOR 4: THE STUDENT'S INSTITUTIONAL CONTEXT

Academic integration into the faculty/department

Students get to know the academics as well as the faculty and university structures: "It's not this scary place anymore," one student explained. Inexperienced supervisors are supported, for example, by listening to what kind of questions other supervisors ask students. Sharing of information about available resources enhances academic integration.

Academic integration into the institution

Cross-disciplinary or cross-faculty CS could benefit PhD students as one interviewee put it: "we may see things from different perspectives, but we can acknowledge a good argument, a valid scientific argument", but master's students might not be ready to handle this environment. Participants indicated that CS could accommodate the differences between disciplines through mutual respect for good academic argument and sound methodology justification. The literature also confirms the outcomes of the empirical research that relate to matters connected to integration into the institutional context. Teitel (1997:79-80) refers to CS encouraging deeper discussions in class, including those on sensitive issues, while Fenge (2012:411) states that it "appears to offer a type of support that is not provided by the normal supervisor/supervisee relationship, and therefore may enhance the overall student experience".

DOES COHORT SUPERVISION FACILITATE DOCTORAL SUCCESS?

The above exposition of the empirical findings and the international literature provides the means to determine whether CS facilitates doctoral success when the four factors of Bitzer's framework are used as criteria. The synthesis of the research results and the literature given below within the conceptual framework, presents an answer to this question.

In connection with the personal environment and qualities of the doctoral candidate, both the empirical findings and the literature show that CS is best suited to certain personality types. Through careful planning, CS has the potential to accommodate a variety of thinking styles and to support students' diversity of research knowledge and level of academic abilities. CS also facilitates improved coping with the level of work, and its inherent delivery nature and structure provides motivation.

Relevant to the student's support or social context, academic isolation was shown above to counteract academic isolation. CS also promotes independence and could accommodate diversity in student backgrounds. Financial support is not available directly via CS and the finding of outside funders for cohorts could be explored to further enhance doctoral success.

The student's programme context as reflected in the mode of delivery (PT/FT) could be accommodated in CS through careful planning, although it seems to suit FT students better. Departmental and institutional infrastructure does not always cater adequately for CS. Cohort supervision provides an excellent vehicle to monitor studies, provided it is built into the planning and execution of the sessions. CS also has the potential to promote academic socialisation.

The student's institutional context relevant to the faculty and department is well supported through CS; however, it does not necessarily promote academic integration into the institution, but does have the potential to enhance the overall student experience.

From the above it is clear that CS has the potential to enhance doctoral success in most of the areas related to the four factors of Bitzer's framework. However, it is also clear from the above that CS is not the automatic solution to all the challenges in doctoral studies, as it would only provide the support and development required if it is meticulously planned and executed, with commitment from all participants. Some suggestions towards strengthening the cohort supervision model are provided in the next section.

SUGGESTIONS FOR STRENGTHENING THE COHORT SUPERVISION MODEL TOWARDS PUSHING THE BOUNDARIES OF POSTGRADUATE SUPERVISION

The findings of the empirical research and the consulted literature gave rise to a number of suggestions for strengthening the CS model, in many cases echoing or extending each other. When combining the recommendations from the empirical research with those from the literature, a picture emerges that reflects both a South African context and an international context, thus pushing the boundaries of postgraduate supervision that is relevant world-wide. The recommendations towards further enhancing the CS model of supervision are presented below in four categories, namely student orientation to CS, role of the coordinator, role of supervisors and programme planning.

Student orientation to CS

The empirical research showed that students need to participate in an advance orientation session before joining a cohort group as this could contribute to their benefitting optimally from the model. Students also need preparation in competences in research methodology, theoretical frameworks, academic writing and proposal writing, which could be part of an extended orientation or offered as short learning programmes. As time management is a crucial component of postgraduate studies, students need to be prepared for this aspect as well. Students could find the expectations in the CS sessions overwhelming and they need to be prepared for this as well. Another experience that is likely to occur in CS meetings and which many students might not be familiar with is the vulnerability that comes with exposing oneself in academic debate; they need to know that emotional support is available to cope with such situations. Students also need to be oriented to other aspects of academic debate, such as avoiding destructive competition.

Suggestions from the literature for enhancing the CS model in relation to students do not specifically refer to prior orientation of students; however, the literature highlights a number of matters in which students need to develop competence to benefit optimally from the CS model. These matters deal with the following:

- Deeper discussions that should include sensitive issues. These discussions ought to include strategies for encouraging deeper responses, while participating academics need to flexible when such discussions take place (Teitel 1997:78-80).
- Participation in reflective practice, by reflecting on others' research, reflecting on others' critique of their own research and reflecting on their own competence to critique (De Lange et al. 2011:23-25).
- Being part of a community of practice that supports learning, offers the student a place of safety with a sense of belonging, a sense of learning and access to community supervision (De Lange et al. 2011:25). The community of practice is also referred to as 'cohortness', which "captures the shared journey that students take through the group supervision" (Fenge 2012:407).
- The ability to access the wisdom of many voices through a cross-pollination of ideas that could contribute towards transformative learning (Fenge 2012:409) is also crucial in CS. Linking with this, is McDonald and Kēpa's (2012:154) reference to the positive gain from drawing from the pool of collective expertise.
- Carson (2012:178) recommends having early discussions with individual students about "developing the 'identity-trajectory' of the candidate" as this would assist the student in deciding whether CS would suit her/his particular orientation. Fenge (2012:407) also identifies student identity as important in the CS model.

- Finally, Santicola (2013:257-258) highlights the fact that commitment and discipline are key attributes for the doctoral candidate to attain success in the CS model.

Role of the coordinator

A second aspect that was highlighted in the empirical research towards improving the CS model of supervision is the role of the cohort coordinator. The coordinator needs to be aware in advance of the challenges that might arise and be prepared to meet them. These could include the mediation of diverse personalities and the interaction between them; mediating methodology issues; being competent in planning and executing a variety of appropriate activities; being able to deal with diverse opinions that could confuse students; managing a safe space for students and inexperienced supervisors in which to test and experiment and being skilled in bridging interdisciplinary issues. The coordinator must also be an experienced supervisor and be prepared to accept and cope with the additional load.

The literature confirms that the coordinator plays a key role in the handling of sensitive issues, facilitating the development of a culture of honest talk and strategies to solicit deeper responses about such issues in the CS sessions (Teitel 1997:78-79). The coordinator also needs to ensure that there a time and place set aside to clarify who will take responsibility for cohort conflict (among students, among academics and between students and academics), to develop guidelines for behaviour and decision-making (Teitel 1997:80-82). Tuckwiller and Childress (2012:52) foreground matters which the coordinator could take up towards improving CS, namely facilitating CS students to interact with academics who are not part of the cohort as well as with each other both on and off campus; also working on supervisor and administrator commitment. They also point out that it is necessary to acknowledge the possibility that students and supervisors could have a second-class mind-set in the group. I believe the coordinator has a role to play in this regard as well.

Role of supervisors

A third matter to be considered for strengthening the CS supervision model, as identified in the empirical research, is the crucial role of the participating supervisors and their advance orientation to participating in such a model. Their buy-in and commitment to the model are essential and they should be afforded freedom of choice regarding participation in the model. Their participation and support during the meetings are of utmost importance. They need to be respectful of what the student brings, be sufficiently critical to shift students' thinking, cooperate towards creating a safe space and shifting the group forward and avoid destructive criticism. A quick turn-around time regarding feedback to students is also important. The CS offers (experienced and inexperienced) supervisors the opportunity to expand their repertoire of methodologies and theories, to learn about creating a safe space for students and asking students appropriate questions, to gain insight into what is good enough and what is cutting edge and to understand how to push the boundaries.

The literature confirms that the supervisors have a pivotal role to play in the CS model. Fenge (2012:411) states that the role of supervisors is "crucial in facilitating a creative environment in which the students feel safe to share in a collaborative learning experience". Attributes that are essential in participating academics include flexibility, using conflict as teaching moments, buy-in and contributing to improving the model through reflection (Teitel 1997:78-82). De Lange et al. (2011:21-25) refer to their contributing to a supportive practice in the cohort, which includes respectful engagement (by modelling) and a high level of participation to enhance eventual emancipation. Tuckwiller and Childress (2012:52) also highlight supervisor commitment.

Programme planning

The fourth and final aspect that the empirical research showed to be crucial in CS is that of programme planning. Information overload should be avoided when planning the sessions so as not to overwhelm the students. Scheduling of sessions should as far as possible suit supervisors and students. University rules could be challenging as they have an impact on the start and end dates of meetings, the day of the week and the frequency of the sessions. The programme should be planned to include a balance in the nature of items, for example an overload of expert presentations and sufficient time for each student's work. The programme should be extensive enough to support students until they complete their studies, while not holding them back. It could also be worthwhile to consider the benefits of smaller groups with related topics in comparison to larger interdisciplinary groups. I am of the opinion that one of the risks that need to be hedged against in smaller groups is that of plagiarism as students might be tempted into this when they have access to each other's work. It is also crucial to accommodate a balance between student needs, supervisor needs and quality requirements in the programme.

The literature stresses the importance of thorough planning and organisation (De Lange et al. 2011:21). Teitel refers to the need to provide time and space for informal connections among students (1997:77), to include content on sensitive issues (1997:80) and to develop a curriculum map for the programme and a portfolio that describes each component as it is delivered (1997:82-83). Recommendations to improve admission to the CS programme have been made by Carson, who states that "tighter controls around student eligibility and admission" (2012:177) are required and that there is a need "for a developed admission process that did not rush supervision issues" (2012:177). Santicola identified attributes of students that are likely to benefit most from CS (2013:258-259); these could play a role in developing an appropriate screening prior to admission. The group size is crucial, as too large a group would not provide sufficient opportunity for meaningful and all-inclusive academic engagement, while too small a group would not serve the purpose of diverse opposing academic debate. The optimal size for the cohort group is reported to be six people (Fenge 2012:408); however, factors such as diversity of student research topics and methodologies, as well as number of students per supervisor, would co-determine the efficiency of any particular group. Tuckwiller and Childress recommend that attention to the physical context is crucial (classroom environment, access to accommodation and travel), as are the concepts of convenience, travel costs and flexible scheduling; also the availability and effectiveness of support and resources (2012:52). The same authors recommend improvement of CS through careful design and delivery (content, timing and sequencing of programme, adult learning and teaching techniques, flexible delivery and organisation) (2012:52).

CONCLUSION AND SUGGESTIONS FOR THE WAY FORWARD

The CS model of postgraduate research supervision clearly has "great value in developing scholarship and reflective practice in candidates, providing support and supervision and sustaining students towards the completion of their doctorates" (De Lange et al. 2011:27). The essence of the suggestions made above can be summarised as follows:

- Accommodating diversity is at the centre of success.
- There is no one-size-fits-all in cohort supervision.
- Careful planning is essential.
- Special attention should be given to the selection of the CS coordinator, as this person's role is crucial.
- Orientation of supervisors and students ahead of the first CS session is recommended.
- Commitment and participation by all parties are crucial.
- The need to create and maintain a safe space is very important. The supervisor should not be positioned as the 'knower'.
- CS for master's students provides excellent preparation for doctorateness and thus for eventual doctoral success.

The recommendations from the empirical research and the confirmation and extension of these recommendations in the literature provide particular pointers towards enhancing the modalities of cohort group supervision, thus further facilitating doctoral success. By combining the recommendations of the empirical research with those in the literature, an international picture emerges. This could be significant for master's and doctoral quality and throughput rates, while it could also inform the development of theory relevant to cohort supervision. Important follow-up research would include reviewing the cohort supervision model with the purpose of enhancing supervision capacity building towards similar practical and theoretical improvements in the model.

REFERENCES

Bitzer EM. 2011. Doctoral success as ongoing quality business: A possible conceptual framework. *South African Journal of Higher Education*, 25(3):425-443.

Carson S. 2012. Risky business: Managing creative practice postgraduates. In: M Kiley (ed). *Narratives of transition: Perspectives of research leaders, educators and postgraduates: Proceedings of the 10th QPR Conference*. Canberra: The Centre for Higher Education, Learning and Teaching, Australian National University. 76-91.

Chisin AV & M'Rithaa MK. 2012. 'I participate, therefore I learn': A process of co-creative graduate supervision in design research in Cape Town. *Image & Text: A Journal for Design*, 20:88-109.

Conrad L. 2003. Five ways of enhancing the postgraduate community: Student perceptions of effective supervision and support. Paper presented at the Learning for an Unknown Future 26th Annual HERDSA Conference, Christchurch, 6-9 July.

De Lange N, Pillay G & Chikoko V. 2011. Doctoral learning: A case for a cohort model of supervision and support. *South African Journal of Higher Education*, 31(1):15-30.

Dysthe O, Samara A & Westrheim K. 2006. Multivoiced supervision of master's students: A case study of alternative supervision practices in higher education. *Studies in Higher Education*, 31(3):299-318.

Fenge L. 2012. Enhancing the doctoral journey: The role of group supervision in supporting collaborative learning and creativity. *Studies in Higher Education*, 37(4):401-414.

Holloway EL & Alexandre L. 2012. Crossing boundaries in doctoral education: Relational learning, cohort communities, and dissertation committees. *New Directions for Teaching and Learning*, 131, Fall:85-97.

Manathunga C. 2012. Supervisors watching supervisors. *Australian Universities' Review*, 54(1):29-37.

McDonald M & Kēpa M. 2012. My doctoral sisterhood. Paper presented at the 5th Biennial International Indigenous Conference, Auckland, 27-30 June.

Samara A. 2006. Group supervision in graduate education: A process of supervision skill development and text improvement. *Higher Education Research and Development*, 25(2):115-129.

Samuel M & Vithal R. 2011. Emergent frameworks of research teaching and learning in a cohort-based doctoral programme. *Perspectives in Education*, 29(3):76-87.

Santicola L. 2013. Pressing on: Persistence through a doctoral cohort program in education. *Contemporary Issues in Education Research*, 6(20):253-264.

Teitel L. 1997. Understanding and harnessing the power of the cohort model in preparing educational leaders. *Peabody Journal of Education*, 72(2):66-85.

Tuckwiller BL & Childress RB. 2012. Benchmarking progress in a doctoral cohort: A follow-up study of student perceptions. In: F Kochan, L Searby & M Barakat (eds). *Southern Regional Council on Educational Administration 2012 Yearbook: Gateway to Leadership and Learning*. Auburn: Auburn University. 124-138.

Watts JH. 2010. Team supervision of the doctorate: Managing roles, relationships and contradictions. *Teaching in Higher Education*, 15(3):335-339.

Wisker G, Robinson G & Schacham M. 2007. Postgraduate research success: Communities of practice involving cohorts, guardian supervisors and online communities. *Innovations in Education and Teaching International*, 44(3):301-320.

Zhao F. 2003. Transforming quality in research supervision: A knowledge management approach. *Quality in Higher Education*, 9(2):187-197.

THE JOURNEYMAN AS A METAPHOR FOR DEVELOPING SKILLS IN POSTGRADUATE EDUCATION

EXPERIENCE, FEEDBACK AND ROLE MODELS

Khalid El Gaidi

INTRODUCTION

The number of PhD students has increased considerably during the last two decades in most countries in the world. In Sweden, it has nearly doubled during the same period while the number of supervisors remains almost unchanged. This change in ratio means that the PhD students have less time to spend with their supervisors in labs, less time for feedback and less time for jointly writing papers and developing a sense of quality in research than they had two decades earlier (UKÄ 2013:2). The decrease in available time for each PhD student to spend with his or her supervisor means that an important part of the informal, though important, close relationship between the two is now reduced to a strict minimum. Demands for efficiency drive the formalisation of the supervision process, which risks undermining the ground for efficient skills development.

To push the boundaries of PhD education, we need to devote special care to the resulting situation. The new conditions call for deepened insight into different components of knowledge, what role experience plays in the students' development and what kind of communication is needed to enable us as supervisors to use interaction time with PhD students more efficiently. Failing to do so and given the time restrictions, there is a risk that the skills transferred to coming generations of researchers will be watered down.

The purpose of this chapter is therefore to analyse PhD students' endeavour and suggest ways that may enable more efficient skill development, interaction and communication between a supervisor and a supervisee in research education.

The journeyman metaphor in this chapter belongs to a medieval system of production in Europe and may need some further explanation. Young apprentices entered trades at the age of ten to fourteen and would work for about seven years before they developed the skills necessary to qualify as a journeyman. If the piece of work (chef d'oeuvre) presented to the guild was accepted, they were given the journeyman's letter. The craftsman was now supposed to travel around in neighbouring countries for a further seven to ten years to work under the supervision of other masters in order to improve his skills even more. After this journey, he (gender intentional) would settle down and work on a masterpiece. If approved by the guild, he was allowed to open his own workshop and have apprentices (Sennett 2008:58).

The use of journeyman as a metaphor is motivated by the fact that skills in the workshop were the focus of the training and its aim was production. Learning is only a bi-product of the activity. As we will see later, training, communication and feedback were adapted to skills development. A few very isolated skill-dependent trades, such as conservatories of music, currently still practise the apprenticeship/journeyman model of education.

In the following, I will discuss the difference between skills and science, give a structured taxonomy of knowledge, proceed with a discussion on how a sense of quality is acquired, deal with critical aspects of skill and science, reflect on methodology and end with some concluding remarks.

FROM SKILLS TO SCIENCE

As a craft, skills are another form of knowledge. They are not science but an imperative prerequisite to producing it. Unlike scientific knowledge which is completely explicit, most of the skills are tacit. They are acquired by working together with more proficient practitioners, obtaining accurate and timely feedback as well as closely studying role models' artefacts.

Better than anyone, Nobel Prize Laureate Peter Medawar, in a reflective text, has captured the essence of skills:

> … any scientist of any age who wants to make important discoveries must study important problems. But what makes a problem "important"? And how do you know when you see it? The answers don't come from reading in a book, nor even by explicitly being taught them. More often, they are conveyed by examples, through the slow accretion of mumbled asides and grumbled curses, by smiles, frowns, and exclamations over years of a close working relationship between an established scientist and his or her protégé (Kanigel 1993:xiv).

Most of the focus in postgraduate education is directed towards the tangible end-product of education: papers and theses. Every year, a number of books are published on how to write scientific papers and dissertations, adding to the huge number already on the bookshelves. The question is how helpful these books are for developing writing skills in postgraduate education.

When working with artificial intelligence and expert systems at the Massachusetts Institute of Technology (MIT) in the sixties, Hubert and Stuart Dreyfus developed a five-stage model, known as "from novice to expert", on how people acquire knowledge and skills in different knowledge areas. The novice is someone who is starting in a trade. After a while, he or she proceeds to advanced beginner and then to the competent stage. The two remaining stages are the skilled and the expert (Dreyfus & Dreyfus 1986:16-51).The most interesting aspect of this model is that the knowledge development in the three first stages is accomplished by learning the rules (how the most common problems are solved) of the domain and trying to put them into practice. The skilled and experts already master the rules in practice and what they are interested in is the challenge of unsolved problems. This is mainly achieved intuitively.

Books for developing skills like scientific writing are filled with mechanical rules of writing. These may be helpful for learners in the early stages of the model. To move beyond this, writers should be encouraged to be creative and see the general in the specific and vice versa (Sennett 2008:247). The question is how this creativity is achieved.

Most of the 'how to' books on writing, however, ignore the fact that skills belong mainly to the tacit domain. Skilled people can demonstrate their skill but it is most of the times hard for them, if not impossible, to explain it. Skills are thus acquired by working responsibly with concrete tasks in concrete situations and obtaining adequate feedback from more proficient practitioners and by trying to emulate masterpieces produced by role models. In the same way, apprentices develop their craft skills under the supervision of a master to become journeymen. This is why a close relationship between a PhD student and a community of practice is of major importance. The language used to develop the craft is also specific. It is by concrete stories of how named journeymen and masters succeeded or failed to solve a specific task, not through abstract information that a sense of the quality of the trade is conveyed (Benjamin 1990:653).

Writing is but one example of all the skills necessary to develop to become an independent researcher. Before reaching the top skill of writing up, students have to acquire a range of other skills at different stages of the research process. Some of the questions that arise in this connection are:

- How do we formulate relevant research questions?
- How do we arrive at the hypothesis to test?
- How do we design experiments?
- How do we discern patterns?
- How do we interpret experimental results?
- How do we develop scientific creativity?
- How do we assess quality in research?
- How do we develop ethical judgment?
- How do we develop independence in research?

Most of these skills and attitudes are reflected in the objectives of PhD education around the world. Skills and attitudes, as mentioned above, are not science in themselves but a necessary prerequisite to producing new scientific knowledge. Being another kind of knowledge, they require another kind of pedagogical communication to help PhD students to acquire them. Giving the student a book on scientific writing and expecting him or her to produce well-written scientific papers will result most of the time in frustration rather than well-written papers. The same applies to all the other skills and attitudes.

A THREEFOLD VIEW ON KNOWLEDGE

What, then, is the problem? The problem is that unlike scientific knowledge, skills cannot easily be fully described in words. Compare the answers to the following questions:

- How high is Mount Everest?
- Can you play tennis?
- How does the oboe sound?

These questions belong to different kinds of knowledge in the following taxonomy:

- Propositional knowledge
- Skills
- Familiarity

Giving 8 848 metres above sea level as an answer to the first question lets us know all there is to know about this question.

This does not apply to the second question. What does a "Yes" as an answer stand for here? That you can hit the tennis ball with the racket? Or that you can challenge a professional tennis player, say Rafael Nadal, in a competition? The "Yes" can mean everything and nothing. Your proficiency in tennis should be "shown" rather than "told" to convey a meaning. In the absence of an opportunity to show your proficiency, concrete examples of your achievements will do. An adequate answer to the third question calls for the ability to imitate the sound of the oboe. This is almost impossible for most people without an instrument. Even with an instrument, it takes some training to produce a clear high C on the oboe. But many amateurs of classical music will recognise the sound of the oboe if they hear it. They know it but cannot express it because it is tacit. In an investigation to find out if the Vienna Philharmonic Orchestra had a special "timbre", the researcher carried out many blind tests with different categories of people: laymen, amateur musicians and professional musicians. His conclusion was that the Vienna Philharmonic Orchestra indeed had a specific "timbre" that only a professional musician could identify when listening to the same instrument played by a member of the Vienna Philharmonic Orchestra (Bertsch 2002).

In the first category of this taxonomy (Johannessen 1999:88-90), propositional knowledge refers to the scientific knowledge that is explicit and that can be completely described in written form. The case is slightly different for the second question. Playing tennis is a skill and you have to show what you are able to perform to exhibit your skill and to give your "Yes" an experiential meaning. Familiarity associated with the third question is the ability to distinguish qualities among a series of similar artefacts. To be able to tell which sound belongs to the oboe takes some listening training. If the task, then, is to judge whether the oboe has the Vienna Philharmonic Orchestra timbre, the prerequisite is probably that you have played the same instrument at a professional level for years to be able to distinguish it (Bertsch 2002).

If we confine ourselves to the second question, what is important here is not only having the skill to play tennis but most importantly how we acquire that skill. The same applies to acquiring the skill of speaking a foreign language or writing scientific papers.

Reading a book about how to write scientific papers will probably help novice students structure their first step into the skill of writing up to a certain level and no more. These kinds of rules are to be found in all imaginable skills, whether they refer to grammar for language, the way chess pieces may move on a chessboard, or traffic signs.

However, the verbal mastery of these general rule sets does not make the owner proficient in the knowledge areas. It takes more than grammar to be a good writer, more than knowing how chess pieces are allowed to move on the chessboard to be a chess master, and more than knowing what traffic signs mean to be a good driver. The written rules of a knowledge area are called regulative rules (Janik 2002:273-284).

Learning regulative rules may bring us up to the competency level but no more. A car driver with a fresh driving licence is a competent driver allowed to drive cars in the streets. Few, however, would consider our new driver to be proficient in driving cars. Car accident statistics show that young drivers are overrepresented in car crashes during the first few years of driving, a fact that insurance companies very well know. They charge them a higher premium for car insurance.

Regarding the two remaining stages of the novice-master model, the skilled and masters are known for being able to identify and solve problems intuitively. They know the rules of the trade, but what interests them is not already known and solved problems, but how to identify and solve new problems. They not only follow the rules, they create new ones along the way. The problem is that the kinds of rules they create are implicit in their artefacts, whether it be driving a car, writing a scientific paper, or playing tennis. The created rules, being implicit, make it hard if not impossible for novices and advanced beginners to distinguish and to learn from them. The kinds of rules they create are called constitutive rules. Their number is infinite and, therefore, it is hard to systematise and write them down. Most of the time they are implicit in the artefact, woven into narratives and studied as elements of style connected to role models; for example, books of or about world famous tennis players or violin virtuosos. Musicians, for instance, study for different masters and this record is often given in their curriculum vitae to show what tradition they represent.

Harriet Zuckerman, who studied Nobel Prize laureates, found that they had nothing in common with each other except that most of them seemed to come from labs led by former Nobel Prize winners (Zuckerman 1977:138-143).This conclusion is in line with Peter Medawar's cited above.

Now, if reading books about writing scientific papers does not help much in developing writing skills above a certain level, what should be done? There are three main areas for skills acquisition: working together with more proficient peers on authentic tasks in specific situations, receiving initiated and timely feedback from more proficient practitioners on writing and closely studying prototypical papers of role models and emulating their styles (Sennett 2008:100).

One of the most efficient ways of learning skills is to work together with more proficient practitioners. Writing the first papers in collaboration with supervisors and post-docs provides the experience of sharing praxis. When co-authoring, PhD students gain a feeling for what is required by seeing all the thousands of small tacit decisions taken by researchers in the process of writing: why this word and not the other, why this argument and not the other and why this structure and not the other. In this process, constitutive rules of writing are imparted. The questions of the novice PhD students help the supervisor to put into words part of their skills and become aware of the knowledge they possess but seldom reflect on. Authentic tasks for developing skills, like presentation skills, are necessary since they give a sense of responsibility and sharpen the mind of the PhD students.

Working and receiving initiated feedback on what has been achieved is probably the single most important aspect of developing skills. To then develop their own styles, students benefit from closely studying masterpieces and discussing their elements in seminars.

DEVELOPING A SENSE OF SCIENTIFIC QUALITY

Even at preschool, children are proficient in their native language and can discriminate between those who speak the local dialect and those who do not. They master sets of rules such as pronunciation, grammar and syntax. No one has ever taught them these rules but the children have inferred them by experiencing an infinite number of occasions for learning the language in real-life situations and receiving feedback in the form of either words or body language when people do not understand what they mean. Unlike foreign languages learnt in school, the native language is used with confidence and without hesitation. On the other hand, learning a language, say Urdu, by relying solely on the words written in a book, without any feedback from the community of practice, will rarely lead to any intelligible use of the language at all.

The difference between learning a language, a skill, in the two situations described above is that the native language is learnt in a natural environment rich in authentic use in concrete situations, feedback and role models where all the tacit knowledge is transmitted down to subtle regional and dialectal nuances. The foreign language, on the other hand, is learnt from a book, which will not be able to contain or notate all the subtleties of language use. The mastery of the native language makes everybody an expert in a knowledge area: the use of their native language. As such, even preschool children are able to differentiate between the dialect spoken at home and other dialects from regions in the vicinity. This is the essence of familiarity, the attribute necessary for judging quality.

Inferring from learning the native language, we can conclude that the human brain is constructed to unconsciously create general rules and construct concepts when working with concrete situations, but not the other way round. Learning from concrete situations will enable learners to use their knowledge and skills without hesitation in new situations. Learning from abstract general rules, on the other hand, will not necessarily lead to recognising and handling problems in real life.

Helping PhD students develop a sense of quality will mean exposing them to a variety of situations in science and the production of knowledge that give them authentic experience of quality. Concrete authentic situations where aspects of quality variation in research are experienced would include closely studying both good and bad papers in seminars, attending defences of theses and reflecting upon them in the research group, shadow-reviewing papers, with due authorisation, in parallel with senior researchers and comparing results. Like learning one's native language, the knowledge is given a shared experiential meaning.

Role models, emulation and critical thinking

What I have been describing so far is how important a close relationship is in a research community of practice, including supervisors, for skills development in PhD studies. I can hear virtual voices asking: Doesn't this close relationship in research groups undermine critical thinking – the hallmark of science? My short answer is "No", if it is done properly.

The use of "journeyman" as a metaphor for skills development in PhD studies has multiple layers. On the one hand, it stresses the "close relationship" between a master and an apprentice, authentic responsible work, stories associated with successes and failures of named individuals in the guild when dealing with special tasks, and rich and timely feedback. On the other hand, it also imparts an appreciation of the quality required.

Few skill-based domains of learning with a master-apprentice relationship remain today in our formalised information society. One that is still in existence, however, is conservatories of music.

To understand how skills are developed, the researcher conducted a study at the Royal Conservatory of Music (KMH) in Stockholm, Sweden. In one master class, students were required to play a piece of Baroque music (El Gaidi 2007:169-172). The teacher was not satisfied with the way the students played; she wanted them to play in the French style, not the Italian. The students looked puzzled. She went on to explain that the Italian way speeds up the tempo while the French expands the sound in the room. The explanation did not dissipate the puzzling fog from the four students' faces. She was compelled to use an analogy: "If the Italian way of playing is prose, the French way is poetry." The students looked even more puzzled. When she exhausted her words, she grabbed the violin and showed what she meant by playing the passage as she wanted them to play. The fog dissipated and their first attempt showed that they were on the right path, to the great satisfaction of the teacher.

The second class was a quartet playing a piece of classical music. But the quartet was doubled by the teacher of each instrument. The tandems played in exactly the same way. The students had to adjust not only to the other instruments in the quartet but primarily to the teacher's way of playing. The third class was an octet. The group had a one-week practice assignment prior to class. The first thing the teacher said when starting the lesson was, "Could you please play through the piece so we have an opening bid?" The teacher listened attentively and when they had finished, he said, "Good, let us make some music out of this. By the way, somebody played an F-sharp in this passage, and there shouldn't be one." Magnus the cellist admitted immediately, "It was me". The teacher could hear a single false note. His legitimacy was unquestioned.

These three examples show what it means to work closely together, share practices, give feedback and talk about the artefact. This way of learning transfers not only the factual knowledge but also the style and the way of approaching the music that the master conveys to his or her disciples in the sessions.

But where is the critical thinking in all this?

The title "journeyman" gives us a hint about where to look for it. What journey? And why? When, after several years, the apprentice had his workpiece approved by masters in the guild, it was time for him to go off on a journey to other countries (in Europe) and work in the same trade under other masters for at least a year with each.

Working with the second master in a new country and mastering his style of solving problems in the trade not only gave the journeyman a new way of seeing his trade but liberated him from the style of his first master, of which until then he had hardly been aware. Additional mastery of subsequent masters' styles added new layers to the journeyman's frame of reference and independence. The system of a "journey" is thus the backbone of solid critical thinking in a journeyman's development. Back in his original country, it was time to settle down and prepare his masterpiece composed of elements of different masters' skills to form his own style. This process is a way of developing creativity.

It now becomes apparent that what we, in present-day academia, call 'post-doc' is nothing but a journeyman's system. This system could be used more consciously and systematically to foster independence in PhD students even before they have defended their thesis.

In modern-day science, there are many stories about how these elements have been transferred, not by scientific information, but by post-docs working in the labs of prominent scientists. One of these stories deals with Richard Feynman's diagrams.

Richard Feynman, a prominent young physicist, was involved in Los Alamos in the 1940s. He has contributed substantially to atomic physics, solid state physics and gravitational physics. After the Second World War, he started to use small diagrams to keep track of the various mathematical equations he used to solve the tedious work of calculating the movements of atoms. Diagrams were a visual representation of the movements of particles over a period of time. Feynman presented his diagrams at the National Academy of Science in 1948.

But despite the presentation and despite the fact that the diagrams solved complicated calculations that physicists were struggling with around the world, they were not used. Their use during the first six years that followed was connected to Feynman's personal friendship with Freeman Dyson, an advocate of the Feynman diagrams who was working at the Institute of Advanced Studies in Princeton, New Jersey. Four of the five researchers that used these diagrams were post-docs with Freeman Dyson and had a personal relationship to him. In the Soviet Union, it took at least one year for the physicists to study the diagrams and many years to use them, and in Japan, it took much longer.

The spreading of the Feynman diagram is proof that even in theoretical sciences like physics there is a large portion of tacit knowledge that only spreads by working together and understanding the advantages and the limits of the use of such diagrams (Kaiser 2005).

METHODOLOGY

Basic data for the study reported in this chapter was collected in a series of seminars. The researcher met with three experienced supervisors in five dialogue seminars of five hours each to reflect on what skills and attitudes are required for research and how to scaffold their development in PhD education. The participants had to complete reading and writing assignments for each of the five meetings. At the meeting, the participants read their text in the seminar and a dialogue followed. Minutes of the dialogues were written for each meeting. These minutes and the texts were later analysed and interpreted by the researcher using a hermeneutical method (Little 2008). Additional data was collected from a supervisors' course taught by the researcher at the Royal Institute of Technology in Stockholm, Sweden (KTH). More than five hundred supervisors have taken the course and each has produced at least three texts.

Another important aspect of the methodology concerns what the researcher is looking for in the data and how the findings are communicated. Let me give an example: one supervisor reported that a paper had been iterated 34 times between himself and his PhD student. "Being clear" in his feedback, the supervisor expected the PhD student to amend the paper in accordance with his instructions to make it acceptable for submission. And each time he reviewed the paper, he could see that the student had not understood.

Thirty-four iterations is probably an extreme case, but a number of iterations are quite common. What, then, is the problem? The problem, as pointed out by Wittgenstein, is that we only understand language propositions through our experience. Rules do not come with (rules) describing how they should be used (Wittgenstein 2009: para. 202). This means that if we do not share experiences we have no way of understanding each other properly. That is why the proposed way of writing papers together, sharing experiences at the beginning of PhD studies, giving timely and accurate initiated feedback and closely studying prototypical papers written by role models is important.

This idea is also valid for communication, whether it is scientific or informal. The use of authentic experience and concrete examples when communicating with PhD students makes the communication stringent and reduces the area of (mis-) interpretation, thus making communication more effective.

The other aspect of communication is that what a person understands as criteria for quality is what he or she is able to produce. No other understanding is possible. Remember the master classes in music and how the teacher, who was not able to "explain" what she meant by the French way of playing, was instead compelled to "show" the students before they understood. PhD students' understanding of writing quality is evidenced by what they are able to produce, nothing else. If supervisors wait until they see what their students produce as a result of their feedback, they will be spared much frustration.

These two aspects of communication are universal and apply to all communication in all situations. They concern the relationship between language propositions and experience, the theme of Wittgenstein's later work, "Meaning is use" (Wittgenstein 1977:317).

The use of experience and concrete examples in the social sciences should not be looked upon as less worthy since it is anecdotal. It is necessary to give abstract generalisations a strict meaning. This is the difference between the two kinds of language used in the former skill-based workshop and the industrial method of production widely dominating today. The former used "concrete stories" and the latter "abstract information", as pointed out by Walter Benjamin (Benjamin 1990:653). This seems to be the root of much trouble in learning and communication in general today.

A final and important aspect of the methodology is the use of analogical thinking. Finding good analogies and praxis helps shed light on the practice one is studying. Using, for example, the teaching practices from the Royal Conservatory of Music in Stockholm was a source of more than one insight.

CONCLUDING REMARKS

It is not by chance that the objectives of PhD education in Sweden (and most countries in the world) are divided into three categories: scientific knowledge, skills and attitudes. These categories belong to different kinds of knowledge. Each has its specificities and requires special attention in communication and development.

Among the skills and attitudes enumerated in the educational objectives, one can find communication, critical thinking, creativity and ethical judgment. By experience, we know that many more than the skills like those enumerated above are needed to conduct successful scientific research. Most of the time these skills are taken for granted and not mentioned at all. In this chapter, I have only written about skills. Attitudes such as those in ethics are not addressed – they will be the theme of a paper to come.

To properly help PhD students develop the skills they require, and with the present-day time restrictions, we as supervisors have to recognise the different nature of skills, develop knowledge about how to acquire them, design adequate experiences and provide the students with opportunities to reflect about their learning. Failing to do so may lead to much frustration and perturbed communication – and ultimately failure.

REFERENCES

Benjamin W. 1990. Paris, 1800-talets huvudstad: Passagearbetet (Das Passagen-Werk). (Paris, capital of the nineteenth century – The Arcades project).

Bertsch M. 2002. *Can you identify the Vienna Philharmonic Orchestra compared to the Berlin or New York Philharmonic?* [Accessed 13 May 2013] http://iwk.mdw.ac.at/lit_db_iwk/

Dreyfus HL & Dreyfus ES. 1986. *Mind over machine*. New York: The Free Press.

El Gaidi K. 2007. Lärarensyrkeskunnande – Bildningochreflekteradeerfarenheter. Stockholm: Dialoger.

Janik A. 2002. Dialoger. In: P Tillberg (ed). *Tyst kunskap, regelföljande och inlärning*. Stockholm: Industriell ekonomi och organisation Yrkeskunnande och Teknologi. 273-284.

Johannessen KS. 1999. *Praxis och tyst kunnande* (Praxis and tacit knowledge). Stockholm: Dialoger.

Kaiser D. 2005. Doing physics with Feynman's diagrams. *American Scientist*, 93:156-164.

Kanigel R. 1993. *Apprentice to genius*. Baltimore, MD: John Hopkins University Press.

Sennett R. 2008. *The craftsman*. New Haven, CT: Yale University Press.

UKÄ (UniversitetsochHögskoleämbetet). 2013. *UKÄ-rapport*. [Accessed 13 May 2013] http://www.uk-ambetet.se /statistikuppfoljning/arsrapportforuniversitetochhogskolor.4.782a2988 13a88dd0dad800011775.html

Little D. What is hermeneutic explanation? [Accessed 21 January 2014] http://www-personal.umd.umich.edu/~delittle/Encyclopedia%20entries/hermeneutic%20explanation.htm

Wittgenstein L. 1977. *Bemerkungenüber die Farben (Remarks on colour)*. Oxford: Basil Blackwell.

Wittgenstein L. 2009. *Philosophical investigations*. Malden, MA: Blackwell.

Zuckerman H. 1977. *Scientific elite: Nobel laureates in the United States*. New York: The Free Press.

PART FIVE

SUPERVISION ACROSS CULTURES

A COORDINATED FRAMEWORK FOR DEVELOPING RESEARCHERS' INTERCULTURAL COMPETENCY

Cally Guerin, Michelle Picard and Ian Green

INTRODUCTION: ACADEMIC MOBILITY

While the concept of the wandering scholar is not new, the speed and frequency of academic mobility have rapidly gained momentum in the 21st century (Kim 2009). Linked to the notion of the 'borderless' university (Cunningham et al. 1998; Hearn 2011; Watanabe 2011), scholars today expect to study and work in more than one country, to present their research at international conferences, and to collaborate with colleagues from all around the world. The result is a multicultural academic workforce in many universities for whom boundaries between national cultures are increasingly being erased and where all members require high levels of intercultural competence.

The contemporary version of cross-border, transnational academic mobility is marked by "interlocking relations of the spontaneity of mobile individuals; national and supranational policy frameworks; and institutional networks of universities in the global cyberspace of knowledge flows" (Kim 2009:400). The result is a complex picture of permanent and temporary relocations and continuing movement. These relocations are played out by individuals travelling to other countries for part or all of their undergraduate, postgraduate and doctoral studies, in self-funded or government-organised programmes. The length of stay might be from permanent or long-term migration through to temporary stays for specific study programmes or post-doctoral fellowships, to brief sojourns abroad for research collaborations and conference attendance. For others, transnational campuses of universities require episodes of short-term, intensive teaching in other countries (Pherali 2011) alongside ongoing remote relationships with colleagues and students on those campuses.

Discourses around academic mobility in the past have described the 'brain drain' phenomenon, with permanent movements from some countries to others, notably from regions with developing economies or plagued by political unrest, and the associated 'brain gain' of the receiving nations. However, in recognition that this is not necessarily a single movement, 'brain circulation' acknowledges the exchange of knowledge that results from the diasporic research and academic networks established by these cross-border movements (Chen & Koyama 2012). Increasingly for scholars, 'home' might not be tied to a single nation-state or culture. Rather, "[h]ome needs to be understood … in terms of a plurality of places, institutions and epistemic communities; that is to say, more and more academics find themselves 'at home in motion'" (Fahey & Kenway 2010a:568). It is important for academic mobility to be understood not only as physical movement, but also as intellectual movement and flexibility.

In Australia, as elsewhere, the face of higher education has changed dramatically in the last decade owing to the forces of internationalisation and globalisation. Consequently, researchers need to be capable of operating effectively in intercultural milieux and of thinking in a 'worldly' way (Fahey & Kenway 2010b), that is, with an acute awareness of their social, historical and geographical situatedness. Any notion of 'assimilation' is outdated in these contexts, and even the concept of 'acculturation' can be fraught with ambivalence, as researchers seek the skills and outlooks required to work in an increasingly "flexible and fluid global world" (Chen & Koyama 2013:2). Even for researchers remaining relatively static in terms of place, interdisciplinary research work has resulted in a need for intellectual flexibility. This increasingly mobile, fluid research environment necessitates programmes that push the boundaries of postgraduate supervision and provide insight into interdisciplinarity and intercultural communication for both research students and their supervisors.

At the University of Adelaide we have responded to these changes by developing and implementing a framework for researcher development at all levels that includes the skills to conduct an 'ethnography' of personal and disciplinary academic practices. The framework includes a specific programme for international research students (the Integrated Bridging Program-Research (IBP-R)), mixed international and local thesis writing groups, and a supervisor development programme (Exploring Supervision Programme (ESP)) for both local and international staff. The latter programme looks explicitly at issues relating to the multicultural academy. In the next section we explain each of these programmes and the ways in which they work towards developing intercultural competency in researchers through explorations of boundaries around cultural diversity.

INTEGRATED BRIDGING PROGRAM-RESEARCH

"You are the vanguard of internationalisation!" We always greet international research students in this way when they attend the induction session of the IBP-R and point out their importance to the University of Adelaide and the global academy. However, despite the fact that international students have high PhD completion rates in comparison to other students and are usually high-performing students who have often overcome significant odds to take up the challenges of studying abroad (Harman 2003), international students do not necessarily have the English language skills or intercultural competencies required. Likewise, local research students do not necessarily have the intercultural competencies to interact meaningfully with international students. For example, Clifford (2011) illustrates the significant challenges of developing intercultural competencies in local students who do not experience international exchanges.

A common approach to integrating international students is to appoint local mentors, and to provide international students with academic language and learning support. In contrast, at the University of Adelaide we provide all international research students with a concurrent programme that systematically develops two important aspects of intercultural competence: knowledge and skills (Deardorff 2010). The stated aim of the IBP-R is to explicitly unpack "the specific discipline-related expectations of academic writing and oral presentation" (IBP-R 2013).

The IBP-R focuses firstly on developing the academic and generic skills that have increasingly become part of what Nerad and Heggelund (2008:313-314) dub "the global PhD", including the socio-linguistic knowledge and skills of grammar, appropriate citation and attribution, and communication, which assist the student in presenting the required piece of original research in the form of a written thesis and/or dissertation and in oral presentations. This explicit teaching of socio-linguistic knowledge (Deardorff 2010) empowers international students in their interactions with local supervisors and peers. The programme also explicitly develops self-awareness (Deardorff 2010) so that the student can interrogate his or her own discipline, assumptions and abilities and develop intra-cultural competence. Therefore, although the IBP-R pedagogy is characterised by explicit teaching of generic writing, language, citation and presentation skills, the programme focuses on helping students to unpack the conventions of their disciplines and become 'ethnographers or researchers' (Paltridge 2003) of their disciplines.

This is in line with work undertaken by disciplinary researchers such as Downey et al. (2006:107-110), who defined the "globally competent" engineer as someone who has the "knowledge, ability, and predisposition to work effectively with people who define problems differently than they do". These 'differences' in thinking are defined very broadly by Downey et al. (2006) and the IBP-R. Consequently, IBP-R students are assisted in exploring differences and similarities between people of the same disciplines with varying experience, people of related disciplines, other disciplines, lay people versus academics, and so on. The combination of socio-linguistic knowledge and self-awareness assists students in the development of internal outcomes (including flexibility, adaptability, an ethnorelative perspective and empathy) and external outcomes (effective and appropriate communication in an intercultural situation) (Deardorff 2010:88-89).

Rather than placing the local student in the position of the 'knower' and the international student as the 'outsider', the aim is for the international student to develop confidence and skills in a collegial environment with other international students. The explicit development of skills and knowledge in a supportive environment allows the international student to model positive intercultural attitudes (respect, openness, curiosity and discovery) (Deardorff 2010:87) in their interactions with their supervisors and colleagues.

Although many international students have significant language and research challenges, and require systematic language and learning support, others may have few if any language issues and may even be widely published pre-enrolment at the university. Despite the variety of language needs and skill levels, all benefit from the development of intercultural competency in the programme as attested to in positive Student Experience of Learning and Teaching (SELT) surveys where the programme has received a consistent 90% or higher agreement on all measures over its 20 years of existence, and enthusiastic feedback from participants and their supervisors. Because of the variety of language needs and skill levels, the programme includes an initial diagnostic exercise, following which advice is given to students as to recommended participation options (full or negotiated participation) and the specific workshops which would best meet their individual needs. The diagnostic exercise and individualisation of advice and of the programme have developed as a result of student and supervisor requests for explicit advice in open-ended questions in student evaluations of the course and has increasingly been formalised in the formal candidature milestones as part of the movement towards a more structured PhD programme within Australian universities.

Full participation in the IBP-R means that, in the first semester of their candidature, each student attends all twelve of the broadly disciplinary seminars which focus on writing, presentation and intercultural communication skills, and at least eight out of the fifteen workshops that focus on generic research communication skills, language issues and candidature management. Each student also completes two drafts of the research proposal, receiving formal feedback from their supervisors and IBP-R lecturers, and does a practice run of the research proposal presentation, to be delivered at the six-month point in their home discipline. Negotiated participation means that the student attends just those seminars and workshops pertinent to their needs and completes one draft research proposal with feedback from the supervisor and IBP-R lecturer.

One of the explicit 'ethnographic' skills taught in the IBP-R is that of genre analysis, namely identifying the "routine and formulaic nature" of written and spoken texts including their audience, structure, content and language features (Fairclough 1995:86). IBP-R participants are provided with ethnographic tools such as the use of disciplinary and topic-specific corpora (large bodies of text) and concordancers (electronic search tools) in order to explore disciplinary language in its context. This helps them to understand the similarities and, conversely, the huge variety, between texts, both within and across disciplines.

As Deardorff (2010) notes, the development of intercultural competence is a process which requires explicit attention and ongoing development. The IBP-R is a first step in the process towards empowering international students as competent global scholars. On completion of the IBP-R, intercultural competency is further enhanced in structured peer interactions, such as the disciplinary thesis writing groups.

Thesis writing groups

Thesis writing groups can play an important role in facilitating international students' learning, not only in relation to English language skills, but also in relation to negotiating the academic culture in which they find themselves operating. The difficulties for English as an Additional Language (EAL) students of undertaking doctoral study and research publication in English are well documented (see, for example, Bitchener & Basturkmen 2006; Hirvela & Belcher 2001; Wang & Li 2008). Alongside this, much of the extant research indicates that universities are often not good at integrating local and international doctoral students (Cotterall 2011; Robinson-Pant 2009; Trice 2005). Writing groups can be used to respond to both of these concerns, while simultaneously influencing the formation of scholarly identities, creating communities of practice and developing collaborative research cultures (Aitchison & Lee 2006; Boud & Lee 2005; Parker 2009).

Writing groups create authentic situations for students to work and learn together. International doctoral candidates can employ the intercultural skills learnt in the IBP-R in their research community; local students in these groups also have opportunities to develop their intercultural competency. By working together for mutual benefit, genuine collegial relationships develop, dissolving the boundaries of cultural difference and preparing individuals for careers in an internationalised, globalised academy; indeed, research on this topic indicates that cultural and disciplinary diversity can be integral to the success of thesis writing groups (Bastalich 2011; Cuthbert, Spark & Burke 2009; Guerin et al. 2012). In this section, the content covered in the thesis writing groups is outlined, then we reflect on how writing groups can enhance intercultural competency for both international and local doctoral students.

Structure of thesis writing groups

Periodically an email invitation is circulated to all research students, offering to help set up thesis writing groups. Interested students are asked to gather a group of peers (usually 8-12) and arrange a time and place to meet. These groups are intended to be student driven, with input from the Researcher Education team in only the first five sessions, becoming self-managing after that.

- **Session 1: Thinking ahead to the final product.** The first session of the writing group invites research students to consider the final thesis. Discussion focuses on the overall structure of the thesis, identifying differences between traditional format and theses by publication as relevant, as well as exploring issues related to formatting requirements and options.
- **Session 2: Effective writing strategies.** This workshop explores writing strategies to enhance coherence and cohesion at paragraph and sentence level. These exercises focus on topic sentences, paragraph and sentence structure, and ways to locate the reader in the context to ensure clear communication of ideas. Students use each other's writing for the exercises, thus taking the first steps towards sharing their writing and receiving feedback from peers (Aitchison & Lee 2006; Boud & Lee 2005).
- **Session 3: Introductions and conclusions.** This session draws participants' attention to three levels of introductions: to the whole thesis; to chapters or sections; and introductory or topic sentences at the paragraph level. The structure of introductions is examined, and the importance of matching introductions and conclusions is emphasised.
- **Session 4: Argument and voice.** The fourth session focuses on constructing persuasive arguments and common logical errors that can disrupt effective argumentation. It also explores notions of authorial voice, an issue that is generally underexplored in doctoral education, but which new research is suggesting might be a 'threshold concept' for many research students (Guerin & Green 2012).
- **Session 5: Providing feedback on writing by our peers.** In this session one or two group members submit current work for peer critique. Participants are invited to

express opinions about what they admire and to offer suggestions for improvement; the authors are required to listen without interrupting to explain or defend their writing. The feedback is unstructured – participants can raise any issues that occur to them, from comments on structure, grammar and vocabulary, to queries relating to content and methodology, through to more general research topics such as software programs or publication procedures.

After this, the sessions are led by the students themselves. A programme is planned in advance so that participants know when to submit their writing for critique. Anyone unable to attend in person must provide written comments in advance.

Benefits in learning intercultural competency: Writing skills

As expected, thesis writing groups provide valuable opportunities for EAL students to develop their writing skills in English. Although many may be experienced writers in other languages, the conventions of academic writing in English pose new challenges (Hirvela & Belcher 2001). Group discussions are used to make disciplinary conventions explicit, articulate reasons for choices, and offer suitable alternatives. In airing a range of opinions, participants become aware of the acceptable possibilities available to them, continuing the ethnographic investigations of their discipline introduced in the IBP-R. Through ongoing peer critique, individuals receive constructive feedback on their writing during candidature, providing the extended time required for developing language skills at this high level.

It is interesting from the point of view of intercultural competency that this learning is a two-way process (Guerin *et al.* 2012). Unlike most local students, many EAL doctoral students have attended formal English lessons for extensive periods and possess a good understanding of grammar and the language to discuss it; this means they can articulate concepts of which local students sometimes have only shadowy knowledge. Conversely, local students begin to appreciate how to communicate effectively with linguistically and disciplinarily diverse readers, learning where misunderstanding can occur. Comprehending issues relating to language use is crucial in the contemporary academic world, where researchers hail from all corners of the globe; understanding the degree of academic mobility (Hoffman 2009; Pherali 2011) in the academy is essential for successful dissemination of research.

Benefits in learning intercultural competency: Academic culture

The broad range of cultural and linguistic backgrounds of staff and students at the University of Adelaide provides an ideal site in which to prepare doctoral students for the kind of intercultural interactions they can expect in their academic lives. By working closely together, both local and international students can start to appreciate the significance of different attitudes and behaviours created by cultural diversity, and can be encouraged in writing groups to reflect on this diversity from an ethnographic perspective.

One important issue is the amount of 'air time' different members of the group may have in general discussions. Local students, confident and experienced at interacting in this particular academic environment, may tend to dominate the conversations; conversely, EAL speakers can feel that their voices are silenced (Guerin et al. 2012). It is also possible for EAL students to feel that their contributions are misunderstood or ignored – as we know, Australian universities are not always receptive to culturally different forms of knowledge (Singh & Meng 2011).

The skills of peer review are often new to both local and international doctoral candidates, and generally require explicit preparation and practice in a safe environment. Local and international students alike describe the learning curve of discovering the appropriate forms of critique and feedback in academic circles (Guerin et al. 2012). Some find it extremely uncomfortable to openly air criticism of another's work. Thesis writing groups can thus provide opportunities to learn to participate in peer review with sympathetic and like-minded colleagues. For those who are confident about operating in this way, the recognition that this is a culturally inflected aspect of academic life can encourage awareness of the importance of tact and compassion when offering feedback.

Cultural – and also disciplinary – diversity in thesis writing groups allows participants to discover the range of norms in different academic contexts and develop the skills required to negotiate those areas competently with a 'worldly' way of thinking encouraged by an ethnographic approach to their cultural context. Attitudes, knowledge and skills related to intercultural competency are all potentially enhanced in this environment, preparing doctoral students for careers as competent global scholars in the 'borderless university'.

The Exploring Supervision Programme

Background

For the best part of the last two decades, in keeping with the Australian university sector's increasing impetus towards internationalisation, cross-cultural training programmes have been prominent on the agendas of the country's higher education institutions. At the University of Adelaide, for example, the 'Exploring Supervision' programme – a series of three half-day workshops for research degree supervisors – has been running since 2001. For the first six years of the programme's existence, one full four-hour session was devoted entirely to international and cross-cultural issues. Called 'Working with International PhD students', this session ran through a range of policy and procedural issues related to international research students, worked through some supervisory case studies, summarised some cross-cultural communication theory (see, for example, Scollon & Scollon 2001) and suggested some rules of thumb for coping with cross-cultural situations in a research and communication context (as per Ting-Toomey & Chung 2005).

While we are not suggesting there was anything intrinsically wrong with that workshop, it became clear to us by 2007 that it was already somewhat out-dated, and that the internationalised, multicultural university had outgrown it. No longer could the focus be exclusively on the international, EAL research student, constructed as dealing with an Anglo supervisor; just as challenging were the problems faced by international supervisors, as they dealt with students, colleagues and research administrators with an array of linguistic and cultural backgrounds – a changing demographic by no means limited to the University of Adelaide (see, for example, Green & Myatt 2011; Jiang et al. 2010). At the same time, working cross-culturally was no longer considered unusual, but had rather become a routine, day-to-day matter; the potted anthropology that we had dispensed in the 'Working with International PhD students' workshop was no longer novel, but rather had become the conventional wisdom of most working supervisors. In addition, the majority of supervisors clearly felt that they had achieved an effective cosmopolitanism, in the sense of Sanderson (2008), in respect of their research students' working environment, with no cultural divides in the workplace once students had been settled in properly. The supervisors' sense of their own affirming cross-cultural experience left our original workshop looking like a very tired and passé offering indeed.

As a result we radically restructured the workshop, taking the spotlight away from cross-cultural research interactions *per se*, and giving it the simple, brief title 'People', promoting it as exploring "higher degree supervision from a 'people' perspective, asking supervisors to respond to the key interpersonal challenges that supervision presents, and addressing a range of communicative, social and cultural issues". The workshop now functions interactively, with an emphasis on small-group discussion, aiming to build from the collegially mediated experiences of our participant supervisors a systematic method for understanding the nature of person-to-person interaction, as grounded in sets of particular behavioural, conceptual and interpretational conventions. In other words, we try to facilitate supervisors' insights as ethnographers of their own research environments. Discussion of cross-cultural factors is designed to emerge naturally from these ethnographic considerations; at the same time, in this dialogic setting, transnational cross-cultural issues emerge side-by-side with other parameters of diversity: gender and sexuality, age, indigeneity and ethnicity, class, sub-cultural affiliation, ideology, and so on. Indeed, these parameters often vie with the cross-cultural dimensions in their perceived relevance to and influence research degree supervision.

Collaborative critique

To achieve this ethnographic attitude we have developed a teaching approach that we are calling 'collaborative critique' – an approach that is collaborative in that participants work together to create meaning, and their combined efforts are directed at critically assessing and evaluating aspects of their shared environment.[1] Building on the 'reciprocal peer learning' framework for academic development advanced by Boud (1999), and sharing broad affinities with the reflective and experiential approaches to supervisor development espoused by Brew and Peseta (2009), Halse (2011) and Manathunga, Peseta and McCormack (2010), collaborative critique highlights the sharing of personal experience and collegial reflection, but privileges the learning gained from structured environments where critical discussion is embraced. However, while Boud (1999) advocates essentially teacherless collective learning by groups of academics, we continue to maintain a role for a facilitator, as someone with the responsibility to feed in data, questions, scenarios, and so on for the group to consider. The facilitator guides the collective direction for discussion and analysis, and challenges and provokes the group to confront uncomfortable issues. Unlike undergraduate versions of peer review, however, we encourage a collaborative, critical response to the materials under discussion.

We are not attempting to teach specific content; rather, the aim is to encourage supervisors to engage in a collegial critique of their own experiences, assumptions, actions, values and behaviours in their supervisory roles and relationships generally, and particularly in relation to cultural diversity. We provide some hypothesised circumstances, and together the workshop participants explore their responses to the situations. Given that our aim is to promote understanding of research cultures in an environment strongly influenced by high levels of academic mobility, and by increasing engagement in multi-disciplinary enquiry, diversity in attitudes and experiences within the group is welcomed. By responding to the scenarios presented and pooling their individual understandings and experiences, participants work together to formulate auto-ethnographies of their own workplaces (Anderson 2006).

---

[1] A more detailed description of this pedagogical approach can be found in Guerin and Green (2013).

There are no 'correct answers' here; instead, the purpose is to examine the complexity surrounding issues such as multiculturalism in the workplace and develop more nuanced understandings of participants' contexts. The process of collaborative critique allows participants to consider the issues in relation to their own specific disciplinary contexts, which may vary significantly from other members of their workshop group. Through explanation and debate they construct strategies to negotiate this terrain, drawing on their own and each other's experiences to understand events, identifying issues that require attention, and establishing their own set of values and acceptable interpersonal behaviours. Schools and disciplines within a single university will probably always have their own particular research cultures, and we are not suggesting that collaborative critique seeks to resolve this into a unified, monocultural environment. Nevertheless, there are advantages in arriving at some broadly shared understandings of the basic principles of best practice in supervision, particularly given the increasing focus on interdisciplinary research in the contemporary academy that pushes at the boundaries of disciplinary conventions.

Many academics in this transnationally mobile community are reluctant to discuss problems regarding intercultural relations, preferring to present a smooth surface of cosmopolitan success to the rest of the academic community, apparently adopting the 'happiness' discourse critiqued by Ahmed (2012). Elsewhere we have examined the significance of this attitude in relation to notions of an imagined community of the global discipline, where it is assumed that shared disciplinary values and beliefs somehow confer an unproblematically cosmopolitan set of sociocultural beliefs and behaviours on members of that discipline (Guerin & Green forthcoming). While we laud the success of academics to work harmoniously together, we are concerned that this is sometimes at the cost of ignoring – even silencing – inconvenient differences rather than a celebration of diversity (Ahmed 2012). Sometimes workshop participants can find the discussions of cultural difference uncomfortable and unsettling. A major challenge for our 'People' workshop is to create a learning space in which participants are free to explore the meanings of a culturally and disciplinarily diverse population in their research environment in order to develop appropriate intercultural competency in supervisory practices (Bennett & Bennett 2004; Scollon & Scollon 2001).

The ethnography of supervision that is built through collaborative critique explores the tensions between disciplinary homogeneity and cultural diversity, and between learnt cultural behaviours and individual personalities in the research supervision relationship. Through this discovery process, supervisors are able to develop more nuanced strategies for negotiating effective relationships with a diverse range of students. Thus far this approach has been positively received by the participants in the Programme and workshops on the whole, as attested to in formal programme evaluations and other forms of participant feedback. However, we will refine the Programme on an ongoing basis to ensure that it continues to encourage and support supervisors in crossing boundaries in their supervision practices.

CONCLUSION

Our programmes work across all levels of researcher education to provide a cohesive, coordinated framework for developing intercultural competency. A full semester course (the IBP-R) provides explicit opportunities to develop the knowledge and skills of intercultural competency for doctoral candidates new to the University of Adelaide. These competencies are then consolidated in thesis writing groups where international and local doctoral candidates work together, forming strong collegial relationships and promoting first-hand understanding of cultural (and disciplinary) diversity. Alongside this, the supervisor development programme (ESP) encourages academic staff to critique their own workplace in order to understand the intercultural competencies required in their specific situation. Thus, a systematic approach to developing intercultural competency is provided for the individuals who together make up this research environment marked by increasingly complex border crossings and mobility.

REFERENCES

Ahmed S. 2012. *On being included: Racism and diversity in institutional life*. Durham: Duke University Press.

Aitchison C & Lee A. 2006. Research writing: Problems and pedagogies. *Teaching in Higher Education*, 11(3):265-278.

Anderson L. 2006. Analytic autoethnography. *Journal of Contemporary Ethnography*, 35(4):373-395.

Bastalich W. 2011. Beyond the local/general divide: English for academic purposes and process approaches to cross-disciplinary, doctoral writing support. *Higher Education Research and Development*, 30(4):449-462.

Bennett JM & Bennett MJ. 2004. Developing intercultural sensitivity: An integrative approach to global and domestic diversity. In: D Landis, J Bennett & M Bennett (eds). *Handbook of intercultural training*. 3rd edition. Thousand Oaks, CA: Sage. 147-165.

Bitchener J & Basturkmen H. 2006. Perceptions of the difficulties of postgraduate L2 thesis students writing the discussion section. *Journal of English for Academic Purposes*, 5:4-18.

Boud D. 1999. Situating academic development in professional work: Using peer learning. *International Journal for Academic Development*, 4(1):3-10.

Boud D & Lee A. 2005. 'Peer learning' as pedagogic discourse for research education. *Studies in Higher Education*, 30(5):501-516.

Brew A & Peseta T. 2009. Supervision development and recognition in a reflexive space. In: D Boud & A Lee (eds). *Changing practices of doctoral education*. London: Routledge. 126-139.

Chen Q & Koyama JP. 2012. Reconceptualising diasporic intellectual networks: Mobile scholars in transnational space. *Globalisation, Societies and Education*. doi: 10.1080/14767724.2012.690305

Clifford VA. 2011. Internationalising the home student. *Higher Education Research & Development*, 30(5):555-557.

Cotterall S. 2011. Six outsiders and a pseudo-insider: International doctoral students in Australia. In: V Kumar & A Lee (eds). *Doctoral education in international context: Connecting local, regional and global perspectives*. Sebang: Universiti Putra Malaysia Press. 50-63.

Cunningham S, Tapsall S, Ryan Y, Stedman L, Bagdon K & Flew T. 1998 *New media and borderless education*. Canberra: Australian Government Publishing Service.

Cuthbert D, Spark C & Burke E. 2009. Disciplining writing: The case for multi-disciplinary writing groups to support writing for publication by higher degree by research candidates in the humanities, arts and social sciences. *Higher Education Research and Development*, 28(2):137-149.

Deardorff, DK. 2010. Intercultural competence in higher education and intercultural dialogue. In: S Bergan & H Van't Land (eds). *Speaking across borders: The role of higher education in furthering intercultural dialogue*. Paris: Council of Europe & International Association of Universities. 87-100.

Downey GL, Lucena JC, Moskal BM, Parkhurst R, Lehr JL & Nichols-Belo A. 2006. The globally competent engineer: Working effectively with people who define problems differently. *Journal of Engineering Education*, 95(2):1-17.

Fahey J & Kenway J. 2010a. International academic mobility: Problematic and possible paradigms. *Discourse: Studies in the Cultural Politics of Education*, 31(5):627-640.

Fahey J & Kenway J. 2010b. Thinking in a 'worldly' way: Mobility, knowledge, power and geography. *Discourse: Studies in the Cultural Politics of Education*, 31(5):627-640.

Fairclough, N. 1995. *Critical discourse analysis*. Boston, MA: Addison Wesley.

Green W & Myatt P. 2011. Telling tales: A narrative research study of the experiences of new international academic staff at an Australian university. *International Journal for Academic Development*, 16(1):33-44.

Guerin C & Green I. (Forthcoming). Cultural diversity and the imagined community of the global academy. *Asia Pacific Journal of Education*.

Guerin C & Green I. 2012. Doctoral voices: Threshold concepts in research supervision. Paper presented at the Tenth Quality in Postgraduate Education (QPR) Conference on Narratives of Transition, Adelaide, 17-19 April.

Guerin C & Green I. 2013. 'Collaborative critique' in a supervisor development program. *Innovations in Education and Teaching International*, 50(4):1-11.

Guerin C, Xafis V, Doda DV, Gillam M, Larg A, Luckner H, Jahan N, Widayati A & Xu C. 2012. Diversity in collaborative research communities: A multicultural, multidisciplinary thesis writing group in public health. *Studies in Continuing Education*, 35(1):65-81.

Halse C. 2011. 'Becoming a supervisor': The impact of doctoral supervision on supervisors' learning. *Studies in Higher Education*, 36(5):557-570.

Harman G. 2003. International PhD students in Australian universities: Financial support, course experience and career plans. *International Journal of Educational Development*, 23(3):339-351.

Hearn J. 2011. The world university – Teamwork in a time of financial turbulence. In: K Yu & AL Stith (eds). *Competition and cooperation among universities in the age of internationalization*. Shanghai: Shanghai Jiao Tong University Press. 3-12.

Hirvela A & Belcher D. 2001. Coming back to voice: The multiple voices and identities of mature multilingual writers. *Journal of Second Language Writing*, 10:83-106.

Hoffman DM. 2009. Changing academic mobility patterns and international migration: What will academic mobility mean in the 21st century? *Journal of Studies in International Education*, 13(3):347-364.

IBP-R (Integrated Bridging Program-Research). 2013. *Integrated Bridging Program-Research*. Pamphlet. Adelaide: Researcher Education and Development Unit, University of Adelaide.

Jiang X, Di Napoli R, Borg M, Maunder R, Frye H & Walsh E. 2010. Becoming and being an academic: The perspectives of Chinese staff in two research-intensive UK universities. *Studies in Higher Education*, 35(2):155-170.

Kim T. 2009. Shifting patterns of transnational academic mobility: A comparative and historical approach. *Comparative Education*, 45(3):387-403.

Manathunga C, Peseta T. & McCormack C. 2010. Supervisor development through creative approaches to writing. *International Journal for Academic Development*, 15(1):33-46.

Nerad M & Heggelund M. 2008. *Towards a global PhD? Forces and forms in doctoral education worldwide*. Washington, DC: University of Washington Press.

Paltridge B. 2003. Underlying philosophies of English language education in Australia. *English Teaching*, 58(1):273-284.

Parker R. 2009. A learning community approach to doctoral education in the social sciences. *Teaching in Higher Education*, 14(1):43-54.

Pherali TJ. 2011. Academic mobility language and cultural capital: The experience of transnational academics in British higher education institutions. *Journal of Studies in International Education*, 16(4):313-333.

Robinson-Pant A. 2009. Changing academies: Exploring international PhD students' perspectives on 'host' and 'home' universities. *Higher Education Research and Development*, 28(4):417-429.

Sanderson G. 2008. A foundation for the internationalization of the academic self in higher education. *Journal of Studies in International Education*, 12(3):276-307.

Scollon R & Scollon SW. 2001. *Intercultural communication: A discourse approach*. 2nd edition. Oxford: Blackwell.

Singh M & Meng H. 2011. Democratising western research using non-western theories: Ranciere and mute Chinese theoretical tools. *Studies in Higher Education*, 38(6):907-920.

Ting-Toomey S & Chung LC. 2005. *Understanding intercultural communication*. New York: Oxford University Press.

Trice AG. 2005. Navigating in a multinational learning community: Academic departments' responses to graduate international students. *Journal of Studies in International Education*, 9:62-89.

Wang T & Li LY. 2008. Understanding international postgraduate research students' challenges and pedagogical needs in thesis writing. *International Journal of Pedagogies and Learning*, 4(3):88-96.

Watanabe, Y. 2011. Building world-class universities in the age of internationalization: The 'E' elements in Nagoya University. In: K Yu & AL Stith (eds). *Competition and cooperation among universities in the age of internationalization*. Shanghai: Shanghai Jiao Tong University Press. 13-22.

13

MORE THAN AGENCY

THE MULTIPLE MECHANISMS AFFECTING POSTGRADUATE EDUCATION

Puleng Motshoane and Sioux McKenna

INTRODUCTION

It is generally accepted that the health of the postgraduate sector is an important factor in a nation's ability to contribute to innovation and knowledge production (ASSAf 2010; CHE & CREST 2009). The knowledge economy is driven by high level skills and so it is unsurprising that the Department of Science and Technology and the National Research Foundation, amongst other national bodies, have introduced a range of initiatives to ensure growth in postgraduate education. The National Research Foundation's 2007 South African PhD Project seeks to double the number of doctoral graduates by 2015, while the Department of Science and Technology wishes to increase doctoral graduates five-fold by 2018 (Badat 2010). In order to remain competitive and to provide solutions to a range of societal ills, we do indeed need to move beyond our current picture of low output and high dropout to a postgraduate system that enjoys an increase in both quality and quantity.

The 2010 Academy of Science of South Africa's (ASSAf) report on doctoral education indicated that South Africa has just 26 doctorates per million of the population and thus compares very unfavourably with other countries; Brazil, for example, has 52 doctorates per million, the USA has 201 and Australia has 264. The ASSAf report argued that "for South Africa to be a serious competitor in the global knowledge economy, and to achieve standards that are internationally comparable, both the quality and quantity of PhDs need to be expanded dramatically" (ASSAf 2010:21). The CHE and CREST report on postgraduate education in South Africa (2009) raised similar concerns about low participation rates at all levels of postgraduate study, and also demonstrated that the time to completion was far greater than indicated in the national funding formula or the notional hours of the national qualifications framework. Those who are able to successfully complete master's degrees do so in an average of 2.9 years and those who successfully complete doctoral degrees do so in an average of 4.7 years (CHE & CREST 2009:13).

This chapter argues that any serious attempt to develop postgraduate education at a national or even institutional level needs to include an increased focus on the role played by issues such as institutional ethos and research culture in supporting the supervision process. There is a need for careful consideration by policy makers and institutional management of the ways in which structural and cultural issues affect postgraduate supervision and how these can be fostered to improve the postgraduate supervisory process. If the production of postgraduates is going to improve, it is important to have a holistic picture of the various mechanisms affecting education at this level.

While the existing research offers a sophisticated picture of the roles played by supervisors and postgraduate students, and provides invaluable advice to these key stakeholders, we believe the literature insufficiently addresses the ways in which, among other issues, institutional differentiation and institutional history are crucial structural issues in determining the supervision context. Until research on the postgraduate sector shifts its boundaries to include these issues in the spotlight, we argue that ambitious national goals, such as the goal to increase doctoral output to 5 000 by 2030 (NPC 2011), will remain unrealised.

Any growth in the postgraduate sector needs to be underpinned by a framing of the context that incorporates the roles and capacity development of supervisors and postgraduate students but also goes beyond that. This chapter outlines one possible theoretical framework that we believe could drive such broad-based conceptualisation of postgraduate education. It then very briefly raises just two of the possible areas, institutional differentiation and history, that such an approach would include in its gaze and suggests that these are among the many mechanisms currently constraining postgraduate education.

CRITICAL AND SOCIAL REALISM

Bhaskar's Critical Realism (2008) contends that our experiences of the world are mediated through our biased and incomplete conceptual understandings and we are therefore never completely aware of the mechanisms from which events and our experiences thereof arise. The partial and relative way in which we engage with the world often results in what Bhaskar refers to as the "epistemic fallacy" (2008:36) whereby we conflate what we 'know' of the world with what 'is'. The responsibility of research in the open system of the social world, where we cannot contain and manipulate all the possible variables as we could in a laboratory, is to move beyond a relativistic description of multiple interpretations and instead endeavour to offer an "explanatory critique" of what mechanisms might be causing a particular effect. Such an explanatory critique may be incomplete and fallible, but "the arduous task of science [is] the production of the knowledge of those enduring and continually active mechanisms of nature that produce the phenomena of our world" (Bhaskar 2008:37).

Taking this to an attempt to understand the constraints and enablements of postgraduate education would entail a rich interrogation of the ways in which students and supervisors enact the pedagogy and experience this educational process. But it would also include shifting the boundaries beyond these multiple ways of being and asking questions about what the world must be like for postgraduate education to happen in the way that it does.

What is it about our economic, social, political and cultural structures that enable postgraduate education to exist as a phenomenon? Why are state and industrial structures demanding an increase in postgraduate education and what specific forms of such education do these structures value? How does today's globalised world and knowledge economy affect the ways in which postgraduate education occurs? How do unjust legacies and on-going inequities affect those who enjoy access to and success in postgraduate education? These large questions about the structure of the world are central to the realist concern with how complex events, such as postgraduate education, and the multiple experiences thereof come into existence.

While Bhaskar's Critical Realism provides an ontological philosophy of all aspects of the world, Archer (1995, 1996, 2000) concerns herself specifically with the phenomena and underlying mechanisms of the social world. She describes the social world as comprising the domains of 'people' and 'parts'. The 'people' are understood in terms of agency, which refers to the capacity of individuals to act independently and to make their own free choices (Archer 1995). By contrast, the 'parts', which comprise structure and culture, refer to those factors of influence (such as social class, institutions, legislation, funding, customs and policy) that determine or limit the extent to which agency can be activated.

She argues against conflating the domains of the people and the parts and calls doing so the "fallacy of conflation" (2000:6). She distinguishes between upward, downward and central conflation, all of which she believes are problematic. In 'upward conflation' the powers of the 'people' are held to orchestrate those of the 'parts' (2000:4). In 'downward conflation' the 'parts' are seen to organise the people (2000:5), while in 'central conflation' autonomy is withheld from both levels because they are mutually constitutive and not considered in their own right (2000:6). When Archer (1996) discusses 'structure' or 'culture' in relation to 'agency' she is talking about a relationship between two aspects of social life. She demonstrates that however intimately they are intertwined, they should nonetheless be analytically distinct.

Archer (1995:133) argues that much research is guilty of some or other form of conflation – where too much power is accorded to one domain and there is a blind spot as to the causal tendencies of another domain. According to Archer (1995:15), social realism demands a methodology where an explanation of why things are 'so and not otherwise' depends on an analysis of how the properties and powers of the 'people' intertwine with the properties and power of the 'parts'. In reality the 'parts' and the 'people' exist in a constant interplay but Archer (1995:15) argues that for research purposes, analytical dualism of the 'people' (agency) and the 'parts' (structure and culture) is necessary to be able to identify how the different mechanisms work to bring about events and experiences.

Danermark, Ekstrom, Jakobsen and Karlsson (2002) explain that 'dualism' refers to the fact that social structures and human agency are different strata; 'analytical' to the fact that these strata and the interaction between them cannot be detected in the flow of social action and human experiences, but only by means of social scientific analysis. Archer notes that the notion of analytical dualism was first identified by David Lockwood when he wrote about it in his seminal article, 'Social integration and system integration' where he began by distinguishing the 'parts' from the 'people' and then examining their combinations in order to account for variable outcomes which otherwise eluded theorisation (Archer 1995:170).

Archer (1995) further explains that the 'parts' are temporally prior to the actions of people because individuals always enter a situation where structures and culture pre-exist them. Having entered a social context, with its pre-existing structures and cultures, individuals or groups of people through their actions then reproduce or transform the structure and culture. People use agency to defend their interests or to realise their 'projects', and thereby either effect change on the 'parts' within which they are acting, or reinforce the current properties and powers of these 'parts'. The 'people' in society and the 'parts' of society are not different aspects of the same thing, but are radically different in kind (Archer 1995:15).

To bring the focus of research only on people or on parts in order to understand any phenomenon is to be guilty of upwards or downwards conflation. To consider them as one entwined whole is not problematic on philosophical grounds, for surely agents reinforce and change structures and cultures while being simultaneously constrained and enabled by them, but it is problematic on analytical grounds, for if we consider them as one unspecified co-constituted whole we are unable to explore the relative influence of each. To avoid such errors of conflation in an understanding of postgraduate education in South Africa, we argue that it is necessary to consider both the 'people' and the 'parts' and then to look at the interplay between them.

WHY DO WE NEED SUCH A FRAMEWORK?

While much of the research on postgraduate education is new, this is a rapidly growing area of concern. There is now a reasonably sized body of literature on postgraduate supervision, and this offers a sophisticated picture of the roles played by the agents in the form of supervisors and candidates. This literature details the impact of their emotions, personalities, communication styles and pedagogical approaches, among other things. However, we believe that this literature less frequently engages in the consideration of the 'parts' of structure and culture and the interplay between such 'parts' and the relevant agents. We believe that the focused interest in the agents of postgraduate education could result in upwards conflation, and that there is a need for research that pushes the boundaries to include a consideration of the structures and cultures of postgraduate supervision and how these interplay with the actions of the agents.

Alongside research into postgraduate education, there are also a number of guidebooks that aim to support both supervisor and student in this complex pedagogical space (see, for example, Eley & Murray 2009; Kamler & Thomson 2006; Lee 2009; Murray 2011; Phillips & Pugh 2010; Thomson & Walker 2010; Trafford & Leshem 2008; Wisker 2012). These books provide detailed discussions of what the roles and responsibilities of the student and supervisor might be and how they might best traverse the postgraduate journey together. However, the focus on the candidate and her supervisors means that very little is said about the institutional, national and global context within which the postgraduate study takes place. This is perhaps unsurprising as these books are written for individual candidates and supervisors and so provide advice about the areas in postgraduate education where these individuals have the most agency. The focus on what the candidate or supervisor should or should not do could, however, create the impression that good practice, in terms of throughput and retention for example, is the result of actions taken by these individuals, rather than being a phenomenon that emerges from the interplay of a myriad mechanisms.

In South Africa, there are likewise a number of key texts on postgraduate supervision that offer a wealth of insights into how the supervisor can improve her practices and assist her candidates in achieving excellent research. Works by Mouton (2001), Wadee, Keane, Dietz and Hay (2010) and Hofstee (2010), for example, offer support for issues of communication between candidate and supervisor, different approaches to supervision, and ways to support strong research design. They pay little attention though to the context within which the supervision takes place or to the ways in which external structures affect the supervision process. These silences might imply that power over how the process develops is primarily or even exclusively in the hands of the supervisor and candidate.

The pressures from the state and other bodies to increase the postgraduate sector come in various forms. At an individual level, much weight is given to supervision success in research rating processes, and at an institutional level the funding formula is structured in a way that greatly incentivises postgraduate output in universities. But we argue that good supervision alone cannot make much impact on the current low levels of postgraduate participation and throughput. Until we consider the impact of structural and cultural mechanisms alongside those of agency in the enablement of growth in postgraduate education, we are unlikely to see significant progress. We believe that calling on Archer's framework would be one possible way of pushing the boundaries of research on postgraduate education such that we look at the full context of interacting enabling and constraining mechanisms.

WHAT MIGHT BE INCLUDED IN SUCH A FRAMEWORK?

The analytical dualism called for by Archer's social realism is a trick of analysis only. While acknowledging that the effects of structure, culture and agency are simultaneous and mutually affecting, the role of the researcher is to momentarily unravel the complex interplay of multiple mechanisms in order to show the effects they have on each other. This would necessitate looking at postgraduate education within the cultural context of, for example, institutional ethos and the structural context of, for example, national policy. However, it would certainly also necessitate seeing how such structures and cultures 'rub up against' the agents involved in the postgraduate processes. The rest of this chapter provides a very introductory discussion of the kinds of agential, structural and cultural mechanisms that would need to be taken into consideration if postgraduate education is to be considered from the viewpoint of analytical dualism.

A CONSIDERATION OF AGENCY

There is a growing body of work that considers the ways in which supervisors and postgraduate scholars engage and what form the pedagogy takes. Research articles on postgraduate education abound (for example, the collection of articles edited by Fataar 2012; the 2000 special edition of the *South African Journal of Higher Education* edited by Bitzer and the special edition of *Perspectives in Education* edited by Herman 2011), and entire conferences are now dedicated to this issue.[1] These journals and conferences are concerned with a broad range of issues including approaches to supervision, completion rates and student satisfaction.

The main, though certainly not exclusive, focus of such work has been on the agency of supervisors and postgraduate scholars. Archer argues that there are three kinds of agents and that we need to look at people and their "personal projects" in the light of the kinds of agency they are able to claim (2007:4).

Primary agents (Archer 2007) are typically unable to exercise much agency due to their disempowered position in society in relation to socially scarce resources. Primary agents are subject to "involuntary positioning" (Mutch 2004:433) as a result of external factors such as the demographics of age and gender. While it is an exercise of agency to undertake postgraduate studies and requires a strong commitment to a 'personal project', most scholars are, we would argue, primary agents. They are positioned by their novice status in the academy and they are largely subject to the norms and values of the supervisors, the institution and the discipline. In South Africa, and elsewhere, they may also be disempowered through their uneven access to academic discourses.

Social actors (Archer 2007) are individuals who can claim a strong identity because of their association with a particular role or position in society. The supervisor may well be considered a social actor who is able to exercise a number of powerful personal properties by virtue of her institutionally (and socially) recognised position. Research into postgraduate education undertaken in this framework would need to look at how the role of 'supervisor' is constructed in the institution and the extent to which such construction enables and constrains the actions of the individual embodying the role. It may be that in some circumstances, the supervisors find themselves to be primary agents with little space to enact their personal project because of the ways in which other social actors, such as institutional management, have constructed the postgraduate education processes.

The third group of agents identified by Archer (2007) are corporate agents. These are groups of people who are organised around a common interest. By grouping together and organising, it is possible for those with limited personal power to

---

[1] For example, every two years there is a Quality in Postgraduate Research Conference in Australia and a Postgraduate Supervision Conference in South Africa.

bring about structural changes. Studies of postgraduate education using Archer's framework would need to consider whether collectives of students or supervisors are able to function as corporate agents and how and why this occurs.

Bringing a social realist framework to postgraduate education would thus entail the kind of detailed look at the experiences of scholars and supervisors that is already found in much of the current research (for example Grant 2003; Lee & Green 2009; Leshem & Trafford 2007; Wisker 2010). The framework would also entail a look at other agents whose actions could constrain or enable postgraduate education, such as those working in institutional management and administration.

The focus on the ways in which agents act within and upon the world entails a consideration of their "personal projects" and the extent to which they are able to activate their "personal emergent properties and powers" (Archer 2007). We need to focus on agency because any changes planned through policy or direct interventions are mediated by individuals who creatively enact or resist such changes.

The analytical dualist approach required by Archer's social realism, however, insists that the researcher does not consider issues of agency alone but does so within the context of the structures and cultures that enable and constrain the activation of such agency. We now briefly suggest just two of the structures that would need to be interrogated should such a broad framework be implemented in the analysis of the sector.

THE DIFFERENTIATED STRUCTURE OF SOUTH AFRICAN HIGHER EDUCATION

The White Paper (RSA DoE 1997) outlined the framework for post-apartheid change, that is, that the higher education system must be planned, governed and funded as a single national co-ordinated system. But this system was to look very different to that of the apartheid era. The South African higher education system faced major reconstruction in the form of multiple mergers and incorporations from 2002 onwards as 36 public higher education institutions were reduced to 23. This was done in order to overcome fragmentation, inequality and inefficiency and it was from this process that the current higher education differentiation of institutional type was birthed. The ways in which the structural realities of the resulting sector play into the enactment of postgraduate teaching and learning need careful interrogation.

Badsha and Cloete (2011) report that a broad spectrum of the South African higher education community accepted differentiation as a strategy to bring greater diversity and fitness for purpose into the system. The three institutional types focus on different but overlapping forms of higher education. Traditional universities offer primarily general and professional qualifications in the form of degrees, universities of technology offer primarily vocational qualifications in the form of diplomas and comprehensive universities offer a combination of the two. Such groupings are thus clustered around qualification type and purpose.

Adkins (2009) noted that there are few studies examining the links between the knowledge requirements of different types of universities and their implications for the experiences of students and supervisory processes. Do universities of technology work more closely with industry to solve workplace problems and should this drive specific applied kinds of postgraduate knowledge? Do current drivers of postgraduate output have a deleterious effect on undergraduate teaching and learning? Does the need for strong undergraduate output mean that only some institutions should be encouraged to grow postgraduate output? And if so, on what basis do the state and the higher education sector determine where such growth should occur and how it should be driven?

National drives to grow postgraduate education need to be guided by considerations of the ways in which such differentiation affects postgraduate education in terms of kinds of output as well as quantity. Seventy-four per cent of doctoral graduations come from just seven institutions (Badat 2010:23). Generic capacity-building projects and system-wide funding incentives that fail to take differentiation into account may prove to be counterproductive.

One of the starkest ways in which differentiation plays into postgraduate education is the extent to which there is institutional capacity for supervision. One marker of such capacity is the number of staff with doctorates. Work by the Centre for Higher Education Transformation (CHET) shows us that the percentage of academics with doctorates in traditional universities ranges from 59% down to 16%, in comprehensive universities the range is 37% to 9% and in universities of technology the range is 24% to 5% (CHET 2010). At a system level, only 32% of academics have doctorates (Badat 2010:21). In the old technikon system, lecturers were usually hired on the basis of their industry expertise rather than their academic qualifications (Powell 2011) and this continues to be evident in the qualification profile of different institutions.

Another marker of an institution's capacity to offer quality postgraduate education is its research output. Postgraduate education is reliant not only on having staff with the necessary qualifications but also on having the ethos of valuing research and providing the kind of institutional space that makes it possible. The differing teaching loads between universities of technology and traditional universities, for example, must affect the quantity of research output that is possible (Powell 2011). The research output of the South African higher education system as a whole is low but it is also highly differentiated (CHET 2010). The statistical analysis provided by CHET not only raises questions of capacity to offer postgraduate education but also about whether this should be the goal for all segments of the sector, given our great need for quality undergraduate education.

CHET have done enormous work looking at a range of indicators that could help us to understand differentiation in South Africa, some of which relate to the offering of postgraduate education. It is clear from their analyses that there are three distinct groupings of universities (that they call the red, blue and green group), but that these do not entirely mirror the three institutional types of traditional university, comprehensive university and university of technology. An understanding of differentiation therefore needs to go beyond that of the three types to understand the ways in which this is manifest in the South African higher education system. Such an understanding needs to be fundamental to calls for increased postgraduate output. The structural mechanisms of institutional type, function and capacity are central to where and how such postgraduate education could occur and what is needed to make it happen.

Blunt drivers of postgraduate education can have unintended consequences if mechanisms such as institutional differentiation are not taken into account. The current funding formula, for example, provides financial incentives for postgraduate growth, but does so in a uniform way that undermines the development of differentiation. Academic drift that negatively affects undergraduate education (Badat 2010), acceptance of postgraduate students without the required supervision capacity and the valuing of postgraduate supervision over excellent undergraduate teaching are just some of difficulties that emerge from a drive for blanket growth of postgraduate education.

Singh notes that a differentiated higher education system is generally understood as necessary for "widening participation and increasing user choice, attaining competitive excellence in country or across countries, and making targeted contributions to national and regional development" (2008:245) but she goes on to indicate that contestations about the forms and benefits of differentiation also abound and may be more acute in developing countries. Singh notes that differentiation in South Africa is made more complex by the contextual conditionalities of our past. Differentiation often results in problematic hierarchies of institutions where the main purpose of a particular institutional type is seen to hold higher or lower status but this can assume "a greater socio-political edge in a country like South Africa, given its history of structural inequality and racial profiling" (Singh 2008:247).

We now briefly consider how the issue of institutional history acts as another related mechanism constraining or enabling postgraduate education.

INSTITUTIONAL HISTORIES

All universities in South Africa have been culturally and structurally conditioned by apartheid. Although two decades have passed since the implementation of democracy in South Africa and despite the use of mergers to restructure the higher education sector, the histories of our universities remains very much in evidence and continues to have a bearing on the offering of postgraduate education. Technikons, for example, were developed to play specific skills development roles (Winberg 2005) and Afrikaans-medium institutions were structured to reproduce the ideologies of nationalism (Bunting 2002) but it was the historically disadvantaged institutions that "bore the brunt of apartheid thinking, because of the way material resources were denied to them" (Boughey & McKenna 2010).

Research by CHET indicates that postgraduate output is particularly low in historically disadvantaged institutions (2010), a phenomenon which can be traced to the location and histories of these institutions. Bunting (2002) argues that historically disadvantaged universities were not expected to produce research and that postgraduate education was not deemed to be appropriate for the black student body. Supervision capacity and a research ethos were thus not part of the historically disadvantaged institutions. Research by Boughey and McKenna (2010) suggests that such capacity has not yet been sufficiently developed to redress these structural inequities.

The paltry history of postgraduate education in historically disadvantaged institutions was further constrained by a lack of institutional management capacity and a lack of financial resources. While historically advantaged universities had enjoyed a level of financial autonomy from the apartheid state in that they managed their own budgets, technikons and historically disadvantaged institutions had to have budgets and even staff employment approved by the state (Bunting 2002). They were also not allowed to retain any surplus funds and so did not develop financial trusts in the ways that historically advantaged institutions did, nor did they develop the capacity to manage their own funds.

Historically disadvantaged institutions then experienced shortfalls in student funding with the movement of many of their students to historically advantaged institutions (Scott, Yeld & Hendry 2007) and with the remaining students often being unable to pay fees, despite such fees being notably lower than in the advantaged institutions. Furthermore, disadvantaged institutions could not meet such shortfalls through increased research output or third stream income as these institutions were poorly placed both geographically and in terms of capacity (Boughey & McKenna 2010).

Research that draws on institutional audit portfolios suggests that historically disadvantaged institutions suffer from low staff morale and a concern about academic identity, and that a discourse of demoralisation permeating such universities remains evident (Boughey & McKenna 2010). If academic integrity is understood to emerge from an academic identity (Henkel 2000; Becher & Trowler 2001) then a lack of clear academic project and vibrant intellectual climate could be seen to be a major constraining mechanism in any development of postgraduate education.

Interventions aimed at increasing postgraduate education cannot be aimed purely in the realm of the agency of supervisors and their students. They need to take into account the ways in which structure and culture affect the processes. Supervising postgraduate students in a well-resourced university where one's colleagues are all highly qualified and actively involved in research is quite different from doing so in an institution where one is the only person in the department with a doctorate and where the university offers little in the way of engaged academic debate.

CONCLUSION

This chapter has offered an introductory argument that both our research into and our policy development for the postgraduate sector needs to take careful consideration of structural and cultural mechanisms alongside those of agency. We have recommended that social realism offers one possible theoretical framing for a more nuanced consideration of the sector, demanding as it does that the people and the parts be considered separately as well as their interplay, if we are to make sense of the current low participation and high dropout rates in the postgraduate sector.

Growth in quantity and quality will not occur if interventions developed to this end are guilty of upwards conflation, whereby the capacity development and reward systems are directed at individual supervisors alone rather than at the full range of mechanisms constraining postgraduate education. While the development of coaching, mentoring and communication skills, among others, can have an enormously beneficial effect on the pedagogical practices of individual supervisors, there will be little system-level advancement without engagement with the ways in which the culture and structures of a discipline, an institution and a higher education system affect the enactment of such pedagogical practices.

REFERENCES

Adkins B. 2009. PhD pedagogy and the changing knowledge landscapes of universities. *Higher Education Research & Development*, 28(2):165-177. [Accessed 27 May 2012]. http://www.tandfonline.com/doi/abs/10.1080/07294360902725041

Archer MS. 1995. *Realist social theory: The morphogenetic approach*. Cambridge: Cambridge University Press.

Archer MS. 1996. *Culture and agency: The place of culture in social theory*. Cambridge: Cambridge University Press.

Archer MS. 2000. *Being human: The problem of agency*. Cambridge: Cambridge University Press.

Archer MS. 2007. Realism and the problem of agency. *Journal of Critical Realism*, 5(1):11-20.

ASSAf (Academy of Science of South Africa). 2010. *The PhD study: An evidenced-based study on how to meet the demands for high-level skills in an emerging economy*. Pretoria: ASSAf

Badat S. 2010. *The challenges of transformation in higher education and training institutions in South Africa*. Commissioned report for the Development Bank of South Africa. Midrand: Development Bank of South Africa.

Badsha N & Cloete N. 2011. *Higher education: Contribution for the NPC's National Development Plan*. [Accessed 18 November 2012] http://chet.org.za/files/uploads/reports/Badsha%20and%20Cloete%20NPC%20Higher%20Education%20November%202011%20F.pdf

Becher T & Trowler P. 2001. *Academic tribes and territories*. 2nd edition. Buckingham: Open University Press.

Bhaskar RA. 2008. *A realist theory of science*. 2nd edition. London: Verso.

Bitzer EM (ed). 2000. *South African Journal of Higher Education*. Special Edition on Postgraduate Supervision, 14(1).

Boughey C & McKenna S. 2010. *A meta-analysis of teaching and learning at historically disadvantaged universities*. Commissioned report for the Council on Higher Education (CHE). Pretoria: CHE.

Bunting I. 2002. Funding. In: N Cloete (ed). *Transformation in higher education: Global pressures and local realities in South Africa*. Cape Town: Juta. 73-94.

CHE & CREST (Council on Higher Education & Centre for Research on Science and Technology). 2009. *Postgraduate studies in South Africa: A statistical profile*. Higher Education Monitor No. 7. Pretoria: CHE.

CHET (Centre for Higher Education Transformation). 2010. *Performance indicators in South African higher education 2000-2008*. Cape Town.

Danermark B, Ekstrom M, Jakobsen L & Karlsson JC. 2002. *Explaining society: Critical realism in the social sciences*. London: New York: Routledge.

Eley A & Murray R. 2009. *How to be an effective supervisor: Best practice in research student supervision*. Maidenhead: Open University Press & McGraw Hill.

Fataar A (ed). 2012. *Debating thesis supervision: Perspectives from a university education department*. Stellenbosch: SUN PRESS.

Grant B. 2003. Mapping the pleasures and risks of postgraduate supervision. *Discourse: Studies in Cultural Politics of Education*, 24(2):175-190.

Henkel M. 2000. *Academic identities and policy change in higher education*. London: Jessica Kingsley.

Herman C (ed). 2011. *Perspectives in Education*. Special Edition on Doctoral Education, 29(3).

Hofstee E. 2010. *Constructing a good dissertation: A practical way to finishing a masters, MBA or PhD on schedule*. Amsterdam: EPE.

Kamler B & Thomson P. 2006. *Helping doctoral students write: Pedagogies for supervision*. London: Routledge.

Lee A & Green B. 2009. Supervision as metaphor. *Studies in Higher Education*, 34(6):615-630.

Lee N. 2009. *Achieving your professional doctorate*. Maidenhead: Open University Press.

Leshem S & Trafford V. 2007. Overlooking the conceptual framework. *Innovations in Education and Teaching International*, 44(1):93-105.

Mouton J. 2001. *How to succeed in your master's and doctoral studies: A South African guide and resource book*. Goodwood: Van Schaik.

Murray R. 2011. *How to write a thesis*. 3rd edition. Maidenhead: Open University Press.

Mutch A. 2004. Constraints on the internal conversation: Margaret Archer and the structural shaping of thought. *Journal for the Theory of Social Behaviour*, 34(4):429-445.

NPC (National Planning Commission). 2011. *National Development Plan: Vision 2030*. Pretoria: The Presidency.

Phillips EM & Pugh DS. 2010. *How to get a PhD: A handbook for students and their supervisors*. 5th edition. Buckingham: Open University Press.

Powell P. 2011. A critical investigation into curriculum development discourses of academic staff at a South African university of technology. PhD thesis. Durban: University of KwaZulu-Natal.

RSA DoE (Republic of South Africa. Department of Education). 1997. *Education White Paper 3: A Programme for the Transformation of Higher Education*. Pretoria.

Scott I, Yeld N & Hendry J. 2007. A case for improving teaching and learning in South African higher education. *Higher Education Monitor No. 6*. Pretoria: CHE.

Singh M. 2008. Valuing differentiation as a qualified good: The case of South African higher education. *Higher Education Policy*, 21:245-263.

Thomson P & Walker M (eds). 2010. *The Routledge doctoral student's companion: Getting to grips with research in education and the social sciences*. London: Routledge.

Trafford V & Leshem S. 2008. *Stepping stones to achieving your doctorate*. Berkshire: Open University Press.

Wadee A, Keane M, Dietz T & Hay D. 2010. *Effective PhD supervision, mentorship and coaching*. Amsterdam: Rosenberg.

Winberg C. 2005. Continuities and discontinuities in the journey from technikon to university of technology. *South African Journal of Higher Education*, 19(2):189-200.

Wisker G. 2010. The 'good enough' doctorate: Doctoral learning journeys. *Acta Academica Supplementum*, 1:223-242.

Wisker G. 2012. *The good supervisor: Supervising postgraduate and undergraduate research for doctoral theses and dissertations.* 2nd edition. London: Palgrave MacMillan.

PART SIX

DOCTORAL EXPERIENCES AND IDENTITIES

14

FIRST-GENERATION STUDENTS ASPIRING TO LIVE THE ACADEMIC DREAM

THE ROLE OF SUPERVISOR SUPPORT

Catherine Mitchell

The University of Auckland Clock Tower, 2008. (This image of the University of Auckland has been made available to the public domain via the Wikimedia commons. Use for any legal purpose has been granted by the owner Richard001 via at http://commons.wikimedia.org//wiki/File:University_of_Auckland_Clock_Tower_building_from_front.JPG)

My family including me (at 3 years leaning against my dad) outside our home.

INTRODUCTION

Aspirations, our imagined possibilities for ourselves, can be powerful tools to mobilise individuals from across a range of social contexts towards educational endeavours. For those students at a distance from the university, such as students who are the first in their family to participate in higher education (referred to as first-generation students), aspirations can provide a potent impetus to bridge the gap between their everyday lives and the world of the university. Such aspirations can be focused on gaining an undergraduate university degree or can support an ongoing engagement with higher education through into advanced academic programmes, such as doctoral studies. First-generation students who undertake doctoral study are individuals who aspire to a version of 'the good life' through doctoral work that is, in practice at least, distinctly different from that of their parents and, perhaps, their wider social networks. I wish here to consider the role of supervision in supporting students' capacity to aspire, particularly in terms of becoming an academic. While many undertake doctoral studies with goals that extend beyond seeking the traditional role of the university academic, there are still many doctoral students who wish to take up academic positions. As a current doctoral student, reflecting on my supervision experience to date has led me to contemplate the multifaceted nature of the supervision process. It has also made me think carefully about what I want to learn from my supervisors as I imagine an academic future and, in a more general sense, the potential of supervisors to contribute to students' movement into academia. This consideration will be informed by theoretical writing about aspiration and will also incorporate some auto-ethnographic reflections from the writer as a first-generation student pursuing a doctorate within education.

JOURNEY STARTING POINTS

When I look at the old photo above of myself, as a toddler, and my family outside our modest working-class home in small-town New Zealand and the emblematic, and much used image of the University of Auckland's Clock Tower building, I am struck by the difference between these two sites. I am also aware of the space between these two worlds, a space represented in mere millimetres on a page in this book. Yet, as I reflect on my journey from my home to university as the first person in my family to participate in higher education, I recognise the considerable distance between these two places across a range of social, cultural, economic, and even physical dimensions. This reflection draws me close to my hopes and dreams and the promises of gaining a university education that were so central to my efforts to succeed despite the challenges I faced. In my case my dreams involved the desire to occupy a particular space within the university as an academic, a dream that continues to spur me on my present doctoral pathway. I also recognise, beyond my own experiences, how undertaking doctoral study is a choice deeply imbued with aspiration.

In reference to the work of Appadurai (2004), I argue that supervisors can play a key role in helping students, especially non-traditional students, to develop their capacities to aspire particularly in relation to becoming academics. In doing so, I would also like to acknowledge the uneasy space supervisors may inhabit in encouraging students to seek academic careers in light of the political, economic and social positioning of the contemporary university and the academics within. I am also very aware of the significant demands placed on supervisors in the modern university which makes it difficult to call for supervisors to 'do or be more'. Nonetheless, it is my view that however we see the numerous roles of the academic, supervisors possess critical knowledge about how the university works, and how to be an academic, because they are insiders within the higher education institutions. If we accept Appadurai's (2004) theorisation of aspiration, supporting this cultural capacity can be highly transformative in terms of social, and individual, development. As many first-generation students may not possess traditional forms of social and cultural capital (Bourdieu 1977:2002) helpful for progression within academia, it is arguably important to focus on developing these students' capacities to aspire in order to enhance their ability to navigate the complex social setting of the university ultimately with a view to creating a more diverse and representative academy.

THE CAPACITY TO ASPIRE

Aspirations, or the desire for a particular goal or ambition to be achieved, are often seen as being powerful as they can contribute to individuals taking action, "to achieve or become something" (Pearsall 1999:76). According to Appadurai (2004:76), the capacity to aspire can be understood as the ability to read "a map of a journey into the future". As such, he characterises this capacity as being navigational in nature, linking intentions, understandings and outcomes. He also maintains that the capacity to aspire is socially constructed. Critically, Appadurai (2004:67) argues that this map is informed by understandings and experiences. As such aspirations cannot be understood in purely individual terms as he says "aspirations are never simply individual (as the language of wants and choices inclines us to think). They are always formed in the interaction and thick of social life". In this way, the capacity to aspire needs to be recognised as a cultural construct and a navigational ability. It is also something that is not evenly distributed:

> ... because the better off by definition have a more complex experience of the relation between a wide range of ends and means, because they have a bigger stock of available experiences and outcomes ... [and] are more able to produce justifications, narratives, metaphors, and pathways through which bundles of goods and services are actually tied to wider social scenes and contexts (Appadurai 2004:68).

Appadurai (2004:69) also describes the disadvantaged in any society as "having more brittle horizons of aspiration" because of their limited opportunities to employ this navigational capacity. Drawing Appadurai's ideas into the context of higher education, Bok (2010:164) argues that "for students to develop their capacity to aspire, other people within their local communities and those that they encounter in their daily lives must have experience navigating particular fields and pathways" and she suggests that "students can access these pathways if they are provided with the knowledge and experiences that enable them to make powerful choices".

The importance of the idea of aspiration is reflected in its use within higher education discourses. As Sellar and Gale (2012:91) observe, it is also a concept that has "figured strongly in recent policies around the globe". Certainly, the term 'aspiration' appears regularly within higher education rhetoric and policy within the Aotearoa/New Zealand context. Analysis of the New Zealand Tertiary Education Commission (TEC) website highlights numerous examples of the use of the term 'aspiration', often linked to discussions of equity. For example, it is used when talking about the importance of "meeting the diverse needs and aspirations of students of all ethnicities, genders, ages and socio-economic backgrounds" (Tertiary Education Commission 2013: para. 1) or in reference to supporting the "development aspirations of Maori" in the Tertiary Education Strategy 2010, although in these cases no definition was provided to address what was meant through employing this term. In many ways aspiration can be seen as a feel-good word and it is often employed with little explanation of its use. This loose usage means the word is vulnerable to co-option into neo-liberal conceptions of studenthood and arguably the potentially corrosive effects of the individualisation it promotes. Certainly, the notion of aspiration has gained prominence in 'third way politics' (Sellar & Gale 2012) with its meaning conflated to economic aspirations which are tightly focused on consumer desire and financial rewards (Sellar & Gale 2012). In contrast, Appadurai's work can be seen as highly valuable because of his desire to repatriate the concept from the world of the rational individual embedded within a frame of economics, to the cultural domain.

Moreover, there are compelling reasons to consider new ways of thinking about students' experiences within doctoral studies given some of the significant challenges faced by students and educators. Doctoral education in recent times has undergone significant expansion which has included a proliferation of different types of doctoral programmes and major increases in numbers of students undertaking doctoral study. For example, in New Zealand between 1999 and 2009 the total numbers of enrolled doctoral students more than doubled, rising from 3 447 to 7 409 students (Ministry of Education 2011). However, it is a cause for concern that there appears to be a consistently high proportion of students who fail to complete their doctorates. New Zealand Ministry of Education (2010) figures show that 62% of doctoral students enrolled in 2001 had completed their PhDs by the end of 2008, revealing that after eight years, more than one in three candidates had not yet completed their doctoral studies. Studies of attrition rates around the world consistently suggest the number of students who do not complete are considerable, with figures estimated to range from an average of 30-50% of all students (Golde & Walker 2006; Green 2009; Lovitts 2001; Martin, Maclachlan & Karmel 1999).[1] With the number of students involved in doctoral education expanding globally (Boud & Lee 2009), it is clear that the number of students failing to complete in actual terms is also increasing significantly. This situation, as a number of writers have suggested, supports the view that doctoral study can be a high-risk undertaking (See Golde 2005; Lovitts 2001). Further, there are questions about which types or groups of students 'succeed', in terms of access to doctoral education and doctoral completions. These questions persist in relation to the kinds of students who move into academic roles. As such it may particularly valuable to seek new ways to engage with students as may be offered by a consideration of aspiration, in its Appaduraian sense, to help more students to achieve their doctoral degrees and reach their postdoctoral goals.

First-generation students and doctoral education

For first-generation students, "researchers have noted and lamented inequities in educational experiences and outcomes" (Lohfink & Paulsen 2005:409). However, analysis of the research undertaken on first-generation students shows that most studies have been focused on students' initial engagements with tertiary education or on the bachelor level of study. The research picture remains less than clear in terms of first-generation students' doctoral completions and progression into the academy as compared with continuing-generation students;[2] there have been few studies in this area. A survey of the literature about first-generation students' access to the professoriate in the US by Kniffin (2007) raises questions about these students' progression into the academy, especially in regard to roles at prestigious academic institutions. In his discussion, Kniffin (2007) refers to data from US National Studies of Post-Secondary Faculty (1999) which, when analysed, revealed that more highly ranked research-focused universities tended to disproportionately employ academics with parents whose formal education included advanced degrees. Kniffin also highlights

---

1 Lovitts's (2001) major study of doctoral attrition in the US and Canada identified an overall doctoral non-completion rate of 30-50%. In New Zealand, recent Ministry of Education (2010) statistics identify an overall non-completion rate of approximately 38%. In Australia, a study by Martin *et al.* (1999) indicated that 47% of doctoral students did not complete their programme of studies across a seven-year time period.

2 Continuing-generation students are those students whose parent or parents studied at university. They can be seen as continuing the family practice of participating in higher education.

the work of Shott (2006) who found in his research on American archaeologists that individual background traits (such as the level of parental education) appeared to be a more reliable measure than scholarly quality in predicting the type of institution an academic will be employed at. There is also significant writing from working-class scholars about the difficulties they have faced within academia that identifies some of the challenges encountered by non-traditional students' movement into academic positions. Examples of this work can be found in journal publications (see Wyatt-Nichol 2012) or in edited volumes of essays such as Muzzati and Samarco's (2006) *Reflections from the wrong side of the tracks: Identity, class and the working class experience in academe,* Dews and Leste Law's (1995) *This fine place so far from home: Voices of academics from the working class* and Tokarczyk and Fay's (1993) *Working-class women in the academy: Laborers in the knowledge factory.* Welsch (2005), in her introduction to a collection of 15 accounts of American working-class and first-generation women, for instance, highlights the sense of distance and difference experienced by these scholars on their journeys into the academy, "where hope and promise are the expected prizes"(xv). She (2005:xv) says:

> When I think of our journeys, I am reminded of many of our forebears who came to this country as immigrants in peculiar clothing carrying treasured possessions in satchels. Although we didn't travel here from foreign lands or have to surrender names, extended families, traditional dress, customs or foods, we too have left home and crossed boundaries into foreign territory.

The research picture provides some indications of differentiated outcomes for first-generation students moving into the faculty roles and broader writings within this area suggest the need to consider more carefully how students from diverse backgrounds can make successful progressions into the academy.

The role of supervision

Supervision, and the roles that supervisors play in supporting students' postgraduate learning is of interest to researchers, many of whom argue that it is a critical part of the doctoral process (see for example Engebretson *et al.* 2008; Grant & Graham 1999; Li & Seale 2007; Salmon 1992). As Amundsen and McAlpine (2009:331) also suggest, for the majority of academics, supervision is a central part of their roles and it "involves intense work with a student". This intense work is focused on supporting the production of a quality thesis along with the goal of transforming the student into an independent researcher (Grant 2003). There exists a variety of supervisory approaches, styles and ways of working shaped by a number of different contextual factors such as institution, discipline and the focus of a research project. Within these varied contexts, there is broad agreement that supervision is multifaceted and far from straightforward. As Li and Seale (2007:512) suggest in their discussion on criticism within doctoral supervision, supervision is "lengthy and complicated" and something that therefore "demands competence, commitment, time, energy and emotion from both parties". Similarly, Wisker, Exley, Antoniou and Ridley (2008) point out that good supervision involves negotiation and dialogue to ensure there are shared understandings which can then support the learning process within this pivotal scholarly relationship.

Bringing aspiration into supervision spaces

If we apply Appadurai's conception of aspiration to doctoral education, then it is necessary to recognise that students who may possess less knowledge about the social context of the university, or perhaps have narrower experiences of it, may therefore have less ability to navigate their way through the doctorate and into academic positions. As such, it is therefore important to think about how these students can be assisted in constructing their navigational maps (Appadurai 2004) of the university. For me, this means bringing students' aspirations into dialogue within the supervision space. This may involve supervisors and students discussing some of the following questions:

- What are the pathways into academic jobs?
- What are possible postdoctoral opportunities for the student(s)?
- How did I navigate into an academic position? How could this be relevant, or not, to my students?
- What assumptions am I making about the students' interests or knowledge about academia?
- What do students need to know about academic roles?
- How would I describe a typical working day or week to a student?
- What are the ways that students can be helped to navigate the complex social world that is the university?

Exploring questions like these may be one useful way to promote conversations with students about their goals for their doctoral studies which may lead to shared ideas and greater understandings of how to navigate the university. In my experience of supervision there have been times when I have felt unsure about the place of questions similar to these within supervision discussions. Despite the highly positive relationships I have with my supervisors, I have wondered if it was acceptable to broach these topics so tied to the future, as a student only approaching the mid-point of her doctoral studies. Would my supervisors think I was not focused on the work at hand? Or, was there really time for these kinds of conversations in our already heavily loaded supervision meetings? Sometimes, my uncertainty grew out a concern for my supervisors because I feared talking about academic jobs might be too burdensome a topic for them given the somewhat limited nature of job opportunities within the university. This resulted in my feeling unsure about whether I knew the things I should, and anxious about whether I was making good choices in my studies because of the gaps in my knowledge about what comes next. Through these reflections, I realised that my lack of knowledge about the steps to take post-doctorate, though related to some distanced time in the future, actually operated in the present to destabilise my sense of agency, and even my sense of belonging within the academy. And, through the subsequent discussions about doctoral student aspirations with my supervisory team I began to expand my thinking, not only about my postdoctoral future but about the direct connections between academic aspirations, navigating within the university and the development of academic identity.

Aspiration and academic 'becomings'

I see the project of academic 'becoming' or academic identity formation as being deeply bound up with students' hopes for, and imaginings of, their future selves. Supervisors' efforts to foster students' academic identities can also function to provide valuable support for the development of students' navigational maps of the university. This is especially true when supervisors make explicit links to how participation in different kinds of academic activities or work can help students extend their understandings about their academic setting. An example of this may be found in supervisors assisting students to operate within a variety of academic settings such as helping students to step into and 'read' the academic space of a conference, and then to understand the myriad ways conference participation can contribute to their learning about academic practices. It may also arise, for example, through supervisors facilitating opportunities for students to speak, and be recognised as legitimate speakers, by other academics within seminar spaces and the like which can develop a student's academic voice. In Appaduraian terms, (2004:68) this support can be seen as helping students to archive experience which may also allow them to produce "justifications, narratives, metaphors" which can contribute to a "more complex experience of the relation between ends and means" within the academy. As I have experienced, the links between navigations of the university in terms of gaining an academic position and the engagements with different kinds of academic experiences may not always be clear to the student. Admittedly, some supervisors may feel reluctant to assume what may be perceived as a broader responsibility for a student's academic identity and their academic aspirations beyond the direct focus on thesis work alone.

Supervision – a 'pedagogy under pressure'

As Grant (2005:ii) argues, "supervision is a pedagogy under pressure". Increasing postgraduate student numbers, expanding academic staff workloads, the imperative to meet student learning needs along with the institutional and governmental demands to improve rates of degree completions mean there are numerous and sometimes contradictory forces that have an impact on the doctoral supervision relationship. Given these demands, engaging with student aspirations may be considered to be another imposition on the already weighty responsibilities of the contemporary supervisor. Moreover, there may be significant reluctance from supervisors to focus on student aspirations, particularly in terms of gaining academic roles, because such discussion have the potential to open up some highly challenging issues about the nature of academic work and the apparently limited opportunities in the modern university that seem to stand in opposition to the continued governmental efforts, and the efforts of the universities themselves, to expand numbers of doctoral students. Many from within the academy have written about how the effects of neoliberal policy reforms on universities across the world have "academics, whether in junior or senior positions ... feeling stressed, frustrated and demoralised" (Bendix Petersen 2009:409). In this setting it is easy to see how supervisors may find themselves in uneasy spaces somewhere between the hopes and dreams of their students, institutional policies to encourage the training of more scholars and their own assessments of the chances for their students to navigate into university positions.

A 'community of scholars' approach

In my call for supervisors to think about student aspirations within their supervisory practice, I wish to make clear that I do not see the individual supervisor as having the sole responsibility for engaging with student aspirations. In conjunction with renewed attention to aspiration in the context of the traditional supervision relationship, I would like to advocate for a 'community of scholars' approach. This could take the format of forum facilitated by a combination of staff and students where there is space for students to discuss their aspirations for academic roles, to explore ways to develop their academic identities and learn about academic pathways alongside their supervisors. Such a forum could be organised in different ways, and may offer access to presentations, workshops and shared discussions on a range of areas such as 'a day in the life of an academic', 'postdoctoral progressions', or 'developing voice'. While some of these topics may be commonly offered to doctoral students within different learning contexts, a key aspect of this approach is that these offerings are brought together in a way that is community-based and explicitly focused on helping students navigate the academy.

This strategy would mean that thinking about doctoral student aspirations is shared and subject to the collective creativity of the academics and students within the school or department. It also means that supervisors with their varied experiences of the university and positioning within it can share the different kinds of knowledge they have, which may mean that students with less established or less well-connected supervisors will benefit from access to a range of insights about academic pathways. I maintain there may also be direct benefits to the supervisors themselves as a focus on aspiration and building students navigational maps may have a positive impact on their students' engagement with their studies and, perhaps, help in fostering a stronger relationship between students, their supervisors and their departments or schools. Importantly, while my attention is on student aspirations for academic roles, I am not arguing for an approach which constructs students as entrepreneurial employment seekers continually involved in presenting their 'CV selves', or indeed, one that supplants the importance of thesis work within a supervision relationship through an all-encompassing focus on the doctoral student job search. Although I recognise some tensions here that require careful attention, my focus on aspiration is targeted towards thinking about how diverse or non-traditional doctoral students can develop their academic identities and their knowledge of the university to enable them to move more easily into academic roles through their relationships with their academic supervisors and community.

CONCLUSION

In this chapter I have sought to push the boundaries of supervision practice by suggesting that there is value in extending the thinking about the supervision relationship beyond the primary focus of thesis production to include greater attention to helping students construct their navigational maps of the university through utilising Appadurai's conceptualisation of aspiration. Supervisors, as university 'insiders', possess important knowledge that can contribute to students' scholarly experiences and academic navigations and this kind of knowledge may be of particular value to students from diverse backgrounds who may not possess detailed social and cultural maps of the university. My call for greater attention to doctoral student aspiration is made with recognition of the potential unease supervisors may face in focusing on student aspirations for the academy in a context of rapid change to academic work and conditions. However, a focus on aspiration, through a 'community of scholars' approach, may be particularly useful in engaging with students' aspirations without placing significant burdens on individual teaching staff, and ultimately may be valuable in helping doctoral students, especially non-traditional students such as those who are first-generation, to achieve their imagined academic futures.

REFERENCES

Amundsen C & McAlpine L. 2009. Learning supervision: Trial by fire. *Innovations in Education and Teaching International*, 46(3):331-342. doi: 10.1080/14703290903068805

Appadurai A. 2004. The capacity to aspire: Culture and the terms of recognition. In: M Walton & V Rao (eds). *Culture and public action: A cross-disciplinary dialogue on development policy*. Washington, DC: World Bank Publications. 59-84.

Bendix Petersen E. 2009. Resistance and enrolment in the enterprise university: An ethno-drama in three acts, with appended reading. *Journal of Educational Policy*, 24(4):409-422. doi: 10.1080/02680930802669953

Bok J. 2010. The capacity to aspire to higher education: 'It's like making them do a play without a script'. *Critical Studies in Higher Education*, 51(2):163-178. doi: 10.1080/17508481003731042

Boud D & Lee A. 2009. Introduction. In: D Boud & A Lee (eds). *Changing practices of doctoral education*. Abingdon: Routledge. 1-9.

Bourdieu P. 1977. Cultural reproduction and social reproduction. In: J Karabel & AH Halsey (eds). *Power and ideology in education*. New York: Oxford University Press. 487-511.

Bourdieu P. 2002. The forms of capital. In: NW Biggart (ed). *Readings in economic sociology*. Malden, MA: Blackwell. 280-291.

Dews CLB & Leste Law C (eds). 1995. *This fine place so far from home: Voices of academics from the working class*. Philadelphia, PA: Temple University Press.

Engebretson K, Smith K, McLaughlin D, Seibold C, Terrett G & Ryan E. 2008. The changing reality of research education in Australia and implications for supervision: A review of the literature. *Teaching in Higher Education*, 13(1):1-15. doi: 10.1080/13562510701792112

Golde CM. 2005. The role of the department and discipline in doctoral student attrition: Lessons from four departments. *Journal of Higher Education*, 76(6):669-700.

Golde CM & Walker GE (eds). 2006. *Envisioning the future of doctoral education: Preparing stewards of the discipline*. San Francisco, CA: Jossey-Bass.

Grant B. 2003. Mapping the pleasures and risks of supervision. *Discourse Studies in the Cultural Politics of Education*, 24(2):175-190. doi: 10.1080/01596300303042

Grant B. 2005. The pedagogy of graduate supervision: Figuring the relations between supervisor and student. PhD thesis. Auckland: University of Auckland. [Accessed 8 March 2013] http://hdl.handle.net/2292/295

Grant B & Graham A. 1999. Naming the game: Reconstructing graduate supervision. *Teaching in Higher Education*, 4(1):77-89. doi: 10.1080/1356251990040105

Green B. 2009. Challenging perspectives, changing practices: Doctoral education in transition. In: D Boud & A Lee (eds). *Changing practices of doctoral education*. Abingdon: Routledge. 239-248.

Kniffin KM. 2007. Accessibility to the PhD and professoriate for first-generation college graduates. *American Academic*, 3(1):49-79. [Accessed 10 November 2012] http://www.aft.org/yourwork/highered/academic.cfm

Li S & Seale C. 2007. Managing criticism in PhD supervision: A qualitative case study. *Studies in Higher Education*, 32(4):511-526. doi: 10.1080/03075070701476225

Lohfink MM & Paulsen MB. 2005. Comparing the determinants of persistance for first generation and continuing generation students. *Journal of College Student Development*, 46(4):409-428. doi: 10.1353/csd.2005.0040

Lovitts B. 2001. *Leaving the ivory tower: The causes and consequences of departure from doctoral study*. Lanham, MD: Rowman & Littlefield.

Martin YM, Maclachlan M & Karmel T. 1999. *Postgraduate completion rates*. Canberra: Department of Education, Training and Youth Affairs.

Ministry of Education. 2010. *Completion of tertiary education*. [Accessed 24 March 2013] http://www.educationcounts.govt.nz/indicators/data/education-and-learning-outcomes/3672

Ministry of Education. 2011. *2009 Tertiary education enrolments*. [Accessed 24 March 2013] http://www.educationcounts.govt.nz/publications/tertiary_education/75361

Muzzati SL & Samarco CV (eds). 2006. *Relections from the wrong side of the tracks: Class, identity, and the working class in Academe*. Lanham, MD: Rowman and Littlefield.

Pearsall J (ed). 1999. *The concise Oxford dictionary*. 10th edition. Oxford: Oxford University Press.

Salmon P. 1992. *Achieving a PhD: Ten students' experience*. Oakhill: Trentham Books.

Sellar S & Gale T. 2012. Aspiration and education: Toward new terms of engagement for marginalized students. In: BJ McMahon & JP Portelli (eds). *Student engagement in urban schools: Beyond neoliberal discourses*. Charlotte, NC: Information Age Publishing. 91-109.

Shott MJ. 2006. An unwashed's knowledge of archaelogy. In Muzzati SL & Samarco CV (eds). 2006. *Relections from the wrong side of the tracks: Class, identity, and the working class in Academe*. Lanham, MD: Rowman and Littlefield.

Tertiary Education Commission. 2013. *Equity funding*. [Accessed 25 March 2013] http://www.tec.govt.nz/Funding/Fund-finder/Equity-Funding/

Tokarczyk ME & Fay E (eds). 1993. *Working-class women in the academy: Laborers in the knowledge factory*. Ameherst, MA: University of Massachusetts Press.

Welsch KA (ed). 2005. *Those winter Sundays: Female academics and their working-class parents*. Lanham, MD: University Press of America.

Wisker G, Exley K, Antoniou M & Ridley P. 2008. *Working one-to-one with students*. New York: Routledge.

Wyatt-Nichol H. 2012. A view from the 50th street gate on Washington avenue: Reflections of a working-class academic. *Journal of Public Affairs Education*, 18(1):17-28.

15 EVOLVING DOCTORAL IDENTITIES

UNDERSTANDING 'COMPLEX INVESTMENTS'

Susan van Schalkwyk

COMMENCING THE CONVERSATION

The metaphor of a journey is often applied to doctoral studies. This journey is characterised by a sense of 'being and becoming' that accompanies the emergence of a candidate's doctoral identity (Green 2005; see also Barnett & Di Napoli 2008). Many students experience this process of identity formation as complex and multifaceted, influenced by individual realities and social contexts (Jazvac-Martek 2009), and fraught with tension and uncertainty (Green 2005). This change in identity is seldom gradual. Often it is marked by moments of dissonance and crisis that lead students to places of change and growth (Di Napoli & Barnett 2008; Jarvis-Selinger, Pratt & Regehr 2012). The doctoral student is expected not only to engage in the process of knowledge acquisition and creation, but to also navigate the developmental journey towards doctorateness (Frick 2011; Trafford & Leshem 2009). Although there is a growing body of research in the field of doctoral education, there remains a need for studies that seek to understand how the identity of the doctoral candidate evolves during the time of study, and why this rite of passage (Andresen 2000) occurs the way it does (Green 2005; Jazvac-Martek 2009). Knowledge about the lived, day-to-day experience of a doctoral candidate is scant. The relationship between student and supervisor is often shrouded in secrecy representing a 'bounded' space that is seldom opened up to scrutiny from the outside. Following on Jazvac-Martek (2009), I argue that drawing on constructs such as identity, and the development thereof, offers a useful lens through which the doctoral experience can be explored.

When describing the supervisory relationship at doctoral level, Owler (1999, cited in Green 2005:154) has suggested that "each individual is revealed to have complex investments in this relationship". In this chapter my interest is in the nature of these "complex investments", particularly on the part of the doctoral student, and the ways in which their investment choices mould their identity as doctoral candidates and eventually graduates. Ultimately I ask what this means for those of us tasked with guiding candidates on their doctoral journeys and how a more in-depth understanding of these investments might enable us to challenge prevailing boundaries in postgraduate supervision.

ASPECTS OF IDENTITY

There is a rich scholarship devoted to understanding, defining and describing identity – a scholarship too extensive to address in any depth in a single chapter. It attests to the multiple dimensions that require attention when considering identity as a construct. In this section I draw on a selection of the scholarship to offer a perspective on identity that provides a space within which this particular discussion on doctoral identity can proceed. In doing this I acknowledge that there are multiple points of departure that others may feel are more relevant, and as a result thereof, would wish to frame the argument differently.

Identity is a slippery term defying tight definition. How one's identity (or identities) comes into being is equally problematic. Much has been written, from different perspectives, about the socio-cultural factors that influence identity development (Barnett & Di Napoli 2008; Bourdieu 1986; Hall & Burns 2009; Jazvac-Martek 2009). However, Clegg's (2008) work, which focuses on the individual and how she exercises agency within a particular context, including when acquiring an academic identity, offers an alternative insight. She draws on the work of Margaret Archer (2000) who describes identity formation occurring through the personification of a particular role (in this case the role of doctoral candidate) and emphasises that there is a necessary investment or intentionality involved in taking on such a role. Archer speaks of our "personal identities" which are shaped during "internal conversations" (2000:318). In these internal conversations our sense of well-being, competence and self-worth influence how we make decisions about who we are and what we will do as we weigh up the nature of the investment and whether we care enough to commit to it (Archer 2000). One might question to what extent our 'being' is indeed so carefully negotiated. Archer has been critiqued for foregrounding what has been termed 'conscious deliberation' above all else and seemingly leaving little space for the unconscious or the reflexive response (Akram 2013). Interestingly, however, she (2000) contends that we have no choice in the place from which we start out. Our heritage is fixed and cannot be ignored, thus influencing the person we choose to become. This becoming occurs in a particular space where the interaction between structure (roles, organisations, institutions, systems) and agency informs the internal conversations alluded to earlier. It could be argued that it is here where our cultural capital, the strength we draw from our heritage (Bourdieu 1986), emerges and leads to the establishment of our social identities which are shaped both by the social context within which we find ourselves and the extent to which we seek to engage in that space. I believe that Archer's work provides a framework within which the development of doctoral identity, at both a personal and a social level, can be considered (O'Byrne 2011) and provides a platform from which we can perhaps shift some of the traditional thinking – the boundaries – that currently informs postgraduate supervision.

What is a 'doctoral' identity? Is it a mantle that the doctoral student draws closer around her as she moves to a place where she gains access or membership to the discourse of a particular disciplinary community? Does it comprise a mix of qualities: intellectual quality and confidence, independence of thinking, enthusiasm and commitment, an ability to adapt to changing circumstances and opportunities (Denicolo & Park 2013)? Perhaps it resides in someone who has made 'an original contribution to knowledge' (Trafford & Leshem 2009)? Frick (2011) provides a summary of doctorateness that highlights characteristics such as being a responsible scholar who is courageous enough to take risks in the pursuit of knowledge and who embraces those traits that could be regarded as typical of such a responsible scholar. It is how candidates experience the pursuit of these characteristics towards the development of a doctoral identity that is the focus of this chapter.

GATHERING THE STORIES

By "learning from [the] lives" (O'Byrne 2011:10) of a number of doctoral candidates who meet on a monthly basis, in two different groups, to engage around issues relating to their doctoral experiences, I have sought to understand the nature of the complex investments that these candidates have made in embarking on advance studies. Known as the 'PhD Discussion Groups', the gatherings were born out of a desire to create a supportive and safe space for doctoral candidates. The first group (Group A), that has been in existence for approximately three years, started with 11 colleagues from my institution who work in a division for academic support. Although their academic backgrounds represent a diversity of disciplines including (higher) education, psychology, educational psychology, sociology, language and applied linguistics, this group does not have 'academic' status as they are employed in what is regard as a 'support' division. Of the original group, two have withdrawn (one because she graduated; the other because she left the university), and three new members have come on board. Approximately nine attend regularly.

The second group (Group B), with 16 members, was formed early in 2012 and is predominantly made up of academics from different professions in a faculty of health sciences including medicine, physiotherapy, occupational therapy, public health and nursing. In this group there is a core of about 10 regular attendees.

While some of the participants are still at the proposal stage, others have already progressed some way on their doctoral journeys. As facilitator of the groups, I follow the work of Boud and Lee (2005) who describe the value of peer learning within a particular research community. Drawing on a reciprocal relationship that sees each member becoming a doctoral peer, the groups have established a unique developmental space among themselves (McAlpine & Asghar 2010).

The data that provides the basis for this chapter has been generated across a period of time. At the end of the first year that Group A was in existence, seven participants wrote reflective pieces describing their doctoral experiences up to that point. This was followed by seven in-depth interviews that were conducted with self-selected respondents from the Group. A year later, a further eight reflective pieces were submitted (including excerpts from one participant's reflective journal) and this was followed up by a focus group interview with nine participants. At the end of the first year that Group B was in existence, members were invited to submit reflective pieces describing their experiences as had been the case for Group A before. Nine responses were received. In addition, seven members made themselves available for in-depth interviews.

Five participants from Group A participated in all four data-collection activities. As I am directly involved in the supervision of one of these candidates, I did not include her in this analysis. Four candidates from Group B were interviewed and completed their reflective pieces. Together these eight respondents are the main protagonists in this work. In Group A, three of the four respondents, who were all at pre-registration phase when the group was formed, are now formally busy with their doctoral studies. All four are women, have families, and could be regarded as mid-career professionals. There are three women and one man in Group B. The male participant is an associate professor in the faculty. Two of the women are at senior lecturer level and have families with young children. The fourth respondent is in her twenties and could be regarded as an early-career professional.

Ethics approval was obtained separately for the study of each group. All interviews were recorded and the subsequent transcriptions and the written reflective texts exposed a rich tapestry of experiences. These were subjected to in-depth thematic analysis and then interpreted against the backdrop of the theoretical framework that I have described earlier in this chapter. My role in this work is, however, as multifaceted as identity itself and also represents a complex investment. I carry the burden of 'guilty knowledge' that comes from conducting research among my colleagues (Williams 2009). My identity, and thus my 'insiderness', has shifted over the three years of the study. Initially I worked quite closely with several of the members in Group A, some of whom reported to me. Later, I moved to a new position within the university where Group B was established, but retained the close ties with Group A through the monthly meetings. I am responsible for either supervising or co-supervising three of the group members and have acted as critical friend or mentor for many of the others. While this enables me to produce rich 'emic' accounts, I acknowledge the impossibility for generating "culturally neutral, 'etic' accounts" (Trowler 2011:2) and remain acutely aware of my responsibility to maintain the anonymity of my participants and be true to their words.

UNDERSTANDING COMPLEX INVESTMENTS

During the process of analysis I first explored the candidates' initial stories about how they saw themselves, and their personal identities, as they entered into the doctoral space. A next step was to consider how they sought to take on this new role of doctoral candidate and to invest themselves voluntarily in a particular social identity – one that they deemed to be expressive of whom they are (Archer 2000). This was followed by a review of the identities that seemed to be emerging as time progressed. Finally I drew on their reflections of how being part of one of the PhD discussion groups has influenced their doctoral journey and, therefore, their identity formation to discern how the group might be of value, and why this might be so.

Initial stories

The candidates' descriptions of who they were, where they started out from, was a clear reminder as to the unique stories – our personal identities – that we each carry within us. For some, doing the PhD was an accepted next step if one worked at a university or if one's father or mother had a doctorate. Others spoke of how they were the first in their family to go to university, and how uncertain they were about taking this next step. Most had not come through a 'traditional' academic track. Apart from one candidate who saw himself as a researcher, all of the group members described having established identities such as teachers, health care practitioners, university staff, and then additionally as wives and mothers. It was evident that they drew strength from these identities and that they provided them with 'cultural capital' towards attaining their educational goals (Bourdieu 1986). Nevertheless, they generally saw these personifications as quite removed from a doctoral or researcher identity:

> "I am an educator, I teach people clinical skills ... I don't see myself as a researcher ..." (Elsa)

For all of the candidates the potential of the doctorate to advance their careers featured as a key reason for embarking on the degree. One noted that this career advancement would have positive financial implications while another felt that the professional growth potential was equal to the benefit at a personal level and the hope of "making a difference in the community". (Delia)

The group member who held a more senior position at the university was already a recognised expert in his field. He felt he had an advantage and it was evident that despite the additional workload that came with doctoral studies, he had decided that he "might as well enjoy it" (Rasheed) while he was at it. He shared an interesting perspective on why he had embarked on the PhD:

> "... eventually it was [member of the university management] who told me that it's like circumcision. It may not make much sense to you and it's painful, but if you don't do it, they won't consider you a man [laughs]." (Rasheed)

Generally there was recognition of the challenges inherent in embarking on an advanced degree which some felt more prepared for than others. In several cases there was a general expression of uncertainty about their ability and competence to complete the PhD, describing a lack of 'academic-ness' and a fear of having to take a stand for their research. The PhD was described as:

> "... this giant mountain looming ahead [I feel] a little bit panic-stricken actually ... I don't feel doctoral at all, no." (Faith)

> "... but I know that I still face a hopelessly long journey to acquire the knowledge that I need, ... I think I am still scared to make myself heard." (Valerie)

This latter quote is instructive. Barnett and Di Napoli (2008:198) argue that "voice is the projection of the identity into the world". Doctoral becoming includes being in a place where you feel you have something worth saying (Clark & Ivanic 1997) and thus there is a need to be heard.

Several of the candidates expressed an overwhelming sense of frustration and anxiety at being trapped in this early stage of their doctoral journeys and not making any progress:

> "... it just feels to me as if I'm going somewhere, and my plane is almost ready to leave. I've got my ticket and I'm packing, and I'm packing, and I'm packing, but I'm not getting on that plane ... My suitcase is really stuffed with things at the moment." (Delia)

Even Rasheed described the PhD as follows:

> "It's sort of like a monster, it bothers you all the time, but the fact that it is the most important thing to complete, in a sense it almost paralyses you from getting on with other smaller things."

It was also evident, however, that some saw the reason to undertake their studies as "a little selfish, for myself ... to prove to myself that I can" (Valerie), which points to an early understanding of the extent of the investment that was being entered into. There was also a sense that the degree would enhance their self-worth even as they described the gap they perceived between their existing skills set and those required for doctorateness.

New roles

Although monthly participation in the PhD groups implied some level of commitment to doctoral candidacy, the extent of investment differed from one person to the next and influenced the level of commitment to the role. In this new role, they articulated challenges that in some instances had been envisaged and were now becoming real, or were completely unexpected. These challenges emerged on different fronts both at a personal level and in their work contexts, often combining, and resulting in concerns about time and space to do what needs to be done:

> "... so I think the biggest thing that is worrying me is that my job is going to get in my way, or the one is going to get in the way of the other and I'm not going to do either properly ... so it is time ... and I've got children living at home still ... I've got an elderly mother as well so I have no idea what is going to crop up ... but that is just going to be how it is ... I'll start and take it from there." (Faith)

For most of the candidates, their family commitments and family ties were points of tension and ambiguity sometimes requiring them to hide emerging identities or constantly shift identities to meet the demands of their loved ones:

> "We are a very close-knit family and I was the first one to go to university ... and my mother also is immensely proud that this child that nobody thought would amount to much growing up in [ ] ... so she tells people,

> I say 'Mommy please don't tell them … because they don't understand, they don't realise how long it's going to take and they are, 'Are you done, are you a PhD?'" (Jackie)
>
> "Another obstacle is of course the whole triangle between being a PhD student or a researcher, having a full-time job and being a mum to two children, and having a husband also. Maybe I should make that four jobs." (Delia)

Now, as they embarked formally on their studies, there was a growing realisation of the risk, the commitment and the investment. Inevitably they described the tensions between their being and becoming:

> "It's like trying to make friends with an unwelcome friend and it takes time. Like an unwelcome guest and you can kick him out, but you know you will blame yourself if you do so, or you can learn to live in symbiosis with him for however long it takes. He has rotten shoes, and does not smell nice, and that challenges you." (Ansie)
>
> "It's putting yourself out there, and that fear of knowing that when you do put it out there, that there's … a high possibility of rejection … you've made a commitment, and you've made other people aware of that commitment so they're going to keep you to it…" (Margaret)

The notion of 'putting oneself out there' was described by others, although sometimes in a more positive sense: "… it helps you to lift your bum off the rock and continue the hike". (Faith)

Nevertheless, there was also a sense of being in a space of their own making, emergent from their internal conversations:

> "Also, because I over-task myself I'm often tired and to me that's just part of my life … To my children as well, when people ask them, 'What does your mother do?' She studies." (Jackie)
>
> "I was wondering why am I keeping on running with this thing, why am I going on. I think it's my internal motivation, the fact that I would like to it." (Delia)

Archer (2000:12-13) describes how these different commitments, these 'ultimate concerns', determine the extent of the investment we are prepared to make and how this influences who we become. However, these commitments "are subject to continuous internal review" taking us back "to the internal conversation which never ceases."

Emerging identities

By the time that the candidates had registered for their PhDs and had made some inroads into their research they appeared to be in different spaces from those described before. Yet, the ebb and flow – the moments of dissonance and crisis interspersed with spaces for growth (Jarvis-Selinger et al. 2012) – that characterises identity development or formation was still evident in how the candidates reflected on their experiences.

Particularly poignant is this series of entries from Ansie's reflective journal:

> "Research is great!"
>
> [On receiving positive feedback] "This makes all the suffering worthwhile."
>
> "I now have three pieces of work out there in other people's hands."
>
> "I have never experienced such a low point in my research life ... I feel terribly alone and there is absolutely no-one I can talk to ... I place myself under so much pressure."
>
> "I have to make a few changes, of course, but the bottom line is my research is important. Over the moon!"
>
> [To cope I must] "minimalise, keep it simple, scale down, say No!" (Ansie)

Jackie described it as "almost like a birthing process ... It's such an important thing, but starting off so fragile and having to go through that pain ... Eventually I'm going to be something."

McAlpine and Asghar (2010:169) remind us that "identity is constituted through thinking, performing, recognizing oneself and being recognised by others as a ... member of a particular community". In Jackie's case this recognition came during an international conference where she was awarded a prize for a presentation on her work, which left her confident to continue despite earlier disappointments.

Moving successfully through to registration was experienced in positive and sometimes unexpected ways:

> "... a phenomenon has happened this year, where I, I'm a lot more confident as a lecturer, I think ... because, I don't know if it is a feeling of self-worth ... perhaps I've been my own catalyst too. I am determined to finish as soon as I possibly can ... I now feel as if I've, in a way, 'set the stage' for the real action to begin ..." (Faith)
>
> "In the past I focused on the day I will get my D, but now I try to focus on the process, because it is still frustration, because everything does not fall into place, but it is also not supposed to fall into place, so I think I understand it better now ... that you grow as the process progresses." (Ansie)

Interestingly, the candidate who was further down the road on his doctoral journey than most others was completing his PhD by publication. He described how focusing on the PhD had led to a drop in his overall research productivity which had previously been quite high and commented that this was a cause for concern – a potentially costly career investment. However, when describing his struggle, it seemed to be less lonely as he clearly saw his two supervisors – his peers in the field – as co-travellers.

Underlying many of the comments are suggestions of the reward emanating from the doctoral investment. In some cases, however, there was a sober awareness of the cost if things did not work out as planned:

> "Patience and perseverance, like that dog, I really feel like I'm holding onto a bone here and not letting go … but one of my biggest fears I think is that I could prolong this process … and then I'll miss out on life." (Delia)

The role of the group

Finally, I reflect on the role of the discussion groups in establishing a doctoral identity among the participants. One is struck by the value that participants attached to being part of a community of doctoral scholars, which is also evidenced in their regular attendance. A more important question is, however, why they experienced the groups the way they did. Three issues appeared to be key: the group provided a safe space, an accountable space and a generative space within which they could test their ideas and draw strength from the experiences of those around them. The fact that they were all on the doctoral journey, despite being on very different versions of it, created a camaraderie that they found invaluable:

> "It was a very supportive group which provided a safe space where any sort of feelings could be shared. No-one, i.e. friends or family, could ever understand the kind of feelings one experiences while doing a PhD." (Margaret)

> "… it is a lonely road, and I'm a herd animal, so I'm only too happy to have somebody else … just a critical friend even, just somebody that you could … just soundboard with, or voice your frustrations with … and one learns a lot, you know, from your experience, or from somebody who is further down the road." (Faith)

> "People learn from one another and they draw strength from other people's difficulties and they know they're not alone, it's not unique." (Rasheed)

The groups were also seen to hold them accountable to themselves and to one another. More than one candidate spoke of how the monthly commitment kept them on track and had been an important contributor to their progress thus far. In the end, the groups provided a generative space where the emergence of a doctoral identity was fostered:

> "I now see myself as a doctoral candidate … I often didn't feel that I am intelligent enough to be here. The group discussions have helped me to realise that I am not the only one with self-doubt." (Jackie)

CONCLUSION

What can be learnt about the doctoral journey and the emergence of a doctoral identity from these stories? What does this mean for our practice as doctoral supervisors and mentors? Do we understand the complex nature of the investments that our students make when they embark on doctoral studies? Jarvis-Selinger et al. (2012) describe identity formation resulting from the necessary interplay between two perspectives which they have termed the individual (which emphasises the notion of development, reflexivity and intentionality) and the collective (which highlights the socio-cultural influences that shape identity formation). This understanding resonates with what has emerged from my study. On the one hand, the students drew strength from being part of the PhD group which they saw as their "community of practice" where they could essentially test their legitimacy in a safe and generative space as they engaged at the periphery of the doctoral community (Wenger 2000:229). Indeed, the value of creating communities of (or for) doctoral scholars has been gaining traction of late, as moves away from the traditional (dyadic) approach to what Bitzer and Albertyn (2011) have described as 'group' and 'team' approaches, are being recognised.

On the other hand, however, this acknowledgement of the socio-cultural dimension of identify formation has not been the main focus of this study. By drawing on Archer's understanding of the development of personal and social identities, a picture of how the doctoral candidate must consciously invest in her or his doctoral studies can emerge. It is evident that for those in the study, that which they valued (their 'concerns') influenced not only the extent of their investment in their doctoral becoming, but also mediated the emergence of their doctoral identities. If we hope to foster this identity, then the need to engage with candidates to understand what it is that is influencing their internal conversations is self-evident and may better enable us to establish nurturing spaces towards this end (Clegg 2008). This may require that we disturb the shroud that obscures the inner workings of the supervisory relationship and in so doing challenge the boundaries that currently define it. Ultimately we ought to be mindful that doctoral studies represent a complex investment on the part of our students, but that it is an investment that has the potential to generate significant capital once it matures.

O'Byrne (2011:13) has argued that as we seek to reach our goals we follow a cyclical pattern that sees the forming of social identities that are "compatible with [our] particular personal identities" and that will enable us to adopt the roles that are based on these identities. Because the candidates in this study are still all on their journeys towards doctorateness, they are still in the process of role personification and investment therein (Archer 2000). This is a process that will continue for some time yet, and beyond the achievement of the doctoral degree. The identities are still emerging, subject to on-going internal review. The eventual cost of the complex investment is, as yet, unknown.

ACKNOWLEDGEMENTS

All those who have attended the PhD discussion groups over the past few years are thanked for their commitment and participation. A particular word of acknowledgement goes to the eight main characters in this chapter. Finally, I wish to express my thanks to Brenda Leibowitz and Julia Blitz for their comments on an earlier version of this work.

REFERENCES

Akram S. 2013. Fully unconscious and prone to habit: The characteristics of agency in the structure and agency dialectic. *Journal for the Theory of Social Behaviour*, 43(1):45-65.

Andresen LW. 2000. A usable, trans-disciplinary conception of scholarship. *Higher Education Research and Development*, 19(2):137-153.

Archer MS. 2000. *Being human: The problem of agency*. Cambridge: Cambridge University Press.

Barnett R & Di Napoli R. 2008. Identity and voice in higher education: Making connections. In: R Barnett & R Di Napoli (eds). *Changing identities in higher education: Voicing perspectives*. London: Routledge. 195-204.

Bitzer EM & Albertyn RM. 2011. Alternative approaches to postgraduate supervision: A planning tool to facilitate supervisory processes. *South African Journal of Higher Education*, 25(5):874-888.

Boud D & Lee A. 2005. 'Peer learning' as pedagogic discourse for research education. *Studies in Higher Education*, 30(5):501-516.

Bourdieu P. 1986. The forms of capital. In: JG Richardson (ed). *Handbook of theory and research for the sociology of education*. New York: Greenwood Press. 241-258.

Clark R & Ivanic R. 1997. *The politics of writing*. London: Routledge.

Clegg S. 2008. Academic identities under threat? *British Educational Research Journal*, 34(3):329-345.

Denicolo PM & Park C. 2013. Doctorateness – an elusive concept? In: M Kompf & PM Denicolo (eds). *Critical issues in higher education*. Rotterdam: Sense. 191-197.

Di Napoli R & Barnett R. 2008. Introduction. In: R Barnett & R Di Napoli (eds). *Changing identities in higher education: Voicing perspectives*. London: Routledge. 1-8.

Frick L. 2011. Facilitating creativity in doctoral education: A resource for supervisors. In: V Kumar & A Lee (eds). *Doctoral education in international context: Connecting local, regional and global perspectives*. Serdang: Universiti Putra Malaysia Press. 123-137.

Green B. 2005. Unfinished business: Subjectivity and supervision. *Higher Education Research and Development*, 24(2):151-163.

Hall LA & Burns LD. 2009. Identity development and mentoring in doctoral education. *Harvard Educational Review*, 79(1):49-70.

Jarvis-Selinger S, Pratt DD & Regehr G. 2012. Competency is not enough: Integrating identity formation into the medical education discourse. *Academic Medicine*, 87(9):1195-1190.

Jazvac-Martek M. 2009. Oscillating role identities: The academic experiences of education doctoral students. *Innovations in Education and Teaching International*, 46(3):253-264.

McAlpine L & Asghar A. 2010. Enhancing academic climate: Doctoral students as their own developers. *International Journal for Academic Development*, 15(2):167-178.

O'Byrne C. 2011. Against the odds: Research development in teaching-focused HEIs. *International Journal for Researcher Development*, 2(1):8-25.

Trafford V & Leshem S. 2009. Doctorateness as a threshold concept. *Innovations in Education and Teaching International*, 46(3):305-316.

Trowler P. 2011. Researching your own institution: Higher education. *British Educational Research Association*. [Accessed 15 July 2013] http://www.bera.ac.uk/resources/researching-your-own-institution-higher-education

Wenger E. 2000. Communities of practice and social learning systems. *Organisation*, 7(2):225-246.

Williams KF. 2009. 'Guilty knowledge': Ethical aporia emergent in the research practice of educational development practitioners. *London Review of Education*, 7(3):211-221.

BEYOND THE END OF THE BOOK
RESEARCH AS OPENINGS INTO NEW SPACES OF THOUGHT AND PRACTICE

Frances Kelly and Barbara Grant

A collection such as the one found in this volume brings together scholars and ideas in an eclectic grouping – albeit responding to an overarching theme. This book provides a space in which, between the arbitrary boundaries of its cover, contributors from diverse geographical contexts including South Africa, New Zealand, Australia, the UK and Europe have been grouped together. Each writer brings something of the ideas and flavour of their own place, as well as an understanding of the practices of postgraduate education that occur there. Each seeks to open our thinking – and perhaps hopefully our practice as well – into new spaces.

The research field of doctoral, and more generally postgraduate, education is itself a heterogeneous space. In various forums (e.g. the triennial meeting of the International Doctoral Education Research Network or IDERN, the Doctoral Education across the Disciplines Special Interest Group [SIG] at the annual American Educational Research Association Conference in the US, the biennial Quality in Postgraduate Research Conference held in Adelaide), diverse scholars – some of whom also participate in other cognate fields – collect in order to exchange ideas and accounts of practice, to further their research agendas and to inform their own localised contexts. Despite (or perhaps because of) significant cross-national flows of knowledge and practice, the theoretical and methodological, and the historical and sociocultural, resources they draw upon are profoundly varied.

One way to read the chapters in this book is to read for the different sociocultural contexts in which research into doctoral and postgraduate education is taking place. If it is possible to characterise some local flavours, it could be argued that the chapters that come from a European context – the UK and Sweden – draw on historical ideas of the doctorate and of learning in a way that differs from the other contributions. Sue Clegg's chapter argues that the doctorate is increasingly understood in terms that bring pedagogy to the fore, rather than knowledge. Her call to 'bring back' knowledge underscores a central dimension of the traditional doctorate since the early 19th century – the research thesis, the contribution to knowledge. Khalid El Gaidi, on the other hand, underscores the learning of the individual in his account of the journeyman as metaphor for postgraduate education, an idea of learning that dates back to European guilds. The South African chapters, while diverse, do to some extent each highlight what inherited ideas and traditions in doctoral education might currently mean in this particular context, which has its own unique history and its own future to carve out. Chaya Herman's chapter addresses this aspect and it was also the focus of an opening plenary at a recent IDERN meeting. Risk, as our colleagues Liezel Frick, Ruth Albertyn and Eli Bitzer show, may be a dimension of doctoral education that is of great interest internationally but it also has particular local meanings and effects in the South African context, where many students come from non-traditional starting points, with a desire that their research will 'solve the world's problems', and with significant 'financial challenges'. The predicament of first-generation students, in particular, in South African higher education may well be of a different order than that of such students in a New Zealand university, for example (as Catherine Mitchell describes). At the same time, the term 'first-generation' masks a wide variety of social positions and there may be more in common between some sub-groups across different national sites (for instance indigenous or colonised students) than there is within those sites.

Another way to read this book on pushing postgraduate boundaries is to trace the pursuit of new directions in postgraduate education research. Catherine Mitchell does this through examining the aspiration to an academic version of 'the good life' amongst first-generation doctoral candidates – to date there have been few such studies and this work is ground-breaking in its application of Appadurai's notion of aspiration to make sense of their experience. James Burford likewise focuses on an overlooked dimension of doctoral education research by addressing affect and emotion in (relation to) doctoral writing. In the process he develops an interesting methodology that invites us to think again about how we conduct research in this field. Alternative methodologies were also the focus of a recent special issue of the Higher Education Research and Development (HERD) journal. As a research community, we show a heavy reliance on interviews or surveys – or often, these days, a blend. Taking a different perspective, Puleng Motshoane and Sioux McKenna show that one dimension of postgraduate education hitherto underexplored involves studying institutions to understand how an individual institutional ethos and research culture supports (or constrains) developments in supervision practices. Such studies offer attention of a focused and detailed kind – along with the suggestion of innovative methodologies — that promises to produce new knowledge about the complexities of postgraduate education.

A third reading of the book takes account of the ways in which some chapters call for boundary-crossing. Terry Evans outlines what boundary-breaking might be, both in disciplinary terms and in terms of our thinking about 'the doctorate' and its parameters. Arguably, one boundary marker of the doctorate is the extent to which it comprises independent work compared to other degrees. The dominant model of the PhD in particular in Australasia, South Africa and the UK is 100 per cent research: this requirement produces difficulties, especially for students who are concurrently in full-time professional work or have little prior research preparation. The emergence of professional doctorates in the last two decades has been one response to this landscape and, in the UK, the development of compulsory research skills courses. Two chapters in this book address the call for forms of taught doctoral education, either through coursework, as in the chapter by Margaret Kiley, Joe Luca and Anna Cowan, or through teaching writing as modelled on a postgraduate writing course, as described by Pia Lamberti and Arnold Wentzel. Both prospects involve thinking differently about the boundaries of supervision, which is also the case with Nonnie Botha's chapter on cohort supervision and Callie Grant's questioning of the traditional one-to-one supervisory relationship in favour of a community-based approach.

Yet another reading of the contents of this book is for the ways in which its chapters investigate the idea of doctoral becoming, the process through which an individual negotiates the (neither-one-thing-nor-t'other) liminal space between their identity as a student and that of disciplined scholar/researcher. Like Mitchell and Burford, chapter contributor Susan van Schalkwyk is interested in the individual doctoral student's identity and becoming. She unpicks the metaphor of the journey, echoing elements of El Gaidi's chapter, to argue that doctoral identities emerge through a complex process that involves both personal and social dimensions. Along these lines, Cally Guerin and colleagues address the transformative process required to remake postgraduates into people who can function interculturally. These discussions prompt consideration of the extent to which postgraduate education legitimately pushes (at) individual boundaries — or promotes threshold crossing of the kind Margaret Kiley and Gina Wisker (2009) have explored. Research at doctoral level, in particular, demands new ways of thinking and being; working at the edge of boundaries, as Evans describes, is productive for individuals (and for research fields) even if it also engenders challenges or even existential shock.

The final kind of reading we would like to address is one we cannot make on behalf of others: it is the way each of us is pushed to think beyond the work described in the chapters of the book. What do we notice as we read? Where are our excitements, our resistances, our confusions, our 'ah-ha' moments, our irritations, our marginal notes? All are traces of newness and are food for fresh thought and action.

In many ways, this book is a bounded space. Yet, in writing a final coda, in pinning the 'tail' onto the book, we have taken the opportunity to reflect on how the boundaries in the book function as openings, or thresholds, that issue invitations to the reader to cross into new ways of knowing, practising and researching doctoral and postgraduate education. In that sense boundaries are not just confines to be obediently kept inside or zealously broken through: they are productive, fertile. As we experienced at IDERN meetings, they set a scene for critical debate: they offer light that casts intriguing shade; they provide the grist to our mill, the irritant for our pearl. As Erica McWilliam suggests in her Preface to the late Alison Lee and Susan Danby's recent book, *Reshaping doctoral education*, "doctoral education is ripe for re-shaping" (2011:xxi). It is over to us as researchers and practitioners in the field to make the boundaries we encounter here (and elsewhere) the starting point for a creative reshaping of the scene of doctoral and postgraduate education so that it better serves our students, our disciplines, our societies, our futures.

REFERENCES

Kiley M & Wisker G. 2009. Threshold concepts in research education and evidence of threshold crossing. *Higher Education Research & Development*, 28(4):431-441.

McWilliam E. 2011. Preface. In: A Lee & S Danby (eds). *Reshaping doctoral education: International approaches and pedagogies*. London: Routledge.

A TRIBUTE TO ALISON LEE

Sue Clegg

The first thing I read by Alison was her wonderful paper with Lesley Johnson and Bill Green (2000) 'The PhD and the autonomous self: Gender rationality and postgraduate pedagogy'. I can still remember the sheer buzz and pleasure of the experience. It leaped out for me because it took the business of theorising the PhD seriously and of putting Doctoral education into a broader context. In the paper they deconstruct the fantasy of the PhD as becoming part of a scholarly elite based on some imaginary past and they locate what they describe as a 'pedagogy of indifference' in the idea of the PhD candidate as 'always already' and I quote as 'having the capacities for which they were to be credentialled at the end of the PhD'. The figure of autonomous scholar as normatively masculine was a trope I recognised from the mismatch of my own experience supervising in a non-elite setting and working with students who were wrestling with research problems that came from their own areas of practice. These students and I did not fit the fantasy and nor did we want to – so the pleasure operated at a number of levels – the textual play and theoretical lucidity which were features of all Alison's writing – the critical edge and a willingness to speak from the margins – and the practice element of speaking to the pedagogical challenges we face and a serious intent to do something about these. I always felt that there was a person who I would recognise as a bold and committed pedagogue in the author of these texts even before I met her.

I think we cannot underestimate the impact Alison has had through her work on doctoral education and what I loved was her combination of rigour and her practical generosity to students and colleagues. Her willingness to build concrete networks that really made a difference and of course the International Doctoral Education Research Network (IDERN) is one such of these as is Doctoralnet. She combined this generous support, evident for example in her work with Malaysian colleagues and

Doctoral scholars with brilliantly provocative theoretical insights. In this brief tribute I'm going concentrate on her writing and this aspect of her enduring legacy

There are at least three areas where Alison has contributed to changing the ways we think about doctoral education – the first is seeing doctoral education as pedagogy – the second is her focus on the significance of writing – and the third is her focus on practice – of course they form a whole but I want to highlight these three features as particularly significant.

PEDAGOGY

The focus on pedagogy unites all of her writing on the doctorate. It is a tribute to her that we can now take the idea of doctoral pedagogy as a given – but as she and Bill Green pointed out in their 1995 paper 'Theorising postgraduate pedagogy' it was not always thus. Indeed as they argued supervision had been understood more in terms of research than teaching. What Alison and Bill did was to challenge this and offer a sophisticated way of understanding pedagogy as coming to know and coming to be. They also moved the debate on by focusing not just on supervision but also on the seminar as the means by which 'what counts as academic work is represented and authorised'. In a quite startling theoretical move they reverse the normal locus of discipline as research and instead bring into focus the seminar, the laboratory, and the classroom as being instrumental in the formation of disciplinary power. And they prefigure their later focus on gender when they note the discursive feminisation of the teacher in contrast to the masculinised figure of the researcher.

The focus on pedagogy is clear and is also central to the book she later edited with Susan Danby (2012) on 'Reshaping Doctoral Education'. This is a wonderfully rich collection and what makes it so useful is that it gives real insight into pedagogical practices across disciplines, in different practice settings, and on different sorts of doctoral programmes. It is extraordinarily to the credit of its editors that they produced such an informative and wide ranging text. Writing about pedagogy in an accessible way is an extremely difficult task – traversing the twin perils of banality and theoreticism – but one of the hallmarks of the series of books Alison was involved with is that they produced really useful knowledge of interest not to just to the specialist researcher but also the Doctoral teacher. These texts create spaces for the teacher to write herself in and to contemplate how their own practice might be amenable to change. By centring on pedagogy Alison, and the colleagues she collaborated with, produced a major shift in how the doctorate is conceived.

WRITING

The edited book on publishing pedagogies (Aitchison, Kamler & Lee 2010) was published two years earlier and is informed by the same spirit as 'Reshaping the Doctorate'. Here the focus is explicitly on writing. The collection includes a fascinating paper by Alison on practice in Sweden where the PhD is typically made up of a number of published papers, not as in the UK where the PhD by publication is a post-facto event, but as a conscious and planned strategy whereby the research is designed with separate publishable elements in mind. The doctoral curriculum as exemplified in this case study includes a structured seminar programme which Alison understands as rhetorical training grounds. Alison also wrote with Claire Aitchison about the need for greater attention to writing in a context where publication has come to be centre stage. They note that policies regarding the efficiency of the doctorate and greatly increased numbers of doctoral students, including those for whom English is not their mother tongue, have coincided with the pressures of research assessment to make writing a major issue. Unlike in North America there is no great tradition in the UK, Australia or South Africa of paying explicit attention to writing and of offering classes. Recent approaches, as Alison and Claire note, have included a shift to understanding writing as a discursive and socio-rhetorical practice. This gives weight to their notion that support for writing should be both socially understood and practiced within a social context. As with her other work on doctoral pedagogy, what we see here is both a focus on theorising practice and also a concrete concern to improve pedagogy. They suggest an approach to working with texts in hands-on ways that develop both writing skill and an understanding of the processes by which knowledge is created in and through writing.

This is extraordinarily useful. In my case it has made me articulate more clearly for my students what I think I am doing when I feedback on their writing and to reflect on how my own writing development has been largely tacit. The one exception to this which speaks directly to Alison's concerns with writing as a social practice was a writing retreat with members of the CAD collective facilitated by Barbara Grant and experiencing and understanding writing differently opens up the space to change doctoral practice. The opportunities for greater attention to doctoral writing are opening up with newer doctoral programmes including the EdD and again what the texts produced and edited by Alison do, is provide both a theoretical language and practical descriptions of what such practices might look like.

PRACTICE

So to turn to the third term that Alison developed and built on in her work on the doctorate, in 'Changing Practices in Doctoral Education' Alison and David Boud (2009) draw on writers such as Schatzski and begin to theorise practice as the core building block of the social – they quote Schatzski in seeing practices as 'embodied materially mediated arrays of human activity centrally organised around shared practical understanding'. Practices are purposeful and people are invested in them and they generate meanings. To think of the doctorate as a practice, therefore, turns our attention to the materiality of the activities of doctoral work, to the networks of activities at local and global levels, and to what is produced – subjects as well as objects. The Chapters in the book give multiple examples of different sorts of practice including research **for** design not just about design which challenge us to think about the nature of our different sorts of knowing.

I know that Alison was increasingly concerned with the practice turn in the social sciences more generally and the methodological implications for how we understand professional life and know-how and how these in turn relate to the role of the university in supporting knowledge production for newly challenging and changing professional contexts, particularly in her work in health related areas. This to me marks a new and exciting shift in Alison's generative and creative theorising and it leaves us with a series of challenges about its methodological implications. One of these is the need for rich ethnographies that address the materiality of practice in different sorts of doctoral settings.

The sadness is that as we research and continue our doctoral practice we won't have Alison there to provoke and challenge us. I loved her for the way she could always ask the question that made me worry away and attempt to become a better theorist and practitioner. And I loved her because we disagreed as well as agreed – our conversations were endlessly productive. But what we can all be grateful for is that we have such a rich and provocative body of published work and that in reading and re-reading her work we can celebrate her enduring contribution to doctoral education.

REFERENCES

Aitchison C, Kamler B & Lee A. 2010. *Publishing Pedagogies for the Doctorate and Beyond.* London: Routledge.

Boud D & Lee A. (eds) 2009. *Changing Practices of Doctoral Education.* London: Routledge.

Green B & Lee A. 1995. Theorising postgraduate Pedagogy. *Australian Universities' Review* 2:40-45.

Johnson L, Lee A & Green B. 2000. The PhD and the Autonomous Self: Gender, rationality and post graduate pedagogy. *Studies in Higher Education,* 25(2):135-147.

Lee A & Danby S. 2012. *Reshaping Doctoral Education: International approaches and pedagogies.* London: Routledge.

INDEX

A

academic
- academic becoming 140, 144, 204, 210, 215-216, 218, 220, 222, 225, 231, 233
- academic boundaries 1
- academic identity formation 196, 210-211, 216
- academic integration 140, 146
- academic integrity 196
- academic isolation 138, 140, 142, 146

agency 115-116, 185, 187-192, 196, 210, 216-217

Alan Fiske 111-114, 116-118, 120

Alison Lee 12, 15, 232-236

Angela Brew 15, 178

Aotearoa/New Zealand 73, 78, 206

Appadurai 204-206, 209, 212, 230

Archer 6, 187-188, 190-192, 216-217, 219, 222, 225-226

ASSAf report 34, 45, 47, 49, 185

Australian PhD programmes 4, 124

Australian Qualifications Framework (AQF) 123, 130

authoritative disciplinary voices 4, 85-86

authority-ranking relationship 112, 114, 117, 119-120

average graduating rate 45

B

backward mapping approach 44, 49

Becher 1, 19, 196

Bernstein 3, 16-20, 85, 114, 119

Bitzer's conceptual framework 5, 134, 137, 139

boundary between undergraduate and postgraduate 4, 86

boundary-riding 3, 25, 28-31

C

cohort supervision 5, 133-136, 138-141, 145-146, 150-151, 231

conceptualisation of the doctorate 11, 27, 46, 55-58, 61

coursework in PhD 124, 126, 130-131

CREST 46-47, 185-186

critical realist conception 20

critical thinking 59, 160-161, 164

D

decontextualised abstract writing 91

Department of Science and Technology (DST) 39, 41, 43, 47-48, 185

dialogical
- dialogical contraction 94-95, 97-101
- dialogical expansion 94-98

dialogue seminars 5, 162

disciplinary
- disciplinary boundaries 1, 4, 25-28, 30, 32-33, 39, 45, 57, 86
- disciplinary knowledge 12, 17-18, 28, 128

diverse student background 138, 143, 146, 208, 212

doctoral
- doctoral experiences and identities 2, 6, 30, 215-218, 224-225, 231
- doctoral graduates by field of study 42
- doctoral graduates by race and gender 42
- doctoral journey 145, 216, 218-219, 221, 224-225
- doctoral output 186
- doctoral persistence 136
- doctoral success 5, 133-135, 137-140, 145-146, 150-151
- doctoral writing 2, 4, 21, 69, 73-74, 81, 230, 235

E

equality-matching relationship 112, 115-117, 119-120

ethnographic tools 173

examining thinking skills 59, 63

expansion
> expansion and risk 2
> expansion of postgraduate education 3, 16, 39

Exploring Supervision Programme (ESP) 170, 176, 180

F

fast-tracking doctoral research programme 48

first-generation students 6, 203-205, 207-208, 230

G

gender in postgraduate education 6, 39, 42, 114-115, 191

Gibbons 2, 17, 44

global PhD, the 171

H

Higher Education Management Information System (HEMIS) 40-43

I

identity formation 6, 210, 215-216, 219, 225

IDERN 229-230, 232-233

institutional boundaries 4

Integrated Bridging Program-Research (IBP-R) 170-173, 175, 180

intercultural competency 5, 169-170, 172-176, 179-180

international
> international competitiveness 13
> international standing 13

intersubjective positioning 93, 95

intertextuality 92

J

joint supervision 135

journeyman as a metaphor 5, 153-154, 160-161, 230

K

knowledge
> knowledge boundaries 2-3, 5, 56
> knowledge economy 12, 16-17, 39, 48-49, 51, 185, 187
> knowledge production 2-3, 15-21, 86, 134, 136, 160, 185, 236

Kuhn 1, 3, 26-27, 31, 33

L

learning in community 109, 111, 113, 115-118, 120

M

market-pricing relationship 112, 117-120

Michael Young 16, 20, 22

Mikhail Bakhtin 91-93

Mode 1 knowledge 1, 16-17, 44-45

Mode 2 knowledge 1, 16-17, 45

N

number of doctoral graduates 40, 185

O

one-to-one supervision 120, 135-136, 139, 142-143

P

part-time status 29, 50, 110, 127, 138, 140

peer learning 134, 178, 218

post-doctoral employability 13, 79

postgraduate
    postgraduate journey 189
    postgraduate students' associations 25
    postgraduate writing 4, 85, 91, 231

practice-based doctorate 18
practices of supervision 80
precarity of academic labour 4, 78
professional doctorate 18, 123-125, 129

Q

quality of supervision 13

R

reflective practice 1, 136, 144, 147, 150
research doctorate 30
Research Training Scheme (RTS) 124

risk
    risk as a reciprocal notion 62
    risk in doctoral education 3, 53-54, 57, 64

role models 153-155, 158-160, 163
Royal Institute of Technology 162
Roy Bhaskar 20, 186-187

S

scientific quality 159
Southern African Development Community (SADC) 41, 45

student
    student colloquia 136
    student selection 63

supervision
    supervising across cultures 2
    supervision pedagogy 134-135
    supervision strategies 2, 4-5, 119
    supervisory capacity 45, 47, 49

Sweden 153, 160, 162, 164, 229, 235

T

teaching intervention 90-91
team supervision 33, 135
Tertiary Education Quality Standards Agency (TEQSA) 123
threshold crossing 231
throughput rate 109-110, 113, 119, 121, 143, 151
timeliness of completion 13
transdisciplinarity 17
transformative learning 121, 147
Trowler 1, 19, 196, 219

U

unreflexive view of the doctorate 11

W

Wetherell's development of affective practice 70-73, 75-78, 81
Wittgenstein 5, 163
workforce 125, 169

www.ingramcontent.com/pod-product-compliance
Lightning Source LLC
Chambersburg PA
CBHW080439170426
43195CB00017B/2827